Charcoal and Blood

Wilbur S. Shepperson Series in Nevada History
Michael S. Green, Series Editor

CHARCOAL AND BLOOD

Italian Immigrants in Eureka, Nevada, and the Fish Creek Massacre

SILVIO MANNO

UNIVERSITY OF NEVADA PRESS   Reno & Las Vegas

University of Nevada Press, Reno, Nevada 89557 USA
www.unpress.nevada.edu
Copyright © 2016 by University of Nevada Press
All rights reserved
Cover illustrations: *Charcoal Burners Atop Charcoal Pit* courtesy of JB Monaco Collection, San Francisco History Center, San Francisco Public Library; and *Tail Light Heartbeats* © 2015 by Rio Asch Phoenix
Cover design by Louise OFarrell
Manufactured in the United States of America

LIBRARY OF CONGRESS CATALOGING-IN-PUBLICATION DATA
Names: Manno, Silvio, 1954– author.
Title: Charcoal and blood : Italian immigrants in Eureka, Nevada, and the Fish Creek Massacre / Silvio Manno.
Other titles: Italian immigrants in Eureka, Nevada, and the Fish Creek Massacre
Description: Reno, Nevada : University of Nevada Press, [2016] | Series: Wilbur S. Shepperson series in Nevada history | Includes bibliographical references and index.
Identifiers: LCCN 2015046482 | ISBN 978-1-943859-00-9 (pbk. : alk. paper) ISBN 978-1-943859-12-2 (ebook)
Subjects: LCSH: Italian Americans—Nevada—Eureka County—History—19th century. | Charcoal burners—Nevada—Eureka County—History—19th century. | Charcoal industry—Nevada—Eureka County—History—19th century. | Strikes and lockouts—Charcoal industry—Nevada—Eureka County. | Massacres—Nevada—Eureka County. | Italians—Nevada—Eureka County—History—19th century. | Immigrants—Nevada—Eureka County—History—19th century.
Classification: LCC F850.I8 M36 2016 | DDC 305.895/1079332—dc23
LC record available at http://lccn.loc.gov/2015046482

∞ The paper used in this book meets the requirements of American National Standard for Information Sciences—Permanence of Paper for Printed Library Materials, ANSI/NISO z39.48-1992 (R2002). Binding materials were selected for strength and durability.

First Printing

To Wilbur S. Shepperson,
who sowed the seed from which this work flourished

*And if a stranger sojourn with thee in your land,
ye shall not do him wrong.
The stranger that dwelleth with you
shall be unto you as one born among you,
and thou shalt love him as thyself.*

—Leviticus 19:33–34

Contents

Preface xi
Introduction 1
1. Italian Emigration and the American Frontier 4
2. Early Italians in Eureka, Nevada 16
3. The Arrival of the Italian Charcoal Burners 23
4. The Eureka Charcoal Burners Protective Association 44
5. The Charcoal Crisis 61
6. Escalation of the Charcoal Troubles 83
7. The Deployment of the Militia 92
8. Veritas's Denunciations 109
9. The Fish Creek Shooting 125
10. The Coroner's Inquest 154
11. The Trial of the Charcoal Burners 180
12. Italian Diplomacy 200
13. Grand Jury Decision 212
    Conclusion 225
    Afterword 233
    Author's Notes 247
    Appendixes 249
    Bibliography 259
    Index 265

Illustrations follow page 140

Preface

In the mid- and late nineteenth century, scores of young northern Italians who had immigrated to America eventually found work as laborers for the mines on the Nevada frontier. The job of most of these men was to gather and prepare the charcoal that was used to fire the smelters. Angered by exploitative systems of labor, in the summer of 1879 these "burners," or carbonari, rose up against the middlemen, teamsters, and smelters who purchased their products. This conflict, sometimes called the "Charcoal Burners' War" or the "Italian War," took place in the town and hinterlands of Eureka, Nevada, and it resulted in the killing of five burners by a sheriff's posse near Fish Creek. More than simply an isolated incident, within this conflict lay broader tensions over immigration and labor and the shifting rules of the frontier West. In the end, this conflict was ultimately a battle over who should count as fully American.

The project began a few years after I arrived in America from Italy. In 1984, as an undergraduate student at California State University–Fresno, I was drawn to the study of immigration history. On one of my countless visits to the university library, I made a significant discovery that would eventually prove deeply rewarding when I encountered a book with the intriguing title *Restless Strangers: Nevada's Immigrants and Their Interpreters*, authored by Wilbur S. Shepperson, history professor at the University of Reno–Nevada. I opened the book to probe the personal stories of the "restless strangers." Like a pirate glancing at a secret map that marked the site of a hidden treasure, I scanned the indexed topics with great curiosity.

One particular entry gripped my attention. It read: "Italian Wars." In the last paragraph of page 125, I learned of the Fish Creek Massacre, and while distraught by the gruesome revelation, I was baffled by the historical silence that had apparently surrounded such a macabre affair all these years. My dismay was echoed by the author's sympathetic lament on the following page:

"The widespread journalistic attention given to the affair, the prejudice and violence engendered...made it comparable to a Sacco and Vanzetti drama; yet in almost ninety years [in 1970], there has been neither an adequate literary nor historical treatment of the Eureka Italians."

Moved by a sense of ethnic solidarity at the slaying of the five Italian immigrants in a remote corner of America so long ago, I sought to understand the complexity of the circumstances surrounding the affair. It became clear that the tragedy was not the typical case of violent confrontation between Anglo-Americans and members of a nationality that they despised in the lawless midst of the western frontier. Rather, it was an intraethnic conflict in which Italian laborers clashed with the economic interests of wealthier countrymen.

As a southern Italian immigrant raised in northern Italy in the 1960s, I had experienced numerous instances of ethnic hatred and injustices at the hands of resentful northerners, who felt threatened by the multitudes of poorer southern immigrants in their midst. Guided by personal insight, I knew that such a disturbing scenario could arise whenever and wherever dismal circumstances of acute economic competition developed, such as in Eureka during the nineteenth century.

Despite countless studies of immigrants in the twentieth-century American West, the anonymity of the Fish Creek incident has persisted. Surprisingly, even Elliott Robert Barkan, in his recent encyclopedic treatment of the western immigrant experience, *From All Points: America's Immigrant West, 1870s–1952*, overlooked the Eureka Italians.

It is my sincere hope that the present work will contribute to remedying the historical void Shepperson bewailed years ago. I approach my inquiry into the "Fish Creek Massacre" with the conviction that by shedding the light of human understanding upon America's darker past, a more enlightened future will emerge, one in which those "restless strangers" still wandering through the "promised land" will at last realize their cherished dreams.

The creation of a book is never a solitary endeavor. Indeed, the project at hand has come to fruition only through the altruistic effort of several individuals and institutions to whom I am indebted. Thanks are due to Nevada historian Phil Earl, whose seminal article on Nevada's Italian War represented a milestone in the saga of Eureka's Italian charcoal burners. I am also deeply indebted to Franklin Grazeola, whose master's thesis provided the initial blueprint for my own work. Sincerest appreciation is also extended to historian Andrew Rolle, professor emeritus of history at Occidental College, for his scrupulous review of the manuscript during its embryonic stage and for recognizing early on the potential of the project. Much gratitude is also owed to Professor Phyllis Martinelli, of Saint Mary's College of California, for her valuable suggestions that lent greater clarity and cohesion to the manuscript.

I would also like to gratefully acknowledge the enthusiastic supervision of Nevada historian Ron James, who patiently tackled the challenging task of reducing substantially the length of the manuscript, providing valuable feedback and vital encouragement at every step. His support was instrumental in moving the project forward and closer to publication. Much gratitude is also owed to Matt Becker, acquisitions editor of the University of Nevada Press, for believing in the merit of the project, and to his successor, Justin Race, who eagerly shepherded the project through to completion. Special words of thanks are also reserved for Mike Green, historian at UNLV and editor of the Wilbur S. Shepperson Series in Nevada History, for his valuable feedback. I am also greatly beholden to Patricia Heinicke, whose professional expertise as copy editor improved greatly the quality of the manuscript, ensuring that the text flowed sensibly, fairly, and accurately. In the last phase of the copyediting process, Annette Wenda's phenomenal skills lent the manuscript its enduring vibrancy.

Appreciation is also due to Mitch Ison, state reference librarian at the Nevada State Library in Carson City, for his unremitting patience in providing innumerable copies of newspaper articles, the crucial primary sources of my research. In the selection of historical illustrations depicting Nevada's frontier days, I am indebted to Kathryn M. Totton, photograph curator with the Special Collections Department at the University of Nevada, for her kind assistance. Many thanks to Susan E. Searcy at the Nevada State Archives for enriching the manuscript by providing an important historical sample of Governor John H. Kinkead's correspondence with General George M. Sabin. Much gratitude is also extended to the staff at the University of Nevada Press, including Caddie S. Dufurrena, marketing and sales manager, and Jinni Fontana, editorial, design, and production manager.

Sincere thanks are reserved for friends in Eureka, Nevada, including Ree Taylor and Colleen Nelson, curators at the Eureka Sentinel Museum, for opening up the Resource Library where I spent countless hours searching through myriad historical records and photographs. Thanks to Albert Biale, who was instrumental in locating the charcoal burners' burial site and the creation of their memorial, and to Wally Cuchine, director of the Eureka Opera House, for having rescued the priceless resources stored at the Eureka Sentinel Museum. Heartfelt gratitude is extended to Connie Hicks, longtime resident of Eureka and passionate local historian, for sharing her detailed knowledge related to some of the historical events covered in the book. Thanks to her on-site collaboration, I was privileged to obtain relevant historical material from Eureka, hundreds of miles away, enabling me to continue my research uninterrupted.

Special thanks are offered to J. R. Monaco, who believed in the sincerity of my effort, granting me the privilege of accessing Louis Monaco's personal correspondence and obtaining vintage photographs taken by his renowned great-uncle while residing in Eureka. Appreciation is also reserved for Rick Monaco, J. R.'s son, for redirecting my search for some of the vintage photographs taken by his illustrious ancestor included in the book to the San Francisco History Center, where photo curator Christina Moretta lent her expertise in obtaining high-quality scans for publication.

Closer to home, I owe a great debt of gratitude to the supportive staff of the Fresno County Central Library, where I spent countless hours deciphering faded newspaper articles. The California Genealogical Room proved itself a treasure trove of historical wealth and became my second home. But more important, the unflagging support offered by historians Bill Secrest Jr. and William B. Secrest Sr. enabled me to retrieve historical records central to the book. With equal appreciation, I also acknowledge the unfaltering help provided by library staffers Melissa Scroggings, Nance Espinosa, and Chris Her.

Special recognition is offered to my "comadre" Teresa Avila and to my "ahijado" Carlos Lugo for their unwavering support. In addition, I am grateful to all my closest friends: Christopher Bettencourt, Thelma Newnam, Donna and Ken Smith, Mary and Brent Roath, Andre Forestiere, Josiah, Dyonisios, and Thanasis Maskaleris, Gregory and Lisa Rowe, Luke and Marium Gunnewegh, Kenneth Scambray, William Greene, PHD, Stephen Blake Mettee, Vincenzo and Charlotte Biancucci, Linda and Terry Scambray, Karen West, Gregory Stephens, DDS; Monet Milgoza; Debra Harrang;

Rocky Guntt; Sam Franklin; Rosie McClain; Ken and Rose Lanier; George Hanson; Sharon Pemberton; Kit and Linda Hausman; Mitsuo and Akiko Fujishima; Jennifer Renzi; Peter Hudson; Laurel Fawcet; Paula Thompson; Jim Schlotz; Janet Capella; Lloyd Carter; Patience Milrod; Jennifer and Kenny Kearns; Donna Palomino; Mark Rivera; Matthew Lozano, MD; Neil D. Kornzweig; Michael Stubblefield, MD; Bob Milovich; Latieshka Simmons; Leon Bueno; Steve Verdugo; Jay Hardiman; Father Finian McGinn; the Rosario "Ric" Forestiere family; and my late dear friend Stanley Griffin. Sincere appreciation is also extended to colleagues and friends from the Rowell School days, with particular affection reserved for my fellow bilingual teachers with whom I shared many years of professional challenges promoting the cause of bilingual education. A special acknowledgment is also extended to all my friends at the Forestiere Underground Gardens for their unfaltering encouragement.

A special "grazie" to my Italian friends Roberto and Lyn Acitelli; Tom Cerbo; Cristina and Lorenzo Tozzi; Giordano Dall'Armellina; Marco Briano; Dario, Joyce, and Roman Bianchi; Nella Magni; Mauro De Molli, MD; Francesco Cuoghi; Lucilla Fondacaro Giardini; and Fulvia Testori, who supported me all along and absolved me for neglecting temporarily their precious friendship.

Thanks also to my faraway relatives: the Dichiera, Iacopetta, and Ritorto families in Adelaide, Australia; the Dichiera, Audino, Blumer, and Cavallaro families in the United States; the Scimone, Pezzaniti, Dimasi, Albanese, and Lanzarin families in Milan; the Manno and Cavallaro families in Calabria, Italy; the Mazzina family in Chiavenna, Italy; and Evelyn Casini in Nice, France, all of whom, though physically distant, are always close to my heart and whose transoceanic support has been deeply felt. Heartfelt appreciation is offered to my late uncle, Franco Panaja, whose fascination with the myth of the American West spurred my youthful imagination.

Ultimately, I thank my immediate family for their patience and understanding for all the time the writing of this book robbed from them. Thanks to my son, Scot, for providing me with food, drink, and love while I sat glued to the computer to breathe life into the book. I hope that one day he will read it and understand why I exerted so much effort and time on this endeavor. An unrepayable debt of gratitude I owe to my parents, Vincenzo Manno and Maria Pezzaniti, who gave me the gift of life and who endured great hardships for their children's sake. Sincere thanks also to my brothers, Piero and Mario, who always challenged my thinking and prodded me to see beyond the limits of my world. Appreciation goes also to my grandsons, Clayton and Jeffrey Bettencourt and Eric Smith, for taking over chores around the house, allowing me to pour extra energy into the book. Last, but definitely not least, I would like to express my heartfelt appreciation to my wife, Carolyn, for her help with and boundless support of my vast endeavor. Final thanks and apologies are extended to those individuals whom my memory has failed to acknowledge.

Charcoal and Blood

Introduction

The United States of America has long been a land of immigrants. No corner of the vast American landscape has been impervious to immigrant settlement. During the last half of the nineteenth century, even remote Nevada drew to its uninviting midst droves of foreign-born settlers, thus transforming the Silver State into one of the most culturally diverse states in the Union.[1]

Fleeing desperate conditions, immigrants settled on the fringes of the austere American frontier in the hope of reaping the material rewards that typically accrued to early arrivals. In 1880 roughly 60 percent of the 7,086 people residing in remote Eureka County, Nevada, were foreign born. Further, a remarkable 19 percent of Eureka's newcomers traced their birthplace to Italy.[2] Frequently, the cultural diversity of Nevada's population fomented labor disputes, thus causing the foreign born to be viewed with suspicion and disparagement by Anglo-Americans. An indication of the intensity of ethnic strife that plagued Nevada in the later decades of the nineteenth century is provided by an episode recorded in Eureka in the autumn of 1872. At that time the city of Eureka, wedged in a canyon between the Diamond and Prospect mountain ranges, was a boomtown, soon to be transformed into the second-largest mining center in the state after Virginia City.

By the early 1870s, Eureka was experiencing a phase of economic expansion, reflected in the establishment of new smelting furnaces. Increased smelting activity demanded a higher production of fuel, namely, charcoal, which, in turn, enabled the fuel producers to raise prices. Hoping to counter the rising costs of charcoal, contractors turned to cheap Chinese laborers to harvest the timber and produce the indispensable fuel. However, this antilabor tactic provoked such antagonism among Anglo-American laborers that by June 1872, the Chinese had been forced to abandon the charcoal-burning enterprise altogether.[3]

Determined to further their profits, the contractors tapped the abundant cheap labor supplied by Italian immigration. Experienced in the age-old trade of charcoal burning and in dire need of employment, Italians flocked to Eureka in unprecedented numbers. By the late 1870s, Italians held a virtual monopoly over the production of charcoal throughout the county.

Although using Italian labor and expertise rather than Chinese was ostensibly promising, this strategy would eventually prove to be equally ill-fated. With a torrent of Italian labor coming into Eureka County, xenophobia latently targeted the Italian immigrant. By the spring of 1876, collective apprehension toward the newcomers had grown so acute as to prompt the *Eureka Daily Sentinel* to express alarm that three-fourths of the migrants arriving into the region were unemployable Italian immigrants.[4]

Earning a meager wage of ten dollars per week, less than half the wages earned by the average miner,[5] the Italian charcoal burners were relegated to the bottom rung of Eureka's economic ladder. The burners were so abjectly poor that they had no alternative but to live in crude, ill-equipped hovels and dugouts, eliciting scorn and suspicion from the higher-paid members of the labor force.

Yet the charcoal they produced was the lifeblood of Eureka's mining economy, ensuring the prosperity of the whole community. By 1878 Eureka's furnaces were devouring more than sixteen thousand bushels of charcoal per day, amounting to an overall cost of nearly six hundred thousand dollars per month. In order to satisfy the insatiable appetite for fuel, the hills around Eureka for a distance of thirty-five to fifty miles were laid barren, stripped of nut pine, piñon, dwarf cedar, juniper, and mountain mahogany, the primary sources of charcoal.

As deforestation progressed, the burners were compelled to tread farther into the wilderness to obtain new sources of timber. Similarly, the teamsters had to travel greater distances to deliver the charcoal to the smelters in Eureka. Obviously, ever-expanding harvesting of timber entailed increased hardships and higher costs. Due to the inflation of transportation costs coupled with by a slight recession in 1879, the major smelters sought to lower the price of charcoal.

On July 6, 1879, approximately six hundred coal burners gathered at Celso Tatti's saloon and formed the Eureka Charcoal Burners Protective Association (CBPA).[6] They demanded thirty cents per bushel of charcoal from the middle-man contractors and threatened to cut off the supply if their demand was not met. Three prominent contractors, Reinhold Sadler, a German immigrant and future Nevada governor, as well as Joseph Tognini and Joseph Vanina, two Swiss Italians, adamantly opposed the burners' demand.

When the burners disrupted the flow of charcoal, warrants were issued to arrest the ringleaders. On August 11 an appeal for military intervention was sent to the governor of Nevada.[7] Determined to subdue the rebellious burners without the aid of the state militia, Sheriff Matthew Kyle dispatched a "fighting posse" to the mutinous charcoal camps.

On August 18, 1879, five Italian charcoal burners were slain, six more were wounded, while fourteen were taken prisoner near Fish Creek.[8] The gravity of the incident prompted the Italian minister in Washington to dispatch the Italian consul in San Francisco to Eureka to investigate what became known as the "Fish Creek Massacre." Although the inquest determined that the sheriff's posse acted in accordance with the law, some still viewed the tragic incident as an abuse of authority. To understand how what started as a legitimate labor grievance degenerated into one of the earliest episodes of violence against a unionized foreign group on the American mining frontier, it is necessary to examine those historical antecedents that compelled scores of Italians to emigrate during the second half of the nineteenth century.

Notes

1. Wilbur S. Shepperson, *Restless Strangers: Nevada's Immigrants and Their Interpreters*, 4.
2. US Department of the Interior, Census Office, *Statistics of the Population of the United States at the Tenth Census (1880)*, 439.
3. *Eureka Daily Sentinel*, between September 17, 1871, and June 22, 1872. Hereafter cited as *Sentinel*.
4. *Sentinel*, March 10, 1876.
5. Shepperson, *Restless Strangers*, 122.
6. *Eureka Daily Leader*, July 7, 1879. Hereafter cited as *Leader*.
7. *Leader*, August 11, 1879.
8. *Leader*, August 19, 1879.

Italian Emigration and the American Frontier

On March 17, 1861, following a series of bloody battles against Austria, the unification of Italy became a reality when the national Italian Parliament was formed under the leadership of Victor Emmanuel II, king of Italy. But a worsening of living conditions for the majority of Italians followed. Public taxes substantially increased, aggravating the burdens already oppressing millions of destitute *contadini* (peasants) who tried to eke out a living from the land.

Toward the end of the nineteenth century, the rural economy prevalent in the Ticino region of northern Italy, where many of Eureka's charcoal burners originated, was on the verge of collapse. The major causes responsible for such a dire economic stagnation included outdated agricultural practices, excessive taxation, and farm contracts unfavorable to the peasantry. With 90 percent of the land concentrated in the hands of a small propertied class, the *contadini* of the upper Milanese were virtually penniless and on the brink of starvation.

With the socioeconomic promises of the Risorgimento (the political movement that led to the unification of Italy) betrayed, thousands of impoverished northern *contadini* looked at emigration as their only chance for future progress. With a renewed sense of personal empowerment gained from their participation in the Risorgimento, multitudes of estranged peasants abandoned their ancestral land in search of better opportunities on the American continent. The painful decision to emigrate was prompted by desperate circumstances aptly summed up by the sorrowful lament: "We plant and we reap, but never do we taste white bread. We cultivate the grape but we drink no wine. We raise animals for food but we eat no meat. We are clothed in rags."[1]

In a conference addressing specifically the phenomenon of overseas emigration, held at the Istituto Lombardo di Scienze e Lettere on June 4, 1868, Ercole Ferrario, an expert on the conditions of the upper Milanese territory, cited several causes of immigration related to the poor agricultural and economic conditions. He summarized his observation by stating that "the dismal poverty afflicting the peasantry, already marked by 1864, increased steadily each year thereafter, worsened by the further impoverishment of the landowners.... [T]hese are the causes of emigration."

Indeed, the early Italian immigrants who settled in the United States before the Civil War and in the decade after originated almost exclusively from Italy's northern provinces.[2] Most of them sought refuge within the Italian enclaves of the main industrial centers of the Atlantic Seaboard and the Midwest. From these grim tenements eventually sprang up thriving and colorful communities known as "Little Italies." Yet a sizable number of Italian immigrants ventured out into the less traveled American frontier. In Eureka, Nevada, their fortunes would become linked with those of the region's mining interests. For decades the experience of ethnic minorities in the American West has been obscured by the "frontier thesis" formulated by American historian Frederick Jackson Turner in the late nineteenth century. Essentially, Turner asserted that the frontier experience had laid the foundations of the American character, with all its defining traits.[3]

Biased in his view of the peoples who settled the West, Turner credited Anglo-Americans as the protagonists of this westward movement while ignoring the multiethnic throngs that put down roots on the American frontier. Historian Patricia Limerick, a major exponent of the "new western history," asserted: "Turner was...ethnocentric and nationalistic. English-speaking white men were the stars of his story; Indians, Hispanics, French Canadians, and Asians were at best supporting actors and at worst invisible." As an example of his ethnocentricity, Turner viewed non-Anglo-Americans, including Italians, as detrimental to the health of the United States: "It is obvious that the replacement of the German and English immigration by Southern Italians, Poles, Russian Jews and Slovaks is a loss to the social organism of the United States. The congestion of foreigners...in our great cities, the increase in crime and pauperism are attributable to the poorer elements."[4]

Intent on rectifying the distorted image of Italian immigrants to America that linked them to pauperism, slum dwelling, disease, and crime, historian Andrew Rolle undertook an extensive study of the Italian immigrant experience in America during the nineteenth and twentieth centuries. Rolle set out to demonstrate that the unique opportunities of the frontier for the more enterprising newcomers spawned circumstances far more conducive to individual success than could ever be imagined by urban immigrants. "The frontier did not coerce...it emancipated," wrote Rolle.[5]

In his endeavor to offset the misunderstood image of the Italian immigrant, Rolle highlighted the triumphs achieved by scores of Italian immigrants across the American frontier while glossing over the adversities faced by throngs of ordinary Italian immigrants. By contrast, elaborating on the experience of Italian immigrants in California during the Progressive Era, Joseph Giovinco stated: "Beneath the surface of the 'model colony' [San Francisco's Italian colony] image is a darker story: of numerous Italian immigrants...who not only did not achieve success and fortune but who found life as difficult and unrewarding as did impoverished immigrants elsewhere in the nation."[6] Although Giovinco is describing a later historical period in the evolution of the Italian community in America, his comment aptly depicts the economic predicament the Italian charcoal burners faced in Eureka, Nevada, during the 1870s.

Although a few Italian Jesuit missionaries and adventurers had explored the Pacific Coast region prior to 1830, it was not until 1840 that a small but steady flow of Italians trickled into California and the Pacific slope. By 1848, seduced by the fertility of California's soil and by the balmy Mediterranean-like climate, Genoese seamen returning home spread glowing reports about this Pacific region. Almost immediately, a small-scale wave of Ligurian immigration to California ensued.[7] These Ligurian seafarers and their families prospered, finding neither ethnic hostility nor economic rivalry in this remote area of the world.

However, it was Marshall's legendary discovery of gold at Coloma, California, in 1848 that drew many more Italians to the Golden State.[8] Eager for quick riches, multitudes set out for California in search of fortune. Undaunted by the greater financial cost and distance involved in reaching California's goldfields, many Italian adventurers shunned the "Little Italies" founded by their conationals in the major eastern cities. The Italian presence in California eventually grew so markedly as to prompt the Kingdom of Sardinia to establish an Italian consulate in San Francisco.[9]

Even the California Gold Rush, with its motley legions of gold seekers, was fraught with ethnic prejudice. The sudden arrival in the Golden State of droves of foreign hopefuls bred resentment among Anglo prospectors. Ultimately, the antiforeigner hysteria that swept the diggings reached the halls of the California Legislature, which in 1850 enacted the Foreigners Mining Tax. The law exacted an exorbitant fee of twenty dollars per month from any foreigner intending to mine the mineral wealth of El Dorado.[10] Among the hordes of foreign miners who became the targets of Anglo discrimination, there were clusters of Italian immigrants. "Many Italians were independent miners, who, together with Native Americans, Latins, Chinese and blacks, had to face the brunt of discrimination. Because of this many were soon pushed away from mining and settled in adjoining towns."[11]

Most Italian argonauts, just like their Anglo competitors, did not strike it rich, and many of these disillusioned gold seekers soon realized that fortunes could be made far more reliably by catering to the survival needs of the forty-niners. Hence, these sons of Italy readily turned to inn keeping, merchandising, truck gardening, wine making, and the building trades to stake their claims. Experienced in these types of Old World activities, many of them prospered. In fact, their success was so impressive throughout California's Mother Lode as to give rise to a popular adage: "The miners mined the gold while the Italians mined the miners."[12]

Ten years after the fabulous discovery of gold in California, the American West was jolted by yet another astonishing mineral strike to the east. The world's richest silver deposit, the Comstock Lode, had slumbered only twenty miles east of the California border until it was revealed to the world in 1859. The immense wealth of the Comstock Lode attracted a vast supply of unspecialized labor, predominantly immigrants. The steady influx of immigrants continued unabated for years, transforming the territory of Nevada into a haven for the foreign born.

The upsurge of new immigration to the United States was directly related to the staggering loss of human lives caused by the Civil War. The fratricidal war between North and South, in which close to a million people were killed or wounded,[13] created an acute labor shortage. To help fill the labor vacuum caused by wartime casualties, the Contract Labor Law was passed on June 4, 1864, allowing employers to recruit foreign workers.[14] In October of that same year, Nevada attained statehood, and for the next fourteen years the Silver State experienced rapid growth. During this era, the mining frontier of Nevada generated high levels of mineral production, accompanied by unparalleled prosperity. Boomtowns sprang up with lightning speed, breeding a social climate of lawlessness wherein the administration of justice often lapsed or came to rely upon sheer force.

In order to attract cheap labor to the mineral regions of the western frontier, some promoters and recruiters resorted to the use of the foreign-language press operating in the major urban centers of the East. Frequently, after reading glowing reports of fabulous mining booms in the West, scores of desperate fortune seekers would plunge into the vast frontier only to resurface bitterly disappointed and penniless.

A powerful illustration of the effectiveness of the foreign-language newspaper as a recruiting device is provided by a brief letter that *L'Eco d'Italia* printed in eastern-based Italian newspapers in 1869. The letter was written by Matteo Caschina, an Italian miner employed in Nevada, after he unearthed a two-pound mass of silver. Addressed to a friend in New York City, the epistle was written with the clear intent of spurring him on to move to the silver fields of Nevada. An excerpt reads: "At Treasure City (9865 feet above sea level) in White Pine County, Nevada there are already numerous Italians, some of whom have purchased lots to build hotels, restaurants, and grocery stores.... [F]ood costs $5.00 a day, but one earns much more."[15]

Caschina inferred that prosperity awaited the more daring immigrants at Treasure City, and countless similar newspaper articles were fraught with gross distortions and exaggerations aimed at alluring unwary would-be miners. Nevada in particular, with its embryonic society, appealed strongly to the foreign born. With much of its territory still unsettled, Nevada brimmed with yet unclaimed opportunities.

Relegated to the bottom of the Comstock social pyramid were those groups found most racially antagonistic to and incompatible with the dominant Anglo-American mainstream: Native Americans, African Americans, Chinese, and Mexicans.[16] These were the peoples that eastern old-stock Americans viewed as a threat to their Anglo-Saxon purity. Soon membership into this category of undesirables included northern Italians, central Europeans, and eastern European Jews.

Following the Comstock Lode rush, waves of late fortune seekers relentlessly probed the desolate Nevadan landscape in search of new untapped wealth. In September 1864, the exploration of Nevada's remote interior rewarded a group of prospectors who stumbled into the rich mineral outcroppings at Eureka. The unearthing of Eureka's mineral riches caused sensational reverberations across the mining frontier, for it turned out to be the first notable strike of silver-lead in the entire country.[17] Although gold and silver were the most avidly sought precious metals on the American mining frontier, only the former was found in its pure state. By contrast, silver almost invariably combined with other base metals such as lead, copper, zinc, and iron, requiring further treatment by smelting. The rich silver deposits at Eureka contained a large percentage of lead.

In his *Eureka and Its Resources*, Lambert Molinelli asserts: "The history of the industrial growth of Eureka District is the history of the first successful treatment in America of argentiferous lead ores." In describing the complexity of Eureka's silver-lead ores, Molinelli explains: "They are self-fluxing. They carry from 15 to 60 per cent of lead, and sufficient iron and silica to obviate the necessity of importing foreign material for smelting purposes. Eureka is the only known mining district possessing this all important advantage."[18] Though comparatively rare, Eureka's self-fluxing silver-lead ores, rich in iron and silica, could be easily reduced to a molten liquid state, thus making smelting simpler. The startling discovery transformed Eureka into Nevada's second most productive mining center of the nineteenth century.[19]

However, Eureka's mineral wealth of silver-lead ores was not readily amenable to conventional smelting methods. In order to profitably develop the intricate amalgamation of silver and lead, some kind of innovative smelting technology was needed. This required professional expertise as well as financial capital scarcely available on this remote frontier.

The challenge of developing a smelting technology capable of reducing silver-lead ore effectively was not confined to Eureka. Throughout the Rockies, wherever silver-lead ores were unearthed, the difficulty was equally felt. According to University of Colorado professor James E. Fell Jr., the enigma was solved by a cadre of competent German metallurgists "who introduced the blast furnace—the proper technology for smelting silver-lead ores...in the West during the late 1860s."[20]

Similarly, the odds of unraveling Eureka's mineral riddle increased dramatically with the arrival of two experienced Welsh smeltermen, R. P. Jones and John Williams. The two metallurgists succeeded in developing a rudimentary but effective apparatus, modeled after the Stedefeldt furnace. The Stedefeldt furnace is aptly described by Ernest Oberbillig: "[It] was a shaft roasting furnace in which finely ground silver ore and salt passed down a shaft against a current of hot air. The result was a 90 percent chloridized product ready to be amalgamized."[21]

Given the complexity of the Eureka ores, the furnaces needed to generate extremely high temperatures to melt the metals. In the absence of a more efficient carbon-rich fuel such as coke, the extreme heat could be created only by burning vast quantities of charcoal placed at the furnace base. As a result, "charcoal was in great demand," explains Nevada historian James W. Hulse. "Hundreds of men made their living in the mountains around the town by gathering wood from the pine and juniper trees and carrying it to special outdoors ovens where it was transformed to charcoal for the furnaces in Eureka. The business of making charcoal was...especially significant in Eureka."[22]

In 1869, five years after Eureka's mineral deposits were first detected and after much trial-and-error mechanical experimentation, a marked increase in the district's overall mineral production was attained. Although far from sensational, the increase in mineral output was significant enough to attract the attention of two major mining companies, the San Francisco–based Eureka Consolidated Mining Company and the London-based Richmond Consolidated Mining Company. By 1871 these two mining enterprises had purchased most of Eureka's mineral claims. The vast capital wielded by the two mining giants and their keen interest in developing Eureka's complex ores signaled the beginning of a new and bright era for the once precarious mining camp.[23]

Within a few short years, Eureka's mining industry saw the value of its mineral production soar from a meager $5,932 in 1869 to an impressive level of more than $2 million in 1872. Remarkable in the history of mining towns on the western American frontier, Eureka mines remained highly productive for more than a decade. The rapid growth that engulfed Eureka prompted the state legislature to accord it county status, and in 1873 Eureka was carved out of Lander County's eastern flank.[24]

By 1875, thanks to the construction of a narrow-gauge railroad that ran from Eureka to Palisade, Eureka had permanently overcome its geographical isolation. The secondary rail line was grafted onto the standard-gauge Central Pacific rail system,[25] thereby accelerating the shipment of the valuable silver and lead ingots to their distant destinations. The railroad also guaranteed a steady influx of immigrant labor into the prosperous county. In 1878, Eureka's most productive year, $5.2 million of mineral wealth was produced, and the city boasted a population of about nine thousand residents.[26] Brimming with prosperity, Eureka became Nevada's second-largest city.

However, Eureka derived its life-giving substance from the sixteen smelters that dotted the city's grimy periphery. Here, amid deafening noise and foul smoke, the ore-processing furnaces incessantly swallowed a daily average of 745 tons of ores extracted from more than fifty active mines scattered across the county.[27] In addition to the volume of bullion production, the intensity of Eureka's smelting activity could be measured by the degree of environmental degradation it spawned. With the smelters constantly spewing out poisonous gases into the atmosphere, Eureka's once pristine alpine landscape was now smothered by a thick blanket of smoke that hung in the air, giving the town a gloomy appearance along with the fitting title of the "Pittsburgh of the West." An account by H.R. Whitehill, the state mineralogist, explains the term: "Heavy black clouds of dense smoke from the furnaces, heavily laden and strongly scented with the fumes of lead, arsenic and other volatile elements of the ores are constantly rolling over the town, depositing soot, scales and black dust, so that [Eureka] resembles very much one of the manufacturing towns in the coal regions of Pennsylvania."[28]

Inevitably, as the smelting technology evolved, the need for charcoal grew more acute. After 1875, wishing to eliminate the cost of shipping the locally produced silver-lead bullions to distant refineries, the Richmond Company decided to build its own refinery. The refining process consisted of reheating the bullion several times to gradually enhance its purity, ultimately obtaining lead and silver ingots of much higher quality. Naturally, the creation of the Richmond refinery generated an increased demand for charcoal. By 1879 the daily consumption of charcoal by Eureka's smelters had risen to 175,000 pounds.[29]

Assuming the proportions of a full-scale industry, the manufacturing of charcoal in Eureka County employed droves of men who earned their livelihood by chopping thousands of cords of wood each day in the mountains around Eureka. Just as the smelting of Eureka's complex lead-silver ores was a costly and elaborate process, so was producing charcoal.

After finding a source of suitable wood, the trees were felled, stripped of their limbs (delimbed), and cut into four-foot logs (a process known as bucking). Next, the wood was transported to the charcoal pits or kilns to be burned (coaled). The wood could be burned in outdoor kilns made of bricks or stone or in earth-covered mounds known as pits. Although pit burning required less capital, less skill, and less time to construct, making charcoal in a kiln was more advantageous. Kiln burning was easier to control, required less labor to operate, burned cleaner and hotter, produced greater and better-quality yields, and cost a lot less.[30] The obvious limitation of kiln burning was its permanency. Whereas pit burning was an itinerant craft plied in close proximity to the source of wood, kiln burning was a stationary trade, growing more costly as distances from the wood supply increased.

Whether charcoal was produced in kilns or pits, its quality entailed great skills. Although kiln and pit burning involved different adaptations of the same tasks, the process unfolded over three phases. First, the kiln was filled with cordwood precisely stacked to ensure thorough and uniform burning (charging). The kiln was initially "charged" through its front entrance. However, when the kiln operator could no longer reach the top of the woodpile, the stacking continued through a smaller opening, typically found at the upper rear of the oven. Charging a beehive-like kiln measuring an average thirty-foot width required "four men and two horses one day."[31]

The second phase of charcoal production, and the most crucial, was burning or carbonizing the wood by eliminating the volatile gases and moisture stored in the carbon-rich wood fiber in an oxygen-reduced environment. The quality of the finished product hinged critically upon the burner's ability to regulate the flow of oxygen through the kiln vents and to assess the kiln's internal combustion from its external effusions. Far from being an autonomous process, kiln burning required the constant and vigilant supervision of the burner in charge until the burning was done. "To burn a pit satisfactorily required no small degree of skill, judgment, and vigilance. The pit had to be watched day and night for almost a week, so great was the danger of the slow smoldering combustion turning into a conflagration, wiping out a burner's earnings, his home or himself. Wind could cause uneven charring or, worse, total destruction."[32]

Not unlike the deft Native American who could accurately decipher the meaning of smoke signals, the burner was also adept at reading the changing hues of the smoke emanating from the kiln. Typically, during the first few days of charring, a thick white smoke billowed from the uppermost row of vents, wood moisture rising as steam. By the fourth day, the white smoke would turn yellowish and then bluish. Blue smoke signaled the apex of combustion and the final phase of burning. Akin to an organist nimbly playing his keyboard to direct the flow of air through the instrument's hollow pipes to fill a cathedral with the truest sound, the charcoal burner manipulates with equal dexterity the three rows of kiln vents to ensure the purest form of carbon.

Twelve hours after first charging the kiln, and at twelve-hour intervals after that, the rows of vents were sequentially opened and closed to direct the fire toward the bottom of the structure. After blue smoke appeared, the top vents were closed and the row of vents below opened. Twelve hours later, after the blue smoke returned, the middle row of vents were closed and the bottom vents opened. At this point, the fire had reached the kiln's floor. Once the blue smoke reappeared, the lower row of vents was also closed.[33]

Once the kiln was completely fired, all vents were plugged with a brick and sealed tightly with a layer of mortar. Then the fiery oven was allowed to cool naturally for two to three days. Eight to ten barrels of water were finally poured from the top of the kiln to douse the smoldering mass below. Usually, the charcoal could be drawn the following day. The final phase of "drawing" or "discharging" the kiln employed two men over a twelve-hour day.[34]

Experienced charcoal burners or colliers were essential if the industry was to produce high-quality charcoal affordably; thus, many of them were frequently imported from the old charcoal-producing regions of Europe.

Notes

1. Alexander de Conde, *Half Bitter, Half Sweet: An Excursion into Italian-American History*, 72.
2. Erik Amfitheatrof, *The Children of Columbus: An Informal History of the Italians in the New World*, 100.
3. Frederick Jackson Turner, *The Frontier in American History*; R. A. Billington, *America's Frontier Heritage*, 12–13.
4. Patricia N. Limerick, *The Legacy of Conquest: The Unbroken Past of the American West*, 21; Turner, *Frontier in American History*, 351.
5. Andrew Rolle, *The Immigrant Upraised: Italian Adventurers and Colonists in an Expanding America*, viii–xi.
6. Joseph P. Giovinco, "'Success in the Sun?': California's Italians during the Progressive Era," 21.
7. Amfitheatrof, *Children of Columbus*, 192.
8. De Conde, *Half Bitter, Half Sweet*, 14.
9. Amfitheatrof, *Children of Columbus*, 14.
10. W. Eugene Hollon, *Frontier Violence: Another Look*, 64–65.
11. Paola A. Sensi-Isolani and Phylis Cancilla Martinelli, *Struggle and Success: An Anthology of the Italian Immigrant Experience in California*, 9.
12. Joseph P. Giovinco, "The Ethnic Dimension of Calaveras County History," 17.
13. Newer estimates place the total death toll at 650,000 to 850,000. See Guy Gugliotta, "New Estimate Raises Civil War Death Toll," *New York Times*, April 2, 2012; and David J. Hacker, "A Census-Based Count of the Civil War Dead."
14. Thomas C. Cochran and William Miller, *The Age of Enterprise: A Social History of Industrial America*, 106–7.
15. Giovanni Schiavo, *Four Centuries of Italian-American History*, 175.
16. Russell R. Elliott, *History of Nevada*, 148–49.
17. Ibid., 105.
18. Lambert Molinelli, *Eureka and Its Resources*, 15, 26.
19. Elliott, *History of Nevada*, 105.
20. James E. Fell Jr., *Ores to Metals: The Rocky Mountain Smelting Industry*, 63, 66.
21. Ernest Oberbillig, "Development of Washoe and Reese River Silver Processes," 43.
22. James W. Hulse, *The Nevada Adventure: A History*, 142.
23. Elliott, *History of Nevada*, 105.
24. Ibid.
25. Ibid.

26. Stanley W. Paher, *Nevada Ghost Towns and Mining Camps*, 181–88.
27. *Nevada State Census, 1875.*
28. Judith K. Winzeler and Nancy Peppin, *Eureka, Nevada: A History of the Town*, 9.
29. Ibid., 7, 9.
30. Thomas Egleston, "The Manufacture of Charcoal in Kilns," 374.
31. Ibid., 393.
32. John Uhlmann and Peggy Heinrich, *The Soul of Fire*, 129.
33. Egleston, "Manufacture of Charcoal in Kilns," 393.
34. Ibid., 389, 395.

II

Early Italians in Eureka, Nevada

By the late 1870s, the labor-intensive enterprise of charcoal making in Eureka County had become the almost exclusive domain of more than a thousand Italian charcoal burners, mostly immigrants from the poverty-stricken Alpine region of northern Italy, where charcoal making had been practiced for at least a century.[1] Mixed with the Italians proper were scores of Italian-speaking Swiss nationals.

In keeping with Nevada's demographic composition during the 1870s, the state labor market evinced a rigid segmentation along ethnic and racial lines, confirmed by the US Census reports for that period. Accordingly, Nevada's variegated workplace revealed the following trends: although oversimplified, one can see the French Canadians specialized in cutting forests, the Chinese were expert railroad builders, the Irish and the Cornish extracted most of the ore, the French and Spanish Basques roamed Nevada's pastures herding sheep, and the Italians and the Swiss produced charcoal.

The previously cited *L'Eco d'Italia* letter, authored by an Italian immigrant engaged as a miner at Treasure City, about forty miles southeast of Eureka, provides an informative glimpse into what might have been the dynamics of Italian settlement in this remote region of the western frontier. According to the letter, a small but rather prosperous group of Italian investors had already acquired parcels of local real estate on which they planned to "build hotels, restaurants, and grocery stores." Given Treasure City's geographical vicinity to booming Eureka, it is easy to imagine a similar Italian business community operating there as well.

With an international business community already established in its midst, Eureka possessed a natural advantage over less pluralistic districts. Thus, Eureka's need for specialized labor from overseas could have been effectively negotiated through local business leaders who had direct ties with their respective countries of origin on the European continent. Shepperson remarked that these foreign-born successful businessmen played important roles since they not only promoted the emigration of their co-nationals but also gave them work.[2] The symbiotic relationship that developed between these labor brokers and their recruits became known as the *padrone system*.

Still other Italian immigrants reached Eureka by the conventional system of chain immigration, whereby an already established family member would invite a next of kin to join him in the new country. Such was the case of Bernardo Merialdo, born in 1857 in Genoa, Italy, who arrived in Eureka in March 1878. Bernardo came at the call of his older brother, who had already made the journey in 1872 and had settled successfully in Eureka. Before immigrating to America, Bernardo held a job in a Genoese tannery where he earned a monthly wage equivalent to $7.50. In Eureka, the older brother procured Bernardo a job that earned him $2.00 a day, a remarkable pay by the Italian standards of that time.[3]

Many other Italian family sagas unfolded similarly during Eureka's early years, as corroborated by Estelle Genzoli, descendant of Eureka's Italians, in a 1992 interview.[4] Industrious Italians could be found in a wide variety of occupations, ranging from ranching to saloon keeping. Indeed, some of the Italian pioneers played such a pivotal role in Eureka's early development that eventually their identities merged with local history. In time, the names of Italian pioneer families such as the Biales, Rogantinis, Ratazzis, de Paolis, Pastorinos, Gibellinis, Dameles, and Rebaleatis became household names in Eureka County, inextricably woven within the fiber of Eureka's past, with their descendants still an integral part of the modern community.

Fortuitously, a thorough historical account of Eureka's early history was compiled in 1879 by Lambert Molinelli, a Eureka resident, real estate agent, and Italian immigrant. Conceived primarily as a promotional publication, *Eureka and Its Resources* represents a valuable historical resource. Although replete with commercially oriented exaggerations and overly glowing prospects designed to attract new residents to Eureka and, more important, new capital, the booklet provides a detailed portrait of Eureka at the height of its prosperity in the late 1870s.[5]

Filled with fascinating accounts of the "Pittsburgh of the West," the booklet also contains an advertisement section that features some of the city's more prosperous business entities operating in Eureka by November 1879, when the book was first published. A brief survey of the commercial listings provides useful clues about Italian participation in the various mercantile enterprises. The section opens with a display for Lambert Molinelli & Co., owned by the pamphlet's author, featuring services ranging from real estate to life and fire insurance. The next Italian entry is the Garibaldi Hotel, owned by John Torre and located on Main Street. Torre is also listed as "a dealer of general merchandise, wines, liquors and cigars."

Next is the Railroad Saloon and Store, owned by Joseph Vanina and also located on Main Street. Vanina's establishment offered "all kinds of merchandise constantly on hand," while also claiming "coal contracting as a specialty." Further, the Capitol Market, on Main Street, lists joint owners P. Roberti and W. M. Sholderer. On South Main Street was to be found the photographic studio owned by Louis Monaco, dubbed by the ad as the "Old Reliable Pioneer Photographer." The section closes with an aid promoting the sale of Molinelli's *Eureka and Its Resources*.

Undoubtedly, the advertisements in Molinelli's book are not exhaustive, as other Italian-owned businesses operated in Eureka during the same period. One such establishment was Celso Tatti's saloon, on South Main Street, which would attain notoriety as the place where the controversial Eureka Charcoal Burners Protective Association first met. Also in 1877 Ferdinando Bonetti and his business partner, Gabriel Morgantini, owned and managed the Stone Saloon on Main Street. Further, as of September 1878, in the town of Alpha, about thirty-eight miles north of Eureka, an Italian entrepreneur by the name of John Canepa owned and ran the Garden City, a multipurpose establishment consisting of a general store, saloon, and hotel.[6]

The prosperity of Eureka's Italian entrepreneurship depended amply upon the multitudes of Italian immigrants who patronized the businesses run by their conationals. Facilitated by a shared language and Old World customs, it is likely that an interdependent relationship between entrepreneur and patron naturally arose. Obviously, distance from one's native soil acted as glue that bound a foreigner to other members of his nationality.

However, such a rapport, as amiable as it might have been, was by no means an egalitarian affiliation. After all, the balance of power is always tipped in favor of those endowed with the means to satisfy the wants of others.

Although late-nineteenth-century Eureka was a melting pot, spiced with a wide assortment of nationalities, the Italian community certainly figured prominently among the foreign born. The Italian immigrants and the city of Eureka came of age together. Indeed, the influx of Italians into the area was initially instigated by the sudden burst of smelting activity that occurred in the early 1870s. Eureka's rich mineral deposits of lead and silver were first unearthed in 1864, when charcoal burning was performed by native-born Americans. Once technical innovations boosted Eureka's mineral output, the need for charcoal increased.

In 1871 many charcoal producers raised their prices from thirty cents to thirty-two cents a bushel. The mining companies threatened to close the furnaces for the winter before paying what they considered the inflated price.[7] By the spring of 1872, with charcoal demand rising sharply, the Eureka Consolidated Mining Company, one of the most prominent smelters in Eureka, yielded to the higher rate. Afterward, a rancher named A. E. Davis was accorded a year's contract for three million bushels of charcoal to satisfy Eureka Consolidated's demand. In an attempt to keep charcoal production costs low, Davis intended to supplant the existing charcoal labor force with the cheaper and plentiful Chinese.[8] However, the capitalistic maneuver was met with such vehement racism by the established charcoal producers that Davis was unable to fulfill his contract. Subsequently, the persecuted Chinese laborers quickly abandoned their new enterprise, permanently forced out of Eureka's charcoal camps. Yet as late as 1877, a few lone Chinese remained engaged in the business of charcoal burning.[9]

In 1869 the transcontinental railroad was completed, releasing thousands of Chinese laborers into Nevada's labor force and provoking Anglo resentment and labor tensions throughout the region.[10] Wandering in search of renewed opportunities, many heeded the silver call that led to Eureka. By 1876 the Chinese in Eureka were the third-largest immigrant group after the British and the Italians, constituting 10 percent of the population.[11]

Amid the union fervor that swept the mining camps of the American West during the last quarter of the nineteenth century, a number of quasi-labor organizations sprang up to protect the interests of the Anglo workers, supposedly threatened by hordes of Celestials. Unexpectedly, in April 1876, shortly after the expulsion of A. E. Davis's Chinese workers, a group of Chinese woodcutters from Eureka was introduced by charcoal contractors to supply coal to the Tybo Consolidated Mining Company, in the mining community of Tybo, in Nye County. To confront what was perceived as unfair Chinese labor competition, the townspeople immediately formed the Workingmen's Protective Union of Central Nevada. Seventy of its most adamant members hastily assembled a committee and, under the cover of night, seized the Chinese competitors and expelled them from the town. Upon discovering the committee's exploit, the dismayed contractors dispatched an armed scouting party tasked with retrieving the ousted Chinese. However, the union persisted in banning the "undesirables" and issued a twenty-four-hour ultimatum to the contractors to release the Chinese from their employment.[12]

Hoping to expedite their removal, the Anglos of Tybo even provided the necessary means of transportation, incurring a cost of $165 for the rental of wagons to transport the unwanted Chinese to Eureka. The charcoal contractors finally conceded when confronted by an unwavering force of 150 armed men who threatened them with expulsion. The assertive action of the Tybo miners waged against the interests of capital not only went unpunished but even elicited praise from the community at large, which lauded the miners for their "magnanimity" in arranging for the Chinese to be transported to Eureka free of charge.[13] In order to prevent a similar conflict, an anti-Chinese club formed quickly in Eureka, where the mining companies, fearing labor troubles, negotiated an agreement with their contractors not to hire Chinese labor. The club sprang into action a few months later when it ousted Chinese graders employed at the Eureka and Palisade Railroad work site.[14] The depth of racial hatred harbored by the citizenry of Eureka toward the Chinese is bluntly revealed by a succinct commentary that appeared in the local press: "The big ditch is again becoming the receptacle for filth and debris. People who kill Chinamen, toss them over into it with no regard to the city's health."[15]

Though left to deal with an acute charcoal production vacuum, the contractors strove to ensure the stability of the price of charcoal. In their renewed attempt, they cast their sight upon another ethnic group just as hard working and cheap as the Chinese, but no doubt less despised: the

Italians. In the words of Shepperson, "The action was to prove almost too successful."[16] In 1875 systematic efforts were made to introduce large numbers of Italian immigrants to Eureka County. Presumably, such a substantial immigration movement could be greatly facilitated through the active involvement of Eureka's Italian pioneers.

Notes

1. Frederick Wallace Reichman, "Early History of Eureka County, Nevada, 1863–1890," 46. Although official historical sources to substantiate the claim that the Italian charcoal burners had brought to the forests around Eureka the century-old craft of charcoal making from their native regions in the Italian Alps are lacking, anecdotal evidence abounds. In his 1992 interview of Estelle Genzoli, descendant of Swiss Italian immigrants in Eureka, Robert D. McCracken asked her why she thought Eureka had been the preferred destination of scores of northern Italians in the second half of the nineteenth century as opposed to other ethnic groups. Genzoli replied, "Because the thing that attracted most of them was making coke [charcoal]." In addition, Genzoli stated, "Some people didn't like to do that kind of work and the Italians would." She concluded by saying, "They'd make the coke because they knew how to do it." Robert D. McCracken, "Eureka Memories: A Series of Interviews with Fourteen Individuals and Families in Eureka, Nevada, 1993," 24.

Additional corroboration is provided by Antonio J. Mendez, author and Eureka native whose ancestors hailed from the charcoal-making region in northern Italy. In his book *The Master of Disguise*, Mendez writes: "My great-grandfather, Cristoforo Giuseppe 'J. C.' Tognini, one of the legends of Nevada's gold bonanza earlier this century, had been born into a big family in the mountain town of Villa di Chiavenna in the northern Italian region of Lombardy. J. C.'s father died in 1872, and the boy struggled to help his family survive before immigrating to America at age fifteen." Mendez further states, "Somehow, he reached the United States and traveled west to Nevada to join two of his brothers. J. C. already possessed a skill highly prized in mining towns: In Italy he'd begun learning the secrets of the *carbonari*, who transformed wood into the high-grade charcoal needed to fire smelters." Extolling the resourcefulness of his adventurous ancestor, Mendez elaborates further: "It was working in the mountains as a young charcoal burner for pennies a day that J. C. gained his intimate knowledge of the land forms and rock formations of Nevada. Still a teenager, J. C. headed off to seek his fortune prospecting in the Comstock Range." Antonio J. Mendez, *The Master of Disguise: My Secret Life in the CIA*, 7–8.

Further evidence that charcoal making was typical in the region where the Eureka charcoal burners originated is provided by Douglas William Freshfield, English mountaineer and author. In recounting his traveling experiences across the Swiss-Italian Alpine landscape of Val Verzasca, Swiss Canton Ticino, Freshfield wrote, "The natives we met, a strong, wild-looking race, were all stone-quarries, woodmen, or charcoal-burners." Farther along his wanderings in the Val Saviore region of eastern Lombardy, Italy, he writes, "We reached Fresiue, a smutty charcoal-burners' hamlet on the banks of the Salarno torrent." Finally, journeying through Val Presanella, also in eastern Lombardy, he notes, "After passing a group of charcoal-burners' huts the ascent ceased." Douglas William Freshfield, *Italian Alps: Sketches in the Mountains of Ticino, Lombardy, the Trentino, and Venetia*, 32, 161, 196.

2. Shepperson, *Restless Strangers*, 30.

3. Peter B. Merialdo, *Memoirs of a Son of Italian Immigrants, Recorder and Auditor of Eureka County, Nevada State Controller, and Republican Party Worker*, 1.

4. In his 1992 interview of Genzoli, McCracken also wondered if such a large number of Italians found out about jobs in Eureka through advertisement in Italy. Genzoli replied confidently: "They didn't have to advertise...It was just by word of mouth." McCracken, "Eureka Memories," 24. Genzoli's reply, while not explicitly attesting to the existence of a padrone system in Eureka, implied a well-established network of chain immigration between Eureka's Italians and their compatriots overseas. However, given the greater expense the prospective workers would have had to pay out of pocket to reach Nevada after disembarking at one of the major eastern ports, the padrone hypothesis seems more plausible.

5. Molinelli, *Eureka and Its Resources*, 15, 26.

6. Dale E. Woolley, *The Dameles and the American Curly Horse*, 86.

7. *Sentinel*, September 17, 1871.

8. *Sentinel*, June 22, 1872.

9. *Sentinel*, March 3, 1877.

10. Elliott, *History of Nevada*, 166.

11. Winzeler and Peppin, *Eureka, Nevada*, 14.

12. *Sentinel*, March 9, April 30, May 6, 11, 1876; Richard E. Lingenfelter, *The Hardrock Miners: A History of the Mining Labor Movement in the American West, 1863–1893*, 123.

13. *Sentinel*, March 9, April 30, May 6, 11, 1876.

14. *Sentinel*, June 10, 1876, January 1, 1877.

15. *Leader*, November 19, 1878.

16. Shepperson, *Restless Strangers*, 122.

III

The Arrival of the Italian Charcoal Burners

Coaxed by *paesani* (countrymen) and padrones, a chain immigration of inflated proportions readily ensued. Yearning for gainful employment, scores of Italian laborers embarked on an uncertain journey, hoping to find work in Eureka, Nevada, where a burgeoning Italian community had taken root.

As typically happens when labor shortages are aggressively advertised, far more laborers heed the call than the needy market can absorb. The resulting labor surplus, while welcomed by employers, is resented by the local workforce, which sees its wages threatened. The sudden arrival of huge numbers of outside laborers into a recently established community tends to produce social strain and even ethnic antagonism. By March 1876, the Italian presence in Eureka County had grown so ubiquitous as to be openly characterized in contemptuous tones: "Three-fourths of the migrants coming into the area are unemployable Italians." Anticipating the discontent of the new arrivals, the *Eureka Daily Sentinel* forewarned, "There were 35 passengers on the train from Palisade last night, 26 of whom were Italian immigrants. If the latter came here looking for work we fear they will be disappointed, as there is already a large number of idle men here unable to obtain employment."[1]

Notwithstanding the volatile character of Nevada's mining economy, throngs of immigrants flocked to the Silver State. In Shepperson's words, "Despite the 'boom and bust' cycle ... the state long remained strangely attractive to the foreign born."[2] However, it is unlikely that these new Italian arrivals would have ventured so far afield, bearing the extra travel costs, unless their employment prospects were good. With so many already out of work, the stream of Italians pouring into a precarious labor market may be explained in terms of a padrone system, or some variant of it, operative in Eureka's economy.

The existence of a padrone system among Italian immigrants on the American mining frontier, though at a slightly later period than in Eureka, is corroborated by historian Thomas G. Andrews. Echoing Italian miners' discontent in regards to mine officials' hiring practices in Colorado, effected through Italian labor brokers, Andrews writes, "A large body of businessmen…have become rich by our [the Italians'] labor." Elaborating further upon the influence wielded by the presumed padrones in Las Animas, a coalfield in southern Colorado, Andrews states, "The Tarabino brothers, who were merchants and saloon owners, and John Aiello, whose diversified enterprises included a bank, a saloon, and a general store, played pivotal roles in bridging the distance between a handful of southern Italian villages and Las Animas." According to Andrews, the enterprising role of labor contractors finds ample support in the "naturalization records and oral histories" of scores of immigrants attesting to "the importance of ethnic mediators between the demand of Colorado coal-mining companies for labor and the supply of work seekers in the labor hinterlands."[3]

Yet business was good. Despite lingering economic stagnation, 1877 witnessed an upsurge of charcoal manufacturing due to an increase of smelting activity. Hints of future prosperity for the community of Eureka surfaced as early as January 14, when the *Sentinel* made the following announcement: "All matters pertaining to mining have moved along satisfactorily, and the general outlook of the district is very promising. Our leading mines never looked better or gave more evidence of depth and permanency than at present time."

The *Sentinel* of May 2, 1877, declared that "sixty tons of ore were delivered at the Richmond works yesterday," while on the same day "twenty car loads of contracted ore were delivered at the Eureka furnace." About a month later, it was announced that the ore dumps at the reduction works of Eureka Consolidated were overflowing.[4] Smelting production at the Richmond Company continued to grow due to an abundance of ore, and on September 24 the company started up a new furnace.[5] In turn, the charcoal industry began to rebound, spawning greater employment opportunities for prospective charcoal burners. That the pace of charcoal production was quickening was corroborated by the following ad: "Coal Burners: By reference to advertisement in another column, it will be seen that twenty-five men can find employment as coal burners by applying to W.C. Reveal, at Bishop & Carpenter's stable."[6]

A newspaper article from May 1877 underscored the resurgence of the charcoal trade: "A team, belonging to Geo. Lamoureux and loaded with 40,000 pounds of charcoal, passed through town yesterday, en route to the Richmond. It is claimed to be the largest load ever hauled into Eureka. The outfit comprises 18 mules and four wagons."[7] Further proof that the charcoal industry was steadily recovering its health was provided by the *Sentinel* on September 15: "The amount of charcoal consumed daily at the furnaces in the district will reach, at the present date, close to 10,000 bushels. This amount will be largely increased as the idle furnaces resume operations." As the year progressed, charcoal production appeared to remain stable: "Pete Hanson [sic], of Pine Station [outside Eureka], informed us yesterday that the coal-burners of that locality were again starting to burn coal, and that there would be a large amount of charcoal made in a few weeks. We [the editors] infer from this that the coal-burners have faith that the furnaces here will be kept running during the winter months."[8]

The economic recovery did little to improve the lives of the charcoal burners. Instead, they were met with an exploitative labor system, low wages, unscrupulous business practices, miserable working and living conditions, and ethnic hostility. This left them vulnerable to the economic downturn that hit Eureka by 1879. Crucial to Eureka's economy, charcoal production required a specialized contract-labor workforce, unavailable locally.

The charcoal manufacturing process entailed cutting the wood, burning it, and sacking the finished product. The meager price the burners commanded for their commodity hardly represented a living wage.[9] By 1879 the plight of the charcoal burners, now numbering about three thousand men,[10] was growing bleaker by the day, while the community around them seemed to grow more opulent than ever. Despite increased labor exertion by the burners to procure timber at ever-increasing distances, the average price for charcoal was only 25 cents a bushel, amounting to a wage of less than a $1 a day for the burners, or less than half that received by mine laborers.

To make matters worse, the 25 cents per bushel paid for charcoal was not the actual amount received by each, but, rather, it was the price smelters paid to the freighting companies for hauling the charcoal directly to the furnaces. In turn, the teamsters who delivered the charcoal would pay the charcoal manufacturer, the owner of the kiln, an average of 13 cents a bushel, an amount from which the charcoal burners finally derived their wages. Although the charcoal burners' meager daily earnings amounted to scarcely half of what even the lowest-paid mine laborer earned, such starvation wages were nonetheless attractive to the burners, for they surpassed the average wage in Italy at the time manifold.[11]

Iniquity was ingrained into the system. While the teamsters earned an average of $4.60 per day,[12] almost five times the amount earned by the average burner, their employers, the contractors who actually owned the freight business, profited handsomely from the charcoal trade. Though not accounting for the capital invested, the supplies used, and the labor employed, the freighting companies reaped a gross daily income of roughly $1,300. This estimate is based on a daily average charcoal supply of ten thousand bushels consumed by Eureka's smelters.

The charcoal burners' earnings were further diluted by an intrinsically flawed system of payment, consisting of a combination of monetary remuneration and credit. Accordingly, a percentage of their wages was issued in the form of purchase orders redeemable for consumer goods only at predetermined commercial outlets in Eureka.[13] Clearly, the issuance of bills of goods for the procurement of the essential provisions amounted to a deliberately orchestrated system of graft. Because creditors could view impoverished burners as high risk, charging them higher prices could seem justified. After all, the burners were at the bottom of the local economy, the most likely casualties in a marketplace perennially in flux, where even the slightest shift could spell financial hardship. The difficulty remained, however, in determining what constituted a fair profit.

The outcome of this arrangement was that Eureka charcoal burners were routinely overcharged at the mercantile establishments manned by their presumed padrones, where food prices ran as high as double the actual price paid by the store owner.[14] Thus, many burners sank inexorably into debt. Had the charcoal burners been shielded from such an exploitative and unscrupulous practice and been allowed to enjoy the fruits of their toil, the despair that vexed their lives might have dissipated harmlessly rather than hardening with the passage of time.

The town's merchants were not the only ones who preyed upon the Italian charcoal burners. In fact, both the teamsters and the smelter operators readily seized the chance to further their economic interests at the charcoal burners' expenses. Unwilling to negotiate directly with the charcoal producers, thus precluding the possibility of obtaining the commodity at an even lower price, the smelter operators dealt exclusively with the teamsters, the recipients of the charcoal contracts. Not only did the teamsters hold a virtual monopoly over the hauling of charcoal to the smelters, but they also exerted much influence upon its price.

Excluded from the straightforward process of negotiating with the smelter operators, the charcoal burners grew increasingly suspicious of the secretive relationship between the teamsters and the smelter operators. The burners' suspicion stemmed primarily from their inability to examine the shipping invoices, which the teamsters refused to disclose.[15]

Not only did the burners object to the secrecy surrounding the shipping of charcoal, but they also distrusted the methods used by the teamsters to measure the quantities of charcoal delivered to the smelters. The precarious business transaction between the charcoal burners and the teamsters started and ended at the charcoal loading site, either at the kiln or at the earthen pit where the charcoal was produced. Here, the charcoal was loaded onto the wagons, either in bulk or in gunnysacks, by the burners themselves. However, the weighing of the charcoal took place at the smelter site, unsupervised by the charcoal burners.

Further, confusion regarding the system of measuring charcoal was widespread throughout the charcoal-producing regions of the West. The lack of a clearly defined standard of measuring charcoal was particularly lamented by the charcoal and furnace men of Inyo County, who, in apparent distress, contacted members of the industry in Darwin and Eureka to ascertain the number of cubic inches constituting a bushel of charcoal or the exact size of a box that would contain ten bushels. Eager to address the issue raised by Inyo coal and furnace men, the *Eureka Daily Sentinel* reported about the system of measuring coal employed at Eureka Consolidated, where "a box holding 82 bushels is used in measuring from the cars," whereas "in unloading from teams at the rack, a box, two feet square, holding eight cubic feet or five bushels of charcoal, is used instead." Probing further the methodology used to calculate the amount of coal, the newspaper stated, "There are 2,748 cubic inches in a bushel of coal, and although not exactly correct, a box 34 inches square and 24 inches deep will hold ten bushels near enough for all practical purposes."[16]

Eventually, on February 26, 1879, a law designed to remedy the flaws inherent in the measuring of charcoal was approved by Nevada governor John H. Kinkead, bringing about the standardization of that crucial unit of measurement and thus accurately determining a bushel of charcoal at 2,747 cubic inches.[17] Upon arrival at the smelter, after each charcoal shipment had been weighed, the smelter operators issued the teamsters a receipt attesting to the specific quantity of merchandise received and the amount of money paid for it. Subsequently, the teamsters proceeded to pay the charcoal producers what can only be termed a "discretionary" sum of money. The circumstances were further complicated by rumors that the teamsters paid bribes to the smelters to keep charcoal prices unchanged.

Obviously, the questionable practices employed by the teamsters would have raised the suspicions of any alert partner, regardless of background or profession. Although the vast majority of the charcoal burners were humble folks, illiterate in both Italian and English, they certainly did not lack the practical intelligence to realize the illegitimacy of the teamsters' deceptive scheme.

The natural circumstances regulating the manufacturing of charcoal induced the charcoal burners to dwell outdoors, in makeshift camps in close proximity to the sources of timber, and under extremely harsh and primitive living conditions. An insightful description of the typical charcoal burner's dwelling was provided by an article published in 1852 in the magazine *Knickerbocker*: "little, miserable burrows made of sticks and turf, which they dignify with the name of 'houses,' but which look more like the den of some mammoth rabbit than anything else."[18] As no remnants of burner-dwelling structures, indicative of stable shelters, have been found in the charcoal camps around Eureka, one can surmise that the above depiction fits the bleak setting inhabited by the Italian *carbonari*.

Engaged in an ever-expanding race for timber to transform into charcoal, the burners first felled the mature pine-nut trees, which would then be burned in earthen pits, that is, primitive charcoal-making technology. Once this first choice resource became exhausted, the burners turned to dwarf cedar, juniper, and black mahogany to produce their charcoal. However, the latter trees required higher burning temperatures before turning into charcoal, for which, following their age-old tradition, the Italian *carbonari* in Eureka constructed slate stone kilns of varying sizes. The beehive-shaped charcoal kilns built by the Italians around Eureka exhibited a sophisticated craftsmanship.

Availing themselves of the slate fragments that dotted the hilly landscape, they erected stony structures infused with much aesthetic appeal. The mortar employed to hold the stones together was made of clay. To scale the rising kiln during its construction, slate steps were strategically placed around the stony outer shell at varying heights. Not only did these small slate platforms protruding from the external walls enable the kiln builders to climb farther, but they also provided access to vents through which the burners could regulate the kiln's internal temperature more safely and more effectively than the pit.[19]

A few stone kilns can still be found strewn around the hills of Eureka, silent reminders of an era gone by. One of the best-preserved stone kilns, built by Italian charcoal burners in the early days of the charcoal industry, is located on the western slope of Diamond Mountain, near Sheep Canyon, in Diamond Valley. Emerging from the engulfing brush, this stony monument, rising skyward like a cathedral in the wilderness, still radiates the artistic sensibility of the masons who crafted it. Forced to endure the hardships imposed by primitive living conditions when charcoal production temporarily ceased, the burners found shelter from the elements in these stone kilns, which became relatively comfortable dwellings.

Making charcoal with a stone kiln was definitely preferable to making it in a pit. Managing a stone kiln was much easier and safer for the burners, and the final product was of superior quality. Further, a kiln, though initially more expensive than a pit, could be used repeatedly and produced charcoal in less time. Transforming wood into charcoal, a process that in nature would be achieved over millennia, could be accomplished in a stone kiln in just a few days. The inherent advantages afforded by a charcoal kiln over an earthen pit were stated in an article titled "Charcoal Kilns" published on August 31, 1877, by the *Eureka Daily Sentinel*: "A great economy of time is gained by using these kilns instead of burning in the old-fashioned way [earthen pits].... [Kiln owners] calculate on their fuel costing them about one half of the usual rates." In addition to yielding charcoal of superior quality, the productivity of stone kilns was 15 to 20 percent greater than that obtained from the earthen pits.[20]

However, whenever building a stone kiln was infeasible, burners would build pits of varying sizes. Although initially they dug a pit only a few feet deep, eventually it evolved into a mound built on flat ground in which burners carefully placed wood either vertically or horizontally. At the center of the pit, rising about three feet aboveground, the burners erected a chimney.[21] The largest pit could hold as much as one hundred cords of wood, generating about two thousand bushels of charcoal. After being smothered with earth, the pit would be lit and allowed to burn for fifteen to twenty days.[22]

In their detailed history of charcoal, *The Soul of Fire*, John Uhlmann and Peggy Heinrich emphasize that burning charcoal in a pit was a complex activity that demanded much expertise and keen alertness: "The need to seal any cracks that developed in the shrinking, shifting mass presented still another hazard, for it was necessary to climb on the pit to look for soft spots, known as 'mulls.' If any were found, the burner 'jumped the pit,' jumping up and down on solid parts of the pile to force the mull closed. Knowing how and when to walk on the huge mound was an art in itself and many a man fell through into the furnace-like heat."[23]

A cursory glance at the newspapers of the period reveals that charcoal burning was indeed a dangerous activity and that work-related accidents were frequently lethal. On November 27, 1878, the *Eureka Daily Leader* carried a grisly headline that announced the death of a forty-five-year-old Italian coal burner named Giovana Angelo Margorali two days earlier. On the night of the twenty-fifth, the victim, presumably in the employ of Joseph Tognini, was watching a smoldering coal pit seven miles from Joe Winzell's ranch, west of Mineral Station. Apparently, Margorali perished as he endeavored to extinguish a fire that had engulfed the coal. The body was discovered the next morning amid the live coals by John Eseere, a coworker. Attempting to pull Margorali out of the fiery pit, Eseere grasped the man's legs, causing the roasted flesh to peel away from the bones. The body was charred beyond recognition. As if to dramatize the hazard of charcoal burning, the paper reported that the heat was so intense that it partially melted the few coins the deceased had in his pocket.

The quantity of charcoal was further determined by weather conditions and wood varieties. Ordinarily, trees intended for charcoal making were harvested and corded in the winter months to be smoldered in summer. In the event circumstances required that charcoal be burned in winter, a higher percentage of wood had to be sacrificed to compensate for the colder temperatures outside the kiln or pit.[24]

Charcoal production was also affected by the varieties of wood available for the manufacturing process. While charcoal has always been made with any type of wood that was readily available, hardwoods such as beech, oak, hickory, maple, ash, and fruitwoods are best suited. On the Nevada frontier, where timber was very scarce, charcoal was obtained from virtually anything the landscape provided, including piñon, pine, juniper, mountain mahogany, and even sagebrush.[25]

If charcoal manufacturing was a potentially risky activity for the burners who produced the vital commodity, transporting the finished product to the distant furnaces was not without its hazards. Instances of full-blown conflagrations engulfing entire carloads of charcoal on their way to market were certainly not uncommon. Uhlmann and Heinrich recount that "before taking off to celebrate the end of a long watch, a group of Nevada burners hitched their wagonloads and four-mule team near their cabins. Returning, they found not only their loads and mules reduced to ashes but their entire campground as well. One such occurrence was reported on the outskirts of Eureka as well."[26]

Transporting charcoal by rail, though more expeditious, often entailed the same risks. In this regard the *Sentinel* of April 5, 1877, reported: "One of Pete Hansen's coal cars, attached to the regular train, was discovered to be on fire Sunday evening just as the train was entering the mouth of Eureka canyon. After ineffectual efforts to extinguish the fire, the train men were forced to cut loose from the passenger and baggage car, and good time was made to the first water tank, and deluging it with the contents, the fire was finally subdued. About two hundred bushels of coal were consumed, and the car was badly burned."

Feeling unwelcome and viewed with suspicion by the townspeople, the charcoal burners inclined to live isolated in the safety of the wilderness, in the company of their own kind. This only furthered their alienation. Speaking a foreign language and practicing foreign customs, the forest dwellers elicited incomprehension and distrust from the host community. As pointed out by Rolle, mere "differentness," especially in the use of foreign speech, was one of the central elements that elicited intolerance among nativists in America, both in the East and in the West.[27]

Clearly, some of the hostility harbored against the Italian charcoal burners of Eureka can be understood as a defensive reaction by an overanxious community that felt threatened by a tidal wave of outsiders rather than as an indictment of their nationality. Yet Eureka was not immune to the antiforeign hysteria common during the latter part of the nineteenth century. Eureka was influenced by the alarmist warnings echoing from the East, where older-stock Americans agitated for stronger restrictions on Asian and south-central European immigrants, whose growing numbers allegedly threatened Anglo-Saxon dominance.

The magnitude of ethnic prejudice felt toward the ordinary Italian of Eureka was unambiguously exhibited by the Oliver Stewart affair in October 1875. Stewart was a nine-year-old boy who said an Italian shot at him for no apparent reason while he was playing near his Pinto home. Infuriated by the alleged audacity of the Italian, the boy's mother immediately confronted and detained the stunned stranger at gunpoint until the local lawmen arrived on the scene and arrested him. After a fourteen-mile walk over the mountains, the presumed culprit was lodged in the Eureka jail. Subsequently, a stiff bail of two thousand dollars was issued, and the poor foreigner, unable to buy his freedom, languished in jail for weeks.[28]

Eventually, the falsehood of the boy's accusation was proved, and the Italian was released.[29] Although dismissed as a childish prank by some, this episode demonstrates how deeply entrenched ethnic prejudice was in Eureka. Indeed, so pervasive was the intolerance for foreigners that even a child could tap the reservoir of bigotry and hatred that flowed just beneath the surface of the community.

Typical of the boomtowns that sprang up almost overnight across the frontier, Eureka lacked a stable societal structure. Hastily built and boasting one of the highest immigrant populations in the entire West, of which 15 percent were Italians, Eureka was a simmering ethnic caldron. In Eureka, as throughout the western frontier, violence was often viewed as a legitimate and efficient means by which to expeditiously restore a disrupted social order. Indeed, force was often invoked as an expedient shortcut to justice, as confirmed by the pervasiveness of the phenomenon of vigilantism throughout the frontier. Eureka boasted its own local chapter, known as the Vigilante Committee 601.[30] The three-digit term was commonly used to designate vigilance committees.

In May 1874 Gus Botto, an Italian gambler and real estate agent who had resided in Eureka since 1871, shot and killed Johnny Brannan in a Eureka saloon over a debt of two dollars. Jailed briefly, he bought his way out of trouble by paying his victim's funeral expenses and was not prosecuted.[31] According to the obituaries published in the *Pioche Daily Record*, Johnny Brannan "made money fighting in saloons."[32] Then, four years later and roughly a year before the shooting at Fish Creek erupted, on the evening of April 6, 1878, Botto was killed at the hand of Jesse Bigelow, proprietor of the Bigelow Opera House in Eureka. Following a misunderstanding over seat reservations for the evening show, Bigelow shot Botto five times, the last two bullets fired at close range, execution style, as Botto lay on the floor.[33]

The trial that followed galvanized the entire community, and Bigelow was acquitted. The *Eureka Daily Leader* of September 7, 1878, carried an illuminating report that perhaps demonstrates the existence of a legal bias against some of Eureka's Italians. While sentencing an Italian named Prini in a later case, Judge Cole seized the opportunity to express his strong views regarding the recent Bigelow trial. The judge stated that by acquitting Jesse Bigelow, the jury had let him escape justice, adding that the preponderance of the evidence in that case had clearly warranted a conviction. In handing down the sentence on Prini, Judge Cole reiterated that "others, no less guilty, had...gone scot free."

Italians differed from Eureka's American population significantly enough to command recognition as a distinct group. Clear evidence that Italians were perceived as a category apart stems from the Wells Fargo list of mail recipients published in the local newspapers as the "Italian list."[34] Whether prejudicial or not, the ethnic distinctiveness of the Italians seems widespread in a newspaper report that branded a destitute family compelled to beg for food on the streets of Gold Hill and Virginia City, to the west of Eureka, subsequently arrested for soliciting, as an "Italian family."[35]

Some facets of the Italians' distinctive character were self-created as an expression of their ethnicity. Thus, the emergence of establishments denoting "Italianness," such as the "Italian Saloon" and the "Italian Ranch,"[36] could be understood as a pathway through which the ill-adjusted immigrant could diminish that pervasive feeling of anonymity experienced in the midst of a culturally alien landscape.

In 1878 Eureka housed six smelters, which collectively fed sixteen furnaces.[37] Operating in concert, the sixteen smelting chambers converted sixteen thousand bushels of charcoal into heat-generating energy each day.[38] The two major smelters alone, the Eureka and the Richmond, consumed a rather equal share of about 60 percent of the total charcoal supply.[39]

The impact upon the forested landscape around Eureka was inexorable. Vast amounts of timber were needed to keep pace with the charcoal demand. The harvesting of ten to twelve acres of a typical forest produced only about one hundred cords of raw wood,[40] which, after being smothered in a charcoal pit or kiln, yielded roughly three thousand bushels of charcoal, enough fuel to "roast" about a hundred tons of Eureka ore. Inevitably, Eureka's forested surroundings grew thinner with each smelting day, widening the treeless radius from twenty miles, as reported in 1874, to thirty-five miles by 1878.[41]

Indeed, by 1879 Eureka's economic equilibrium was threatened by the growing scarcity of timberland. The charcoal burners were thus compelled to wander farther away in search of new wooded land. This added movement also entailed the opening of a network of intersecting new trails and roads through which the timber could be hauled to the charcoal kilns or burning pits for treatment. With the new charcoal camps established farther away, the hauling distance increased proportionally, averaging about forty miles from the charcoal manufacturing site to the smelters in Eureka. Naturally, these added exertions of labor in the production and transport of charcoal would be predictably reflected by a higher price for the commodity, thus impacting the charcoal-based industry.

Eureka's major smelters, challenged by higher fuel costs coupled with a moderate decline in mining, sought to curb their losses. Powerless to determine the price paid for silver to compensate for higher production costs, the smelters would be forced to bear the increased costs themselves. Yet the smelters soon realized that what they confronted was not merely a temporary market anomaly but rather an economic trend likely to become more severe as a result of an ever-diminishing resource vital to their industry.

Contending with the certainty of future increases in the cost of charcoal, on the one hand, and the typical uncertainty endemic to the marketplace, on the other, the smelters faced a serious dilemma. Wishing to retain ample latitude to protect stockholders' dividends while securing a reliable charcoal supply, superintendent Richard Rickard's double-edged strategy of paying a "going price" for charcoal yet also being willing to purchase the commodity when offered at lower rates than the "going price" made definite business sense.[42] With the entire smelting industry paying a standard price in a provisionally charcoal-glutted market, no competitor could accrue an unfair advantage by paying less than the prevailing charcoal price. In other words, all smelters would collectively absorb the higher costs for charcoal without favoring any competing interest.

Nonetheless, an increase in charcoal price was a matter of careful calibration, for the price of a market commodity must always remain competitive. In the eventuality that the price of charcoal, concomitantly with hauling costs, rose beyond the going price, the market almost invariably would have engendered adaptive measures to stabilize itself. Indeed, once a commodity exceeds the price the market is willing to pay, strong economic incentives are created for the introduction of more affordable alternatives.

Searching for a way out of their economic dilemma, Eureka's smelters contemplated the possibility of supplanting charcoal with coke, the solid product resulting from the distillation of coal in an oven. The promising use of coke in the smelting process had been considered years earlier but was deemed overly expensive compared to an abundant and cheap supply of charcoal. However, fearing future charcoal scarcity and confronted by imminent price hikes, the smelting industry was eager to reconsider the use of coke, hoping for a money-saving conversion.

In fact, concrete steps were taken by Eureka's smelters to test the feasibility of coke as a more efficient alternative source of fuel. As reported by the *Eureka Daily Leader* on June 27, 1879, "four carloads" of the surrogate substance were delivered to the Richmond site to carry out a preliminary trial. Aware of the exorbitant cost of coke from past experience, Richmond utilized coke sparingly and in conjunction with charcoal, hoping in this way to lessen its dependency upon a diminishing and costly resource. Foreseeing escalating charcoal prices, the Eureka smelting industry's experimentation with the promising substitute remained ongoing.

Seeking to contain rising operating costs, in February 1879 smelters' owners even contemplated substituting the means of transportation by which the charcoal would be delivered to the furnaces. A proposal was circulated to replace the shipping services provided by the teamsters with the cheaper hauling afforded by the railroad. Although this tentative strategy would have certainly advanced the particular economic interests of the smelting industry, it would have entailed much broader and damaging repercussions upon the entire district's economy.[43]

The feasibility of utilizing the railroad as a means of transporting mineral ore had been demonstrated as early as 1875 when a narrow-gauge railroad had been built to transport ore from the mines around Ruby Hill, a town located two miles west of Eureka, to the smelters in Eureka.[44] Further rail development within the same mining district was contemplated two years later, as reported by the *Sentinel* on September 15, 1877: "Proposed Connection—The railroad Company are figuring on the cost of connecting the new Matamoras furnace with the Ruby Hill road. A short branch would enable them to deliver the ore from Ruby Hill to the works at a much less figure than the expense entailed by wagon transportation, and also prove a convenience in receiving charcoal."

Indeed, the prospect of switching to railroad transport for the delivery of charcoal to the smelters was gaining increasing acceptability, as indicated by the *Sentinel* in January 1877: "Delivered by Rail—Charcoal is now being delivered at the bins of the Richmond Company by rail, the coal cars are brought close to the dumps and emptied in a very expeditious manner."[45]

Already threatened by the extension of the railroad lines for the transportation of ore from the mines to the furnaces, the freight business, which included two prominent Italian contractors, Joseph Tognini and Joseph Vanina, naturally perceived a prospective increase in the price of charcoal as an additional detriment that might further stimulate the expansion of railroad transport. But the freight business represented a considerable part of Eureka's economy, as another *Sentinel* article from January 1877, titled "Hauling Charcoal Exclusively," pointed out: "90 wagons, 360 animals and

30 teamsters are steadily engaged, and the capital invested will reach $80,000. These are employed in hauling directly to the furnaces, and do not include the teams that deliver the charcoal to different points on the railroad for transportation to Eureka.... [W]e find that the various branches give direct employment to 200 men, while as many more derive their support indirectly from the same industry."[46]

Though the rail transport challenged the freighting business, support for the Eureka teamsters predominated. As the *Sentinel* pointed out:

> The wage paid to the employees finds its way into circulation in the community, and the supplies needed, and repairs necessary, support the artisan, enrich the merchant and create a demand for the farmer's products. We are indebted to the fact that Eureka is a terminal point, and not a way station, for a large portion of this trade; and the advocates of the further extension of the narrow-gauge will find that the withdrawal of the freighting business will strand us high and dry on the shores of dullness...cut[ing] off a traffic that is a large element in our standing as a flourishing community.[47]

The *Sentinel* article favored a more balanced distribution of the community's economic opportunities, a stance that transcended the conventional tenets of laissez-faire capitalism. Although transporting charcoal to the furnaces by rail could have been expanded, thus promoting competition, the business sector opted to protect its sectarian interests by backing the freighting industry. While teamsters could haul charcoal with greater efficiency on land routes, shipping charcoal by rail enabled greater quantities to be delivered far more rapidly than the slow-moving teams. Because anything shipped by rail had to be moved by teamsters before and after the journey, an increase in rail transport would boost the freighting system. However, advocates for the freighters acknowledged that not all economic decisions made by a community must adhere to the economic laws of supply and demand.

Indeed, it was readily recognized that the elimination of the teamsters' business would have resulted in a greater loss of consumer revenues to the local economy than it would have accrued from the economic activities transferred to the railroad company. The community-wide rejection of the rail expansion plan revealed a remarkable level of public awareness about the inner workings of the economic engine and the roles played therein by its moving parts. By extension, such a keen collective understanding of economic principles must have also conditioned the civic perception of the plight of the charcoal burners, economic casualties within a fiercely competitive marketplace.

While the Richmond Company was wrestling with the charcoal prices on September 27, 1878, a disastrous fire destroyed three hundred thousand bushels of coal, causing extensive damage to the property. According to the detailed account furnished by the *Eureka Daily Leader*, the fatal spark presumably originated from the forges in the blacksmith shop, and from there the conflagration spread rapidly and engulfed most of the adjacent wooden buildings. The fire also devoured a three-hundred-foot portion of the railroad trestlework. A moderate estimate placed the damage to the building and machinery at fifty thousand dollars and the coal at one hundred thousand dollars. Unfortunately, the property destroyed was uninsured, resulting in a total loss.[48] Subsequently, the Richmond stock dropped substantially in value on the London Stock Market, from fifty-five to forty-five dollars a share.[49]

In spite of the disaster, the *Leader* issued a commentary redolent of boosterism about the presumed impact. "The catastrophe is an unfortunate one for the town, and while it will not effect [*sic*] our prosperity to any great extent, [it] will throw a number of men temporarily out of work. The force of miners employed at the mine will be decreased for a time.... No definite information as to the future intentions of the company can be learned at present.... If the company decides to rebuild at once, and push operations with vigor, no great harm will be done."[50]

However, the newspaper also expressed concern that the company's dissenting faction back in London would seize upon the disaster to further their ulterior ends. In fact, the detractors had been clamoring to shut down both the refinery and the smelting works, claiming that the ores could be shipped to San Francisco, where they could be reduced at a significantly lower cost. Even though the fire had spared most of the machinery and the facilities for working the ores, the gloomy prospect that the Richmond would be shut down hung over the town like an impending storm for some time. However, admitting that under the competent management of Edward Probert the Richmond Company had reaped handsome dividends, the majority of the company's shareholders renewed their endorsement of the effective manager, and, to the delight of the town, the company rebuilt its damaged structures and resumed operations. And only two days after the disastrous fire, the Richmond started receiving substantial deliveries of coal, as indicated by the following entry published in the *Leader* on September 29: "J. Vanini [sic] has contracted with Geo. W. Lamoureux to deliver 500,000 bushels of coal at the Richmond Company's furnaces."

An already fragile charcoal-teamster-smelter system was made even more precarious by a widespread economic slump, and by the summer of 1879 Eureka was afflicted by general discontent. The local press gave voice to the somber mood by describing it as "dull times."[51] The morbid signs of depression were all too visible in the local real estate market, temporarily glutted by a property surplus whereby numerous houses and mines were for sale but without buyers.[52] Unemployment rates were also alarmingly high, with "at least 500 idle men" out of a total workforce ranging from fifteen to eighteen hundred—or a staggering 27 to 33 percent of the total labor force.[53]

Indeed, idleness was a palpable reality throughout Eureka County, concealing a muted anxiety about an uncertain future. Townsfolk were unaccustomed to witnessing widespread joblessness in Eureka, which had generally been a prosperous center of mining. News of Eureka's hard times had spread across the state, as attested by the *Reno Daily State Journal*: "Eureka just now is a good place to keep away from."[54] Sensing a protracted crisis, even Eureka's women of ill repute were abandoning the ailing town in considerable numbers in search of greener pastures elsewhere, because "business was too light in Eureka."[55]

Curiously, in the late 1870s the economic variables influencing the market price of charcoal seemed to contradict those fundamental principles thought to regulate the marketplace. Reportedly, the median price for charcoal in 1874 had been 30 cents a bushel. Although demand for charcoal after that year steadily increased due to significant expansion in smelting activity, and even though charcoal production and hauling costs rose as the sources of timber grew more distant from the smelters, by 1877 the price of charcoal had dropped to 25 cents a bushel.[56] While a portion of the price reduction could be explained by the charcoal merchants paying the burners less to offset the higher hauling costs, many blamed the sluggish economy.

Yet such a substantial drop could not be attributed solely to a stagnant mining economy. After all, 1878 was Eureka's peak year when ore production reached 120,161 tons, generating a gross yield of $5,316,079. Though the following year was marked by a drop of less than 10,000 tons in ore production, 1879 was still the second most productive year in the county's history.[57] According to historian Stanley W. Paher, Eureka's smelting activity peaked in 1880 when 1.25 million bushels of charcoal were consumed.[58]

The insidious cause of the charcoal price plummeting inexorably was overproduction. Indeed, the existence of a substantial surplus of charcoal, created by the burners' relentless production, enabled the Richmond to rapidly replenish its coal bins following the disastrous fire. The oversupply of fuel available for smelting Eureka's ores obviously relieved some of the external pressure exerted by the charcoal industry upon the smelters. Reportedly, the volume of the surplus available on the market four days before the charcoal dispute erupted at Fish Creek on August 18, 1879, was large enough to satisfy the smelters' needs for the following six months.[59]

The charcoal burners compounded their economic woes by flooding the market with charcoal quantities far in excess of the current demand. Thus, the market value of the burners' commodity was destined to drop proportionally to the growing supply. With the availability of a vast backlog of charcoal at depressed prices, the burners were headed deeper into debt. Unaware of their contribution to the cruel cycle and thinking their only option to be continued production, the burners persevered stubbornly in their own financial demise, never realizing that overproduction contributed to their crisis. By insisting on overproduction, the burners demonstrated a lack of basic understanding of those fundamental principles influencing the marketplace. Even in their eventual organized collective effort to improve their situation, they would fail to see that by regulating their production in accordance with the external demand, the value of their commodity might have stabilized itself, while their bargaining power as economic agents in the marketplace might have also increased, at least temporarily.

Apparently, since their early involvement in the charcoal trade, Eureka's burners had equated their aspired economic progress with the volume of their charcoal production, oblivious to the subtle inverse relationship that linked supply and demand. This perceived equivalency, though false, might have predisposed the burners toward their myopic and detrimental mode of production, ultimately leading them to compensate for their lack of "capital reserve" with a commodity surplus with which to confront the internal inconsistencies of a capricious market. The burners' dilemma is aptly summed up by the *Leader*: "2,000 men throng the coal districts, destitute and starving,...who must continue to labor in the production of coal, in order to obtain food. This force, manufacturing the article much more rapidly than it is consumed, naturally overstock [sic] the market, and as they cannot employ capital to aid them in storing it, they but intensify the evil under which they groan."[60]

By contrast, the position of the smelting companies was strengthened not only by the existence of a six-month charcoal supply but, more crucially, because of the vast capital reserves they possessed. In fact, the assets controlled by the smelters would have enabled them to curtail the demand for charcoal at any time, either before or after the charcoal surplus had been exhausted. By halting smelting activities altogether, further accumulation of the superfluous commodity would have resulted, depressing charcoal prices even more. The burners' pursuit of a higher price was further thwarted by a weakening of the nation's mineral market, particularly silver and lead, Eureka's foremost commodities. Indeed, strong production disincentives vexed Eureka smelters, as attested in the local press. "The present low price of lead makes it unprofitable to ship that article," wrote the *Leader*, "and it is piled up like cordwood at the Richmond refinery, lying idle on the hands of the company." Moreover, the newspaper lamented that "the price of silver is also so low that the profits of the company are greatly reduced—so much so, in fact, that some of the stockholders are in favor of closing the mine until silver appreciates in value."[61]

Regrettably, charcoal overproduction had persisted far too long, and a glutted market had been the inevitable result. Thus confronted with a general economic depression and with mounting indebtedness, the struggling burners grew more combative.

Notes

1. *Sentinel*, March 10, 1876.
2. Shepperson, *Restless Strangers*, 13.
3. Thomas G. Andrews, *Killing for Coal: America's Deadliest Labor War*, 116–17.
4. *Sentinel*, June 21, 1877.

5. *Sentinel*, September 23, 1877.
6. *Sentinel*, April 13, 1877.
7. *Sentinel*, May 20, 1877.
8. *Sentinel*, November 14, 1877.
9. *Sentinel*, November 25, 1876.
10. *Leader*, July 9, 1879.
11. Merialdo, *Memoirs of a Son of Italian Immigrants*, 1.
12. *Sentinel*, January 14, 1877.
13. *Leader*, August 6, 1879.
14. Rolle, *Immigrant Upraised*, 93.
15. *Leader*, August 12, 1879.
16. *Sentinel*, October 7, 1877.
17. Phillip I. Earl, "Nevada's Italian War," 57.
18. Uhlmann and Heinrich, *The Soul of Fire*, 133.
19. Franklin Grazeola, "The Charcoal Burners War of 1879: A Study of the Italian Immigrant in Nevada," 29.
20. Egleston, "Manufacture of Charcoal Kilns," 374.
21. Uhlmann and Heinrich, *The Soul of Fire*, 127.
22. Nell Murbarger, "Charcoal: The West's Forgotten Industry," 5.
23. Uhlmann and Heinrich, *The Soul of Fire*, 127.
24. Ibid., 127.
25. Charles D. Zeier, "Historical Charcoal Production near Eureka, Nevada: An Archeological Perspective"; Otis E. Young, *Western Mining*, 113.
26. Uhlmann and Heinrich, *The Soul of Fire*, 130.
27. Rolle, *Immigrant Upraised*, 97.
28. *Sentinel*, October 10, 1875.
29. *Sentinel*, October 17, 1875.
30. James W. Hulse, *The Silver State: Nevada's Heritage Reinterpreted*, 109.
31. Phillip I. Earl, "Murder at the Opera House—This Was Nevada."
32. Patricia A. Scott, "Obituaries Published in the *Pioche Daily Record*, 1872–1878."
33. Earl, "Murder at the Opera House."
34. *Leader*, July 12, 1879.
35. *Leader*, August 14, 1879.
36. *Sentinel*, August 28, July 23, 1879.
37. *Leader*, November 2, 1878.
38. Nevada State Legislature, *Appendix to the Journals of the Senate and the Assembly, Ninth Session (1879): Report of the Surveyor-General and the State Land Register of the State of Nevada for the Years 1877–78*, 7.
39. Nell Murbarger, "Forgotten Industry of the Frontier," 27.
40. Ibid.
41. Nevada State Legislature, *Appendix to the Journals of the Senate and the Assembly (1875): Fifth Biennial Report of the State Mineralogist for the Years 1873–1874*, 35;

Nevada State Legislature, *Appendix to the Journals of the Senate and the Assembly, Ninth Session (1879): Seventh Biennial Report of the State Mineralogist of the State of Nevada for the Years 1877 and 1878*, 27.

42. *Leader*, July 7, 1879.
43. *Leader*, February 15, 1879.
44. Paher, *Nevada Ghost Towns and Mining Camps*, 185.
45. *Sentinel*, January 9, 1877.
46. *Sentinel*, January 14, 1877.
47. Ibid.
48. *Leader*, September 27, 1878.
49. *Sentinel*, September 30, 1878.
50. *Leader*, September 27, 1878.
51. *Sentinel*, July 8, 1879.
52. *Leader*, July 26, 1879.
53. *Leader*, July 17, 1879.
54. *Reno Daily State Journal*, July 24, 1879.
55. *Sentinel*, August 14, 1879.
56. *Sentinel*, July 25, 1877.
57. Reichmann, "Early History of Eureka County," appx. A, 119.
58. Paher, *Nevada Ghost Towns and Mining Camps*, 183.
59. *Leader*, August 14, 1879.
60. Ibid.
61. *Leader*, July 18, 1879.

IV

The Eureka Charcoal Burners Protective Association

Coerced by exploitation, the Eureka charcoal burners mustered the courage to confront the middlemen. In the summer of 1879, the lowest rung of Eureka's economy took the drastic step of founding a union. The union demanded a price of thirty cents per bushel of charcoal. The demand was hampered from the outset by conflicts, confusion, and rumor within the organization and by antiforeign bias and a lack of support for labor interests from those outside the union.

On July 6, 1879, between five and six hundred people gathered at Celso Tatti's saloon to address the crucial issue of charcoal price. This marked the burners' first organized meeting. The gathering, composed of charcoal burners, their friends, and their supporters, represented a preliminary attempt at creating the Eureka Charcoal Burners Protective Association.[1] Among them were two prominent Eureka citizens: Louis Monaco, a well-known photographer, and Lambert Molinelli, a widely admired and successful entrepreneur.

The saloon proved inadequate for the throng that congregated there. Most of them spilled onto the boardwalk and street, unable to participate directly in the event. A consensus was nonetheless reached, and Guido Bassetti was elected temporary chairman of the yet unnamed entity. During the meeting, a negotiating committee was created. Its first assignment was to convey the charcoal burners' demand for a fairer charcoal price to the smelters' superintendents, namely, Richard Rickard, of the Richmond

Mining Company, and H. Donnelly, of Eureka Consolidated, also present at the forum.[2]

Given the opportunity to express their views, both superintendents refuted the burners' request for a higher charcoal price by invoking their responsibilities to their respective companies' stockholders. Enhancing his bargaining position, Donnelly informed the assembly of his previously stipulated charcoal contracts, admitting his determination to shut down the furnaces should the previously contracted rate of twenty-five cents a bushel be rescinded. In a vain attempt to soften the superintendents' uncompromising stance, the burners upheld their inability to subsist at the current rate. Unless a higher price was established, insisted the burners, they would no longer be able to manufacture charcoal.[3]

The meeting was adjourned with the understanding that discussions between the committee and the managers would be resumed the next evening. Perhaps due to the intricacies of the first assembly, the crucial issues of smelter receipts and the problematic redemption of food orders by some local storekeepers were not discussed at that first gathering. The results of the meeting appeared in the newspaper the following day: "Mr. Rickard informed the committee that the Richmond would always pay the going price for coal, but would, in justice to the stockholders, be compelled to take coal at as low a figure as was offered by responsible sellers. Mr. Donnelly stated that he had contracted for his coal, and the furnaces would be closed unless he got it at the contract price."[4]

The superintendents' responses diverged from one another. Rickard's reply was vague, hinting at the possibility of a compromise. Although he seemed to empathize with the charcoal burners' predicament, he asserted his commitment to his stockholders, leaving open the option for his company to obtain charcoal at the lowest price available on the market. By contrast, Donnelly's reply was a categorical refusal to budge from the contracted charcoal price. To reinforce his position, he threatened a closure of the furnaces in the event the price should rise. Nonetheless, although he was upholding the sanctity of the contract, Donnelly had previously demonstrated a willingness to disregard the contract's terms when he purchased charcoal from cash-needy burners that was way below the contracted price.[5]

On the evening of July 7, a second meeting was held by the charcoal burners. This time the gathering took place at a much larger facility, Bigelow's

Eureka Opera House, a comfortable setting with a seating capacity of up to five hundred people. The exact number of participants to this second gathering is unknown. Realizing the importance of class unity for their labor cause to succeed, the union leadership created a recruitment team tasked with urging all charcoal burners to join the association. A name roster was circulated, and by evening's end six hundred new names had been added to the roll.[6]

The participants christened their union the "Eureka Charcoal Burners Protective Association." The organization would become alternatively known as the Eureka Coal Burners Association, frequently reduced to the acronyms CBPA or CBA, and it was sometimes referred to simply as "the association." Certainly, the term *protective* denoted the pragmatic purpose for which the association was created, namely, to protect the shared interests of the charcoal burners.[7]

Ironically, as if presaging future developments, several weeks before the move to unionize the burners, on April 26, 1879, the teamsters formed their own protective organization, named the Eureka Teamsters' Association. Impelled by similar sectarian interests as those proclaimed by the CBPA, the Teamsters' Association provided the following rationale for its creation: "Inasmuch as it is apparent that an effort is being made by certain parties in the town of Eureka to reduce the prices of our labor, and feeling that such effort, if successful, will prove disastrous to those engaged in the business of teaming, we solemnly pledge, upon honor, to conform to the following By-laws."[8]

The association established a scale of prices for hauling charcoal, round-trip, based on the number of days entailed. Starting at a minimum of two days, round-trip, teamsters charged six cents per bushel, raising the price by three cents thereafter up to the fourth day. Longer hauling trips were charged lower rates; thus, five days of hauling cost fourteen cents per bushel, up to a maximum of six days at fifteen cents per bushel. Members pledged not to haul charcoal at lesser prices than determined by the Eureka Teamsters' Association or pay a five-hundred-dollar fine. The roster of teamsters included, among others, future governor R. Sadler, George W. Lamoureux, J. S. Burlingame, R. E. Brown, and Joseph Vanina, later embroiled in the charcoal disputes of the summer of 1879.[9]

On July 7, the Charcoal Burners Protective Association's first administration was formed, with the following officers elected to represent the interests of the charcoal burners: president Joseph Maginni, a saloon keeper; vice president Lambert Molinelli, a department store clerk; treasurer Sol Ashim, co-owner of a clothing store; and secretary Joseph Hausman,[10] a gunsmith.[11] A number of committees were also created to perform specific tasks, including expanding the association's membership to include all the burners of the area and drafting the organization's first by-laws. Notice was also given that anyone wishing to join the association could do so by calling at Sol Ashim's store.[12]

Interestingly, none of the elected officers was a charcoal burner, yet all were presumed to be ardent sympathizers of their cause. The involvement of prominent men like Monaco and Molinelli with the affairs of their less fortunate compatriots seemed motivated by strong altruistic feelings coupled by vigorous ties of national solidarity to see the fate of their fellow conationals improve. Supposedly, once the association's framework had been established and its mission defined, the CBPA would have been able to shield its members from the oppressive conditions of the marketplace. However, this leadership team, though seemingly prompted by munificent motives, would not last. Hampered by irreconcilable ideological differences toward the aggressive tactics favored by some burners, the principled leaders eventually resigned, thus instigating a critical power vacuum that would compromise the effectiveness of the association, whose declared mission was the attainment of a living price for the charcoal the burners produced.

The newly formed association quickly adopted a resolution that no member would be allowed to sell a bushel of charcoal for less than thirty cents. Infringement of the pledge would inevitably result in a fifty-dollar fine. As if to bind the members' loyalty to the association and its cause, the assembly recited an oath pledging each union member to "demand 30 cents per bushel and prohibit delivery or sale at a less figure."[13]

The community at large learned of the burners' actions through the following press release, first published on July 9 by the *Sentinel* and circulated for ten consecutive days: "Take notice, that on and after this date, no coal will be sold to anyone by the members of the 'Eureka Coal Burners Association' unless the same is disposed of at the furnaces for the sum of Thirty cents per bushel, Eureka Coal [sic] Burners Association, Eureka, July 8, 1879." As disciplined as this effort by the association was, its actual influence could extend only to the membership of the association, thus leaving charcoal burners outside the union unaffected by the organizing effort. The association determined that its members needed to receive thirty cents per bushel in order to continue producing charcoal, and unless such a price would be acceded to, the majority of burners would quit their occupation. Although the prospect of a work stoppage would be difficult for the heavily indebted burners, they stated that "it were better to quit at once...than to continue to labor hard, with no prospect ahead but indebtedness and ruin."[14]

At the second meeting, the burners openly accused the smelting industry of being dominated by an unfair monopoly. "The entire business," the burners claimed, "is controlled by a few men." Allegedly, this small faction of entrepreneurs wielded enough power to control prices while coercing the burners to accept a substantial share of their wages in orders of goods from specific merchants in town, leading to inexorable debt, as has been demonstrated. Consequently, the unionized burners further determined that thenceforth they would accept nothing but ready money in exchange for their toil.[15]

The price question was inextricably linked to a less apparent dilemma: teamsters and smelter operators concealed the shipping receipts from the charcoal burners. Suspecting collusion involving price-fixing and weight manipulation, the burners felt ill prepared to deliberate on future charcoal prices until their suspicions had been allayed. Indeed, the intertwining nature of the two issues was confirmed, though retrospectively, in a personal conversation between G. B. Cordano, a presumed spokesperson for the burners' association, and teamster-merchant Reinhold Sadler. Cordano conveyed to Sadler that "the price was not so much, but [the burners] wanted to see the receipts."[16]

The weeks following the association's pronouncement of the thirty-cent pledge witnessed the circulation of a series of nebulous statements attributed to the mine officials. The *Leader* of July 18 reported: "The Eureka Consolidated...will now pay 30 cents per bushel for coal. This action will probably satisfy the Coalburners' Association.... The Richmond Company have contracted for a certain amount of their coal for 29 cents." Sometime later, on August 6, the same newspaper published the following: "It was erroneously reported on the streets to-day that the Consolidated had reduced their offer for coal to 25 cents per bushel." On August 11 the paper informed: "So far as the Eureka Consolidated Company is concerned, their fiat in this coal matter is that they will brook no dictation from any person or association as to where or of whom they shall purchase [coal]." In another section, the daily announced: "There is a rumor…that Manager Probert has decided to close down the Richmond furnaces."

Presumably, such conflicting assertions promoted confusion and heightened uncertainty about the burners' demands. Clearly, if disclosure of the shipping statements would have been granted in the first place, the mine companies would have had no need to resort to subterfuge. More important, the burners would have been enabled to negotiate the price of their commodity with far greater latitude, vastly increasing the probability of reaching a price compromise.

Although it appeared that agreement among the union members on the demanded price for charcoal was unanimous, it soon became evident that the accord rested on weak foundations. The pricing matter grew into a nebulous and divisive issue within the union. As reported in the *Sentinel*, the association convened on August 6 to reexamine the price question and to proceed with the nomination of the association officers. After a much-heated debate, the membership had to contend with the settling of the price issue by voting for one of two proposed options, either twenty-eight cents or thirty cents per bushel of charcoal. Ultimately, the majority of those assembled endorsed the latter.[17]

Although a palpable sense of urgency pervaded the burners' gatherings, not even the slightest intimation of adopting violence to attain their objectives ever surfaced among the assembled. Reflective of the early ineffectual efforts by workers to unionize, the association founded by the discontented burners was hampered by internal strife. While the burners endeavored to build a cohesive union, the dominance of the mining industry grew larger. Conceivably, at some stage in their struggle for a living wage, it became apparent to the burners that the institutional wheels of their association were turning all too slowly to effect the changes they sought. Perhaps it was at this point, disillusioned by the lack of rapid progress, that the more impetuous burners within the association began to ponder a more radical strategy to attain faster results.

In the six days following the announcement of the association's price demand on July 9, the local press fell silent and stopped reporting on the daily developments of the burners' affairs. Surprisingly, no editorial elaborations by either the *Leader* or the *Sentinel*, the latter being considered "the friend of the people," followed the burners' strident meetings, with all of their glaring accusations and salient demands. This was despite widespread recognition that coal manufacturing was an integral component of the county's booming economy, providing employment to about three thousand men.[18]

Considering that newspapers in the nineteenth century were predominantly owned and controlled by corporate interests,[19] the promulgation of news could be directly regulated and censored to favor the ideology espoused by the owners of the press and their allies. Although Eureka's newspapers had mainly expressed a sympathetic tone in covering the burners' struggle, developments might have reached a tipping point at which the publishers thought it expedient to stop reporting altogether, hoping in this way to induce a cooling-off hiatus. Being the earnest boosters of the camp, newspapermen endeavored to shield the reputation of the community from negative rumors, often distorting or even suppressing the truth. The fine line frontier journalists straddled has been aptly articulated by historian David Fridtjof Halaas: "These camp editors then found themselves in the uncomfortable position—whether to report accurately and combat forcefully the lawlessness that they witnessed or to ignore it."[20]

Eureka's first paper, the *Sentinel*, was created in 1870 and was managed by Dr. L. C. McKenney and A. Skillman.[21] A year later, in June 1871, due to increased readership, the *Sentinel* became a daily publication. According to Molinelli, the *Sentinel* was "democratic in politics and devoted to the advancement of local interests." Eureka's other major paper, the *Leader*, began publication in 1878 under the leadership of Fisk and Canfield. The *Leader* was characterized by Molinelli as "republican in politics, newsy, readable, and devoted to the interests of the county."[22]

Aware of the printed page's power to impact public opinion, newspaper owners on the mining frontier grappled with the challenge of providing readers with balanced reporting. Western newspapermen's "self-appointed role was to promote the camp and to convince distant readers of its boundless future.... [T]hey also had a time cherished responsibility to speak out against crime and injustice." The dilemma faced by western newspaper editors ultimately induced them to favor the publication of flattering accounts while curbing the printing of items detrimental to the community's character. After all, "to admit that violence and crime had gotten out of hand was a poor way to induce immigration or attract eastern capital."[23]

Further, it being common knowledge that the Eureka and the Richmond stored a charcoal reserve in the amount of 120,000 bushels to see them through unexpected shortages,[24] both the newspaper interests and the smelting industry probably overestimated the burners' power to impact the local economy. Aware of the burners' extreme financial vulnerability, most sectors of Eureka society seemed to believe that any attempt by the burners to curtail or even stop charcoal production would be short-lived. Clearly, the destitute burners could not depend on any financial reserve to compete with their antagonists and compel them to accept a price hike.

The foremost challenge faced by the incipient Charcoal Burners Protective Association was that of developing a substantial-enough following to lend the organization credibility as well as endowing it with sufficient bargaining power to effect change. The CBPA realized that the attainment of its objectives hinged on its organizational capacity to speak authoritatively on behalf of the collectivity of charcoal burners in Eureka. Indeed, the CBPA's level of political influence and economic impact upon Eureka's charcoal burning industry and, indirectly, upon the county's overall economy would be ultimately determined by the breadth of the association's membership.

However, union activity in the United States during the last quarter of the nineteenth century was a risky enterprise, strongly and vehemently opposed by big-business interests. The attitude of corporate America toward unionism can be aptly summed up by the words spoken in 1902 by George F. Baer, a mine operator, during the formative years of the American labor movement: "The rights and interests of laboring men will be protected and cared for, not by labor agitators, but by the Christian men to whom God in His infinite wisdom has given control of the property interests of the country, and upon successful management on which so much depends."[25] Baer's paternalistic assertions, although made two decades after the founding of the CBPA, accurately reflected the widespread hostility that characterized management's dealings with union organizations during the 1870s, the most turbulent years of the American industrial revolution.

Given the widespread and open hostility toward unionism, labor organizers for the CBPA resorted to any enlisting tactic that promised results. In a display of unorthodox recruiting ingenuity, some of the more musically inclined members of the CBPA resorted to a rather entertaining form of advertising for the charcoal burners' cause, as reported by the *Leader* on August 14: "The fellow who serenades us every evening harping upon a song commencing, 'List, O List,' is informed that he is wasting his vocal efforts. The strain would be better appreciated in the neighborhood of the railroad depot." Presumably, the quarter in the vicinity of the train depot housed a high percentage of laborers, including charcoal burners, who, according to the critic, might have better appreciated the minstrel's refrain. A few days later, the *Sentinel* echoed the same sentiment almost verbatim while adding an admonitory twist: "The fellow is recruiting for the charcoal war."[26] The usage of the word *war* in the journal's editorial, perhaps unwittingly, seemed to presage an ominous outcome.

However, the size of the association's recruitment pool was difficult to establish with certainty. The widespread tendency within the community at large to link any charcoal laborer to the CBPA further confounded the real numbers, ultimately creating a grossly exaggerated estimate of CBPA membership. The error was further reinforced by a series of inaccurate reports that appeared in the press through the summer of 1879. In its July 9 issue, the *Leader* claimed the existence of three thousand charcoal burners. A month later, the same newspaper estimated that two thousand laborers supposedly engaged in the charcoal trade.[27] On July 16, in glaring contradiction with the *Leader*'s previous figures, the *Sentinel* issued a considerably smaller, though oddly specific, estimate of "1,196 members" allegedly associated with the CBPA. The accuracy of such a figure also conflicted with the state mineralogist data, which, gathered during that period, reported that eight hundred laborers were engaged in the manufacturing of charcoal.[28] Clearly, the actual number was difficult to come by.

A more realistic account of the size of the labor force involved in the manufacturing of charcoal could have been gleaned from the tentative list of prospective CBPA members provided by the association's secretary, Joseph Hausman, which included between five and six hundred alleged signatories.[29] But even this account, though closer to the truth, was likely to be inaccurate, for it failed to differentiate between those charcoal burners who were fullfledged CBPA members and those burners who, although strongly sympathetic toward the association's goals, remained passive spectators, perhaps awaiting more propitious developments before pledging allegiance to the association.

The numerical discrepancy revealed by the official data is rendered even more pronounced by an account provided directly by the burners on

September 2 and published by the *Leader*. While the article elaborated chiefly on the fundamental cause of the burners' discontent, which stemmed from their living expenses being double their earnings, the consensus among the burners was that about two thousand men constituted the coal-burning occupation in the district. Incidentally, this same figure was relied upon by Italian consul Diego de Barrilis of San Francisco in his meticulous report to Italian ambassador Albert Blanc in Washington, DC, two days after the shooting at Fish Creek.[30] Given the relentless, ravenous nature of the charcoal trade, which demanded an ever-expanding territory, it is plausible that scores of burners carried on their charcoal activities in extremely remote camps, virtually inaccessible to official assessors unfamiliar with the rugged terrain and unaware of the particular location of such distant sites. Nonetheless, the issue of the public's perception of the size of the charcoal labor force was anything but trivial.

Although the Charcoal Burners Protective Association's mission was clearly implied, its character remained indistinct. One key characteristic of its membership was clear: the coal burners were laborers in the service of a few employers. In his biennial report published in 1879, the Nevada state mineralogist stated: "There are eight hundred coal burners employed in the trade, ninety per cent of whom are foreigners, and about fifty per cent of the latter are American citizens. With a few exceptions, this force is in the employ of less than a dozen firms, two thirds of whom are of foreign birth."[31] Therefore, given their subordinate occupational status and the power differential that distinguished them from their managers, the coal burners' organization was likely intended to operate as a collective-bargaining entity through which to enhance employment conditions.

Reportedly, on July 8, 1879, just two days after the association was born, Joseph Maginni, the association's first president, declared that the goal of the association was the exclusive attainment of a "living price for coal."[32] His statement, reflective of the will of the majority, was far more consistent with the business logic associated with entrepreneurship rather than a labor demand. Characteristically, disgruntled employees would be more likely to advance demands directly linked to wages, benefits, overtime rates, length of the workweek, and piecework rates and not concern themselves with the overall market value of the commodity their wages compelled them to manufacture.

Further, an analysis of the exchange between G. B. Cordano, a presumed spokesperson for the burners' association, and teamster-merchant Reinhold Sadler reinforces the claim that the burners operated as independent agents. In an article that appeared in the *Leader* on August 26, Cordano stated to Sadler that "he was willing at the time (August 10) to accept a compromise at 28 cents, and he talked fair and tried to effect such a compromise with the other members, and after he so tried he came to me (Sadler) and said that the price was not so much, but they wanted to see the receipts."

The advocacy for a rise in the price of a market commodity coupled by a questioning of the legitimacy of certain bookkeeping methods are hardly the typical grievances put forth by employed laborers. Rather, they are in step with a system of free enterprise. In the event the coal burners worked as self-governing artisans, they would have certainly been entitled to market the materials of their labor at will, even if it meant the exacerbation of economic troubles in other segments of the charcoal trade. As independent entrepreneurs, acting in their own self-interest rather than in the collective advantage of their trade, the coal burners would be inclined to seize any competitive edge resulting from the internal dynamics of the marketplace. Such a strategy was supported by the business transaction concluded with Eureka superintendent Donnelly, in the early part of August 1879, when some destitute burners sold their charcoal below market price.

But to say that the coal burners' association was acting as a group of independents is not to argue that their position was a strong one. Indeed, it was perhaps their stance of relative weakness that inclined the coal burners to shift their attention to the price of their commodity rather than directly confronting the businessmen to whom they were indebted. Among those who held the burners' claims, Joseph Tognini and Joe Vanina, prominent Italian merchants and charcoal contractors, loomed large as latent usurers and stealthy padrones. Indeed, the existence of a padrone scheme would explain the subordinate status of multitudes of burners in relation to those creditors who controlled their lives. Thus, if blatantly challenged, the burners' creditors could have retaliated against their debtors by stopping their credit and demanding immediate cash payments for the transportation of their charcoal to the smelters. Desperate for a way out of their predicament, the burners probably reasoned that they would fare better by throwing their weight in the direction of a price hike for their charcoal.

The association's shortsighted aims of bargaining exclusively for a higher charcoal price prevented it from articulating alternative contingency plans of action to advance the burners' class interests. The burners may have exerted greater influence upon the marketplace by withholding their commodity through decreased production. Also, insistence on a higher price for their commodity was bound to result in higher-priced smelter output, inducing the industry toward conversion to a less contentious source of fuel like coke.

Nevertheless, the solution advocated so firmly by the burners through the collective voice of their association was much too feeble to cure what had been a protracted infirmity. That the founding of the burners' association was gravely belated was acknowledged by the *Leader:* "If the coalburners had inaugurated their movement before the Consolidated contracts had been let, or immediately after…[the burners] would have stood some chance of compelling a compliance to their demand for 30 cents or nothing." The editorial ended on a somber note: "Their chance now is extremely slim." While Eureka's mineral production continued to grow throughout the 1870s, the general economy of Nevada was slumping into a twenty-year depression, as a result of declining silver prices triggered by the Mint Act of 1873, disparagingly termed the "Crime of 73."[33] Thus, Eureka's mineral prosperity was impacted by broader economic forces, making it impractical for the local smelting industry to comply with the burners' demand for a higher charcoal price.

By declaring their intent to unionize, the *carbonari* of Eureka crossed a crucial threshold, stepping out of passive anonymity into labor militancy. Already contending with the Ruby Hill Miners' Union, founded in 1873,[34] Eureka mining interests would not welcome yet another organized segment of the general labor force.

In the post–Civil War era, political power was clasped by Republican politicians, loyal friends, and defenders of capital fervently bent on fueling economic expansion built on the freest form of capitalism. In accordance with the nation's business ethic prevalent during the Gilded Age, politicians promoted and protected the interests of the capitalist class over the welfare of working people. On the mining frontier, the capitalist ideology promoted not only the indiscriminate plunder of natural resources but also the brutal exploitation of labor. Impelled exclusively by profit, mining entrepreneurs had no intention of settling the land, but, rather, aimed to drain its wealth and move on to richer lodes, leaving behind depleted mines and worn-out miners.

Far removed from the Jeffersonian ideal, the mineral West spawned more inequality than egalitarianism. Bewildered and disillusioned with the meager rewards of the western frontier, myriad casualties decried the cruelty of frontier capitalism. Giving voice to some of the thorny questions that festered in the minds of many disheartened western pioneers, historian Limerick has asked: "What was a fair profit? What was a just distribution of rewards? Why was it that the man who worked the hardest...often earned the least?" Limerick probed further: "And how much did a man give up—in dignity, in autonomy, in freedom—when his livelihood depended on wages, when other people's decisions controlled his labor?"[35]

Most of Eureka's prominent citizens endorsed the tenets of laissez-faire capitalism, which helped legitimize their ambitions as local mining investors. After all, it was thanks to their massive investments that the district enjoyed prosperity. Among Eureka's leading Republicans could be counted Congressman Thomas Wren (also an attorney), Judge W. W. Bishop, Judge L. W. Cromer, Judge Adelbert Milton Hillhouse, Sheriff Matthew Kyle, Constable Gorman, and teamster George Lamoureaux.[36] Although the most substantial amount of capital invested in Eureka's mining industry was foreign, "nearly every prominent citizen in the district," regardless of political affiliation, had assets invested in local mines,[37] including attorneys George Baker, W. W. and A. C. Bishop, Richmond superintendent Richard Rickard, and Eureka Militia commander General George M. Sabin.

Interestingly, although the approximately two dozen individuals who constituted Eureka's upper stratum represented only a meager 0.33 percent of the county population, they appeared to own roughly 14 percent of the county property.[38] Such an uneven distribution of economic resources was not uncommon in an age in which most men worshipped wealth and a callous public remained indifferent to the frequently dishonest practices by which such wealth was accumulated. The ranks of Eureka's high society included some of the wealthiest Italian moguls, such as Joseph Tognini, Joseph Vanina, and John Torre, pillars of the Italian bourgeoisie of Eureka. Typically, the existence of a substantial ethnic labor force gives rise to an ethnic bourgeoisie, which, according to sociologist Mike Hilton, is both exploitative, in that it benefits from the ethnic worker, and benevolent, in that it solidifies the ethnic community and provides for its social needs.[39]

While the exploitative facet of the Italian ethnic bourgeoisie in relation to the charcoal burners was obvious, its benevolent aspect was less evident. Presumably, spatial distance or physical remoteness among segments of the same ethnic group weakens their ethnic bonds, making exploitation by the dominant side even more compelling. Historian Brian Frehner corroborated such a notion by analyzing the geographic distribution of the Italians who settled in Eureka from 1875 to 1885.[40]

The 1880 census revealed that almost half of the 827 Italians residing in Eureka County were rural laborers who toiled in settlements located at varying distances on the periphery of the town of Eureka. By contrast, 438 Italians were urbanites who worked in town. According to Frehner, the rural Italian labor force was distributed among twenty-one separate sites. In turn, 25 percent of the rural workforce occupied seven distinct sites north of Eureka, while 35 percent of their counterparts dwelled in twelve locations south of town. Further, the rural camps where the Italians plied their trade averaged 31 workers per site, an extremely diluted presence compared to the Italian urbanites settled in Eureka. Frehner identifies the geographic dispersal of the Italians throughout Eureka County as a major obstacle to the formation of their ethnic cohesion.[41]

Evidently, the scattered teams of Italians who labored in almost virtual isolation in the hills surrounding Eureka were deprived of a common ground on which to preserve a shared sense of ethnic community. Except for sporadic encounters with their fellow urbanites, the rural laborers inhabited a desolate world filled mainly with hard labor. Within their geographic isolation, the rural laborers' village-based identity and provincial mind-set solidified. Reminiscent of the medieval European practice of relegating socially inferior groups outside the city's fortification walls, the Italian charcoal burners found themselves spatially excluded. With opportunities to participate in society's mainstream severely constrained, their acculturation process became thwarted, while upward mobility eluded them.

As attested by the tax figures for the period spanning 1875–80, only a small group of Italian entrepreneurs ascended the economic ladder of prosperity, while the bulk of Italian laborers remained confined to the lowest rungs. Although a dozen or so new businessmen joined the ranks of the

Italian elite by 1880, the base of the Italian bourgeoisie remained fundamentally unchanged since 1875, indicating a strong consolidation of wealth among the early Italian capitalists.[42] Clearly, even in its heyday, Eureka did not award prosperity indiscriminately among its equally aspiring suitors.

Eureka's diverse elite was in no way a social anomaly but, rather, reflected a fundamental aspect of American society of that era, deeply immersed in laissez-faire capitalism while impelled by the conservative values of the Victorian age. The dominant zeitgeist of the time being the gospel of the acquisition of wealth by any means, any demand for some measure of economic fairness advanced by the laboring class, often through unionization, was bound to fall upon unsympathetic ears. After all, mine owners claimed they were running the greatest risks by financing their mining enterprises; therefore, it was only natural that they should be accorded undisputed powers in establishing the rules by which the industry operated.[43] In the words of Mother Jones, considered "the most dangerous woman in America" for her charismatic power to organize miners against mine owners at the turn of the twentieth century, "the desperate struggle between labor and capital," she affirmed, "[was] over who would bear the burdens and reap the rewards of American industrialization."[44]

Notes

1. *Leader*, July 8, 1879.
2. *Leader*, July 7, 1879.
3. Ibid.
4. Ibid.
5. Ibid.
6. *Leader*, July 8, 1879.
7. Lingenfelter, *Hardrock Miners*, 32. Though a bold step for the charcoal burners, unionization in Nevada was not a novel idea. This powerful tool of labor organization had been pioneered in the neighboring Comstock, during the early days of the rush to Washoe. In fact, the Comstock miners were the first of their trade to establish a union west of the Mississippi. Gold Hill, a suburb of Virginia City, was the birthplace of the miners' union, baptized the Miners' Protective Association on May 30, 1863. The Miners' Protective Association was founded to guarantee its members a daily wage of four dollars for any mining activity performed belowground. Subsequently, the Gold Hill union's constitution became the prototype after which several other miners' associations throughout the West styled their own.
8. *Leader*, May 3, 1879.

9. Ibid.
10. *Sentinel*, July 8, 1879.
11. Norton B. Stern, "The Jewish Community of Eureka, Nevada," 101.
12. *Leader*, July 8, 1879.
13. Ibid.
14. *Leader*, July 9, 1879.
15. *Leader*, July 8, July 9, 1879; *Sentinel*, July 9, 1879.
16. *Leader*, August 26, 1879.
17. *Sentinel*, August 6, 1879.
18. *Leader*, July 9, 1879.
19. Limerick, *Legacy of Conquest*, 117–18.
20. David Fridtjof Halaas, *Boom Town Newspapers: Journalism on the Rocky Mountain Mining Frontier, 1859–1881*, 77.
21. *Sentinel*, June 1, 1876.
22. Molinelli, *Eureka and Its Resources*, 14; John Gregg Folkes, *Nevada's Newspapers: A Bibliography, a Compilation of Nevada History, 1854–1964*, 58; Molinelli, *Eureka and Its Resources*, 14–15.
23. Halaas, *Boom Town Newspapers*, 77, 85.
24. Murbarger, "Forgotten Industry of the Frontier," 27.
25. Ovid Demaris, *America the Violent*, 146.
26. *Sentinel*, August 17, 1879.
27. *Leader*, August 13, 1879.
28. Nevada State Legislature, *Appendix to the Journals of the Senate and the Assembly, Ninth Session (1879): Seventh Biennial Report of the State Mineralogist of the State of Nevada for the Years 1877 and 1878*, 27.
29. *Leader*, August 22, 1879.
30. Gleaned from Patrizia Salvetti's book *Corda e sapone: Storia di linciaggi degli italiani negli Stati Uniti* (Rope and soap: History of Italian lynchings in the United States), 4. Salvetti's source is the Archivio Storico Diplomatico del Ministero degli Affari Esteri (ASDMAE), Rappresentanza Diplomatica Italiana a Washington (1861–1901), b. 35, f. 60, Piazzale della Farnesina 1 1-00194 (dispatched by the Italian consul in San Francisco to the Italian Embassy in Washington, DC, August 20, 1879).
31. Nevada State Legislature, *Journal of the Assembly, 1879*, 27.
32. *Leader*, July 8, 1879.
33. *Leader*, July 17, 1879; Elliott, *History of Nevada*, 177.
34. Lingenfelter, *Hardrock Miners*, 129.
35. Limerick, *Legacy of Conquest*, 98.
36. *Leader*, October 15, 22, 1876.
37. *Leader*, February 4, 1879.
38. *Leader*, September 12, 1879.
39. Mike Hilton, "The Split Labor Market and Chinese Immigration, 1848–1882," 4–5. In describing the dynamics of the Chinese ethnic bourgeoisie in America,

sociologist Mike Hilton explains: "Native capitalists are seldom equipped to locate and reproduce that ethnic labor force by themselves. Unfamiliarity with the language and customs of Chinese workers made it necessary that white capital rely on an intermediary class of Chinese businessmen for two purposes. First, locating and hiring an adequate number of Chinese workers required that capital act through an intermediate class of Chinese compradors. Second, once obtained, the Chinese labor force had to be provisioned according to their accustomed tastes. This requirement fostered the development of a class of Chinese merchants." The above description of ethnic bourgeoisie seems quite fitting to the Italian padrones of Eureka, Nevada, in 1879.

40. Brian Frehner, "Ethnicity and Class: The Charcoal Burners' War, 1875–1885," 43.
41. Ibid., 48.
42. Ibid., 50.
43. Limerick, *Legacy of Conquest*, 117.
44. Mother Jones, *The Autobiography of Mother Jones*, 191–92, quoted in Andrews, *Killing for Coal*, 4.

V

The Charcoal Crisis

Following the founding of the CBPA on July 8, 1879, Eureka newspapers reported nine incidents in which charcoal teams, destined for the smelters in Eureka, were stopped by riotous burners. During the time leading up to these events, the smelters' actions only exacerbated affairs. The Italian burners of Eureka lived in a period of American history embittered by hostilities between labor and capital, a time dominated by the unbridled pursuit of individual gain, when capitalists rarely exhibited a charitable attitude toward workers in distress.

During this time of unrivaled capitalistic hegemony, Americans lacked the institutional mechanisms to mediate the class-based conflicts arising between the laboring masses and their adversaries. A segment of the working class toiled under deplorable conditions approaching servitude. With power tightly concentrated in the hands of the propertied class, the legislative system through which workers could hope to improve their lot was ineffective at addressing workers' grievances in a substantive way.[1] Thus, many beleaguered workers took various forms of communal action with varying results. The Charcoal Burners Protective Association hoped not only to increase the price of their commodity but also to play a more influential role in negotiating contracts directly with the smelters rather than through the wily teamsters. However, the strategy adopted by Eureka's charcoal burners proved less than effective.

On July 16, 1879, the *Eureka Daily Sentinel* ran a hopeful statement issued by the Richmond Company. Reportedly, the Richmond "expressed willingness" to meet the burners' demand for a higher charcoal price. By contrast, Eureka Consolidated maintained a stoic stance, concealing its true intentions. In the weeks to follow, similar declarations would be circulated, all of which seemed characterized by an underlying elusiveness. Lamentably, the Richmond's "willingness" proved to be nothing more than a stratagem to prolong the burners' growing uncertainty.

On July 17, Eureka's complacency toward the charcoal burners' abiding grievances was rudely shaken. Reportedly, a nonunion and unidentified burner hurried to Eureka to report an alarming development that had occurred at his charcoal camp the night before. Allegedly, thirty-five armed burners had seized control of the charcoal pit, halting all burning activities therein. The event marked the first occurrence of unloading charcoal by the rebellious burners. While no harm was caused to either property or persons, the bellicose intent of the raiders seemed evident. For whatever reason, the authorities did not indict the perpetrators of the raid.[2]

Public reaction to the incident was mixed. The *Eureka Daily Leader* readily condemned the burners' action while admitting its misgivings about the negative impact of higher charcoal costs upon the smelting industry. Indeed, the *Leader*'s editors feared that the furnaces might be compelled to shut down their operations if the burners insisted on a price increase for their commodity. The *Leader* admonished the charcoal burners for failing to negotiate a more favorable price for their product before binding themselves to the terms stipulated in their contract with the smelter operators and with the teamsters.[3]

By contrast, the *Sentinel* was supportive of the burners' endeavors. Although the newspaper did not indicate whether it approved of the burners' aggressive methods, it did specify that the leadership of the burners' association, upon learning of the raid, immediately disassociated itself from the belligerent rioters' actions. Endeavoring to mend its internal rift, they declared that "the Association disclaims any intention of resorting to violence, and says there is no occasion to do so, as all of the burners are in active sympathy with its objects." Furthermore, the *Sentinel*, obviously aware of the substantial charcoal surplus available to the smelters, voiced skepticism about the rumored furnace shutdowns. The *Sentinel*'s editors endorsed unconditionally the burners' right, the same as any other entrepreneur, to obtain the price they deemed fair for their commodity, even if their demand resulted in some unintended hardship for the teamsters.[4]

Although the charcoal burners' cause won much public support, anxiety about the burners' forceful actions and their potentially adverse impact on the mining industry permeated the community. Many Eurekans feared that as business conditions grew unfavorable to the mining interests, as a result of increased fuel costs, the mine owners may opt to take advantage of lower smelting costs offered in California and decide to ship their unprocessed ore to the Golden State.[5]

On August 17, only a day before violence erupted at Fish Creek, the burners' predicament was articulated by Louis Monaco, the spokesperson entrusted to convey their intentions. On behalf of the burners, Monaco wrote: "We admit one point, that we are poor. We cannot afford to hire lawyers or other proficient talents that know it all to keep up a war of pen and ink."[6] Although Monaco explicitly affirmed his personal refusal to support actions taken outside the realm of the law, his words, perhaps unwittingly, carried a veiled allusion at another prospect. Because the burners could not win "a war of pen and ink," perhaps a different kind of war could be won.

The complex circumstances that besieged the burners curtailed their options. Previous negotiations with the mining industry, though short-lived, had ultimately failed to produce the desired results. Dismayed by their fruitless overture, the burners may have shunned a return to the bargaining table at this stage of the crisis. After all, none of the crucial variables affecting the dispute itself had shifted in any favorable directions. The state of the mining economy remained precarious, while the charcoal market was still adequately supplied through accumulated reserves.

Another crucial factor might have blurred the burners' perception of reality—that is, their sense of urgency to reclaim their self-determination. Assailed by an overwhelming threat to their physical survival and lacking the necessary resources to buy time, the burners could not afford to engage, once again, in protracted negotiations, nor could they meet the expenses for legal services. Their indebtedness was deepening daily, while their despair mounted by the hour. Had the circumstances granted the burners a truce from their pressing difficulties, perhaps they would have regained the clarity of mind to recognize the perils that loomed ahead.

Whatever their initial motivation, some burners came to believe that only by breaking the law, no matter how remotely such an approach was related to the eradication of their problem, would their cause gain prominence in the collective consciousness. Precisely because violating the law is viewed by most people as a grave offense, the burners might have reasoned, the community would come to realize the depth of their ordeal and their determination to conquer it by any means.

The burners' revolt in Eureka seemed fueled by the same frustrated impulses that impelled other downtrodden Americans to become radicalized. In describing how the once ethnically cohesive Irish community in Butte, Montana, splintered along class lines as a result of rampant unemployment among Irish workers, David M. Emmons noted that "radicalism reflected their desperation."[7] Similarly, a sizable number of Italian charcoal burners had grown increasingly radicalized as employment prospects dimmed and as their desperation festered.

Although the burners' rationale was flawed, the plan the burners concocted required careful execution. To attempt pulling off such a risky balancing feat against overwhelming odds, the rioters' seething passions had to be contained to be put to the service of expediency. Indeed, the burners must have rehearsed their daring plan at great length before embarking upon the path of lawlessness. Attuned to the burners' covert tactics, the *Leader* of August 15 stated: "The strikers are too shrewd to invite or risk a collision, and in the presence of officers or an armed force they are as meek as lambs, offering no resistance to arrest and denying any connection with the parties who are engaged in breaking the law. Nevertheless, they have determined upon a policy that will make the business of hauling coal unprofitable to the teamsters, and by obstructing teams, overawing the men at the kilns, and terrorizing outside producers, calculate on carrying their point." By adopting lawbreaking tactics to realize their just ends, the burners nullified the legitimacy of their cause, and their culpability was made inescapable.

Conceivably, the audacious raid carried out the night of July 16 at a charcoal camp near Eureka might have temporarily tipped the balance in the burners' favor. In fact, in less than twenty-four hours after the coal burners brought the charcoal camp to a standstill, the *Leader* promptly reported that Eureka Consolidated had annulled all coal contracts. Ostensibly, such a decision signaled a willingness to comply with the burner association's thirty-cent price per bushel, first pledged by the burners on July 8. The editorial also reported that the Richmond reiterated its previous stipulation for a portion of its charcoal supply to be purchased at a rate of twenty-nine cents and renewed its expectation of the fulfillment of that accord.[8]

Looking out for their corporate interests, the Richmond's officials also expressed their readiness to purchase all other charcoal, outside the already contracted amount, at the going market price, provided it did not exceed twenty-eight cents a bushel. The Richmond's spokesperson concluded his statement menacingly, cautioning that unless the company's terms were met, the furnaces would be shut down immediately. The Richmond's threat of closure for the next six months might have had less to do with the burners' demand for a higher charcoal price than with the conditions of the overall economy at that time. In fact, with prices of lead and silver dipping on the national market, and with the Richmond's lead surplus in the amount of several hundred tons, closing down the company's smelter seemed to make perfect business sense, independent of rising charcoal prices.[9]

Public fears were further heightened when an anonymously written letter appeared in the *Leader* on July 18. Signed merely by "a well-posted man in San Francisco," the letter alleged Eureka Consolidated's tentative plan of contracting with California's smelters to process its ore. Eager to expand its business revenues, the railroad company was more than willing to offer the smelting company enticing freight rates to transport ore across the Sierra Nevada and into the Golden State for processing. By such a maneuver, Eureka Consolidated would have reaped a savings of five dollars a ton. The *Leader* remarked on the obvious fact that the company was taking countermeasures to weather the damaging effects of what seemed an imminent increase in charcoal costs.

Nonetheless, to many, Eureka Consolidated's business subterfuge, asserted by the anonymous author, seemed nothing more than a speculative rumor. Indeed, the letter had the appearance of a pretense designed to foment public opposition to the burners' cause. Subsequently, contradicting the tenor of the alarming letter, on July 19 Eureka Consolidated declared its "intention" of honoring the burners' pledged charcoal price of thirty cents a bushel.[10]

Despite these hopeful signs, the association's mission was far from accomplished. All the association had obtained was a mere "intention" without any actual guarantee that the intent would be carried out. As inconclusive as the willingness to honor the pledged price by Eureka Consolidated was, it did ease tensions more than the Richmond's utter silence. Inexplicably, the positions assumed by the two major mining companies in regards to the burners' demands now stood in sharp contrast to their earlier pronouncements.[11] In a mystifying reversal, Donnelly's former unyielding resolve softened into an amenable compliance, while Rickard's earlier unequivocal support faded. The apparently capricious conduct exhibited by the mining companies in dealing with the charcoal crisis greatly eroded the burners' confidence in the ongoing negotiations.

Following the surprising announcement by Eureka Consolidated, the CBPA called a general meeting to appraise the smelter's proposition. On July 20, after the bulk of the membership had gathered, the CBPA publicly announced acceptance of the offer. A notice to that effect was published in the *Sentinel*, alerting all CBPA members not to interfere with those teams transporting charcoal to Eureka Consolidated.[12]

Evidently, not all charcoal burners had been in attendance at the meeting held on July 20. Many burners, precluded from attending the gathering due to the long distances they had to travel to reach Eureka, were still oblivious of the newly attained price agreement. Unaware of the CBPA's official declaration, a number of burners continued to impede the manufacturing and shipping of charcoal.[13]

On the very same day that the CBPA notice was published, July 20, an escalation of the burners' activism was reported by a teamster named Robert Brown who had traveled to Willow Station, intending to fill his team with the order of charcoal he had been contracted to deliver by Reinhold Sadler. Brown was confronted by five armed burners, who prevented him from loading any charcoal, dumping the sacks instead.[14]

Forced to withdraw from the loading station with an empty wagon, an irritated Brown headed back to town, where he promptly lodged charges of malicious mischief against the five burners. Following Brown's complaint, arrest warrants were issued for the "five Italians" allegedly responsible for the dumping of the charcoal sacks at Willow Station. In addition to accusing the perpetrators of "malicious mischief," Brown claimed a financial loss in the amount of $3,850.[15]

Further, Brown extended the blame to include the CBPA and its officers for "passing and causing resolutions to be passed" fomenting militancy amid the charcoal burners aimed at securing thirty-two cents per bushel of charcoal.[16] As a result of the CBPA strategy, Brown claimed he was prevented from fulfilling his contractual obligations to deliver an order of charcoal placed by Reinhold Sadler.[17]

Brown's allegations rested upon the unconfirmed inference that every single burner who took part in the dumping of the charcoal sacks was associated with the CBPA. Although it is likely that some of the strikers were indeed full-fledged members of the association, such a sweeping allegation was never substantiated during the ensuing inquest. Remarkably, although the dumping of Brown's charcoal clearly escalated the burners' struggle, the incident occurred without any violence.

Without delay, on July 21, Sheriff Matthew Kyle and an escort of six deputies left Eureka bound for the charcoal country to apprehend the alleged wrongdoers. At some unspecified point along their trek, the lawmen crossed paths with a throng of Italians wielding an assortment of weapons, including rifles, pistols, and clubs. Despite conflicting reports, the size of the band was estimated between 150 and 200 men.[18]

During the ensuing talk, the burners' leader informed the sheriff that none of the wanted men was at hand; the spokesperson also reiterated that no charcoal loading would be permitted unless officially ordered by the CBPA president. Seizing the opportunity to deliver the news to the uninformed multitude, Kyle disclosed the latest developments between the CBPA and Eureka Consolidated. Undeterred by the revelation, the burners did not relent and kept demanding proof of official authorization. No sooner had the burners' request for official notice been uttered than an envoy dispatched by the CBPA president appeared on the scene, substantiating the sheriff's assertion while directing the burners to resume loading only those teams under contract with Eureka Consolidated. Reassured by the messenger's declaration, the burners readily complied with the CBPA directives while also assuring the sheriff that the burners for whom warrants had been issued would soon turn themselves in.[19]

In fulfillment of the burners' promise, the five indicted strikers surrendered on July 23. Retracting the original charge of malicious mischief, the authorities accused the five burners with threatening to destroy private property, a heavier charge that the defendants unanimously denied. The trial was scheduled for August 5, while bail was set at two hundred dollars for each accused. It is unknown whether the offenders' bail was ever posted or whether they remained in jail until the day of the trial.[20]

News of the burners' ranch raid and Brown's wagon stoppage provoked considerable anti-Italian sentiment among many Eurekans. Indeed, the burners' strong actions sparked condemnation even within the upper Italian circles. Quite likely, some embarrassment was felt by the "better class of Italians" for the disturbance caused by the less cultured *paesani*. The militancy exhibited by the combative burners was firmly censured by the CBPA leadership. Notwithstanding their commitment to the charcoal burners' cause, three of the association's elected officers, Molinelli, Maginni, and Hausman, turned in their resignations in condemnation of the charcoal burners' willful interference with commerce.[21]

Following Brown's stoppage, on July 21 Molinelli felt compelled to respond to critics' allegations of complicity with the rioters. The *Sentinel* carried his exculpatory statement, directed at the "unprincipled curs" who accused Molinelli of masterminding the burners' forays of the previous day. In an effort to redeem his smeared reputation, Molinelli asserted that his role within the association was limited to the function of translator, claiming he was remunerated like any other professional for the services rendered.[22]

However, Molinelli's disavowal of active participation within the CBPA was emphatically challenged by the coal burners, as evidenced by their rebuttal published in the *Leader* on July 23. In the article, the burners claimed that no fees were ever paid to Molinelli for his translation services, adding that the vice president had assumed his high-ranking position within the CBPA with unconditional commitment. Further, the commentary reminded the public that the coal burners, apart from their nationality, were law-abiding citizens compelled to obtain a rate of thirty cents per bushel of charcoal and the right to inspect the furnace receipts, to corroborate the actual selling price of their commodity to the smelters by the teamsters.

Of all the CBPA leaders, Molinelli appears to have been the most enigmatic. Highly regarded by the community as a successful and civic-minded entrepreneur, Molinelli's role as CBPA vice president seemed based solely upon the altruistic desire to aid the needy conationals. Yet Molinelli's close ties to Eureka's business sector cast doubt upon his motives. In fact, among the character references attesting to his impeccable reputation as a department store clerk were those of the superintendents of Eureka's two major mines, namely, Richard Rickard of Richmond Consolidated and H. Donnelly of Eureka Consolidated.[23]

Because the endorsements dated back to December 23, 1878, a well-established relationship with those influential members of Eureka's elite who vouched for him may be inferred. Molinelli's association with the two prominent superintendents who played clear roles in the situation confronting the charcoal burners strongly suggested a conflict of interest. When conflict erupted, Molinelli opted to end his involvement with the CBPA.

Concurrently with the appearance of Molinelli's resignation in the *Leader*, the additional resignations of Joe Maginni, president of the CBPA, and Joe Hausman, the association's secretary, were declared by the *Sentinel*. The reasons for their decision to withdraw from the CBPA were articulated as follows: "We have used our best endeavors to promote the interests of the coal burners, and raise the price of charcoal to 30 cents per bushel, in a peaceable way, and have never countenanced any lawless proceedings or infractions of the laws. We have obtained the price at the Eureka Consolidated, but not at the Richmond."[24]

While the first leaders of the CBPA could explain their departure as being the result of having partly fulfilled their purpose, they almost certainly left because of the burners' outlawry. The existence of an ideological rift between the leaders and the struggling burners is intimated by Grazeola: "The presence of a...department store clerk [Molinelli], and a clothing store owner [Ashim] as leaders early in a movement to help charcoal burners appears incongruous." Notwithstanding the altruistic attitudes of the association officers toward the burners, in reality a class-based gulf separated the CBPA leadership from the rank and file. Because what held such a peculiar alliance together was not readily apparent, the officers' real motives became suspect. After all, as Grazeola points out, "The vocations held by these men were of such a nature that they may very well have held some burner debts."[25] The intimation of internal collusion within the CBPA was bolstered by Sadler and Lamoureux, as they denied any contrivance of burners' receipts. The two teamsters asserted that "a few small fry operators...are anxious to gain favor with the so-called Coal Burners Association."[26]

Further, the resigning officers, aware of an impending lawsuit brought against the association by teamster Brown, had a great incentive to leave their positions to avoid liability for the financial damages incurred by the plaintiff. Indeed, the suit, filed on July 24, cited the CBPA officers in question as defendants, while an indemnity in the amount of $3,850 was also claimed.[27] Brown's lawsuit heightened public apprehension further. Allegations of internal strife plaguing the association were rampant, while an escalation of the burners' belligerency was feared.[28] Perhaps in an effort to increase structural cohesiveness within the association ranks, a general membership meeting took place on August 5. As published in the *Sentinel* on July 24, the association's rank and file expected Maginni and Hausman to remain in office until the next meeting.

The day before the gathering, Eureka swarmed with scores of Swiss and Italian burners. Congregating in Main Street's saloons, the raucous burners' exchanges were described as "very lively."[29] While voicing disparate and fervent opinions, the adamant burners could not reach a general consensus on how best to resolve the spiraling conflict. Nonetheless, the *Sentinel* reported that those closer to the issue deemed a compromise at twenty-eight cents best for all parties concerned.[30]

As if a portent of things to come, the night before the much-anticipated assembly, heated arguments broke out among tense burners, in one case resulting in violence. Dissenting vehemently over the contentious charcoal price, Joseph Zarger and Angelo Proti exchanged blows in one of the local saloons. The scuffle ended with Proti suffering a lethal skull fracture inflicted by his countryman with a billiard cue. Fearing retaliation from Zarger, those Italians who witnessed the fight refrained from swearing a warrant against their violent compatriot.[31]

On August 5, the charcoal burners gathered at the Eureka County Courthouse to hold new elections and fill the hastily vacated seats of the CBPA leadership. Roughly two hundred burners attended the assembly. Before the actual meeting got under way, the previously elected officers turned in their resignations and exited the hall. Notwithstanding the wide range of opinions held by the burners in attendance regarding the adoption of future measures, the new officers were installed with relative ease. The new slate was thus formed: Angelo del Bondio, president; Giuseppe Martinoli, vice president; Guido Bassetti, secretary; Nicola Ratti, assistant secretary; and Severino Strozzi, treasurer.[32] The newly elected officers were all Italians directly linked to the charcoal burning trade and presumably better attuned to the burners' expectations for economic progress.[33]

Commenting upon the association's internal developments, the *Sentinel* admitted its disappointment over the change of leadership, remarking that the former officers were "intelligent, well-meaning men who had the interests of their countrymen at heart, and, while they differed in minor points, would have steered them clear of all pitfalls."[34]

The most pressing issue confronting the assembly remained the charcoal price. While most members insisted on thirty cents a bushel, a portion of the membership favored twenty-eight cents as a fair compromise rate. After a furious squabble, the membership proceeded to cast its final votes, and the will of the majority prevailed. A binding resolution was issued whereby all burners would enforce the avowed thirty-cent price while also demanding the surrender of the furnace receipts.[35]

What remained undetermined was the strategy by which the association intended to bring nonunionized burners into compliance with the adopted resolution. Perhaps the CBPA believed that once the thirty-cent rate went into effect, the uncommitted burners would willingly join the cause to reap the rewards attained by the union. Whatever its reasoning, the association was unable to formulate a contingency plan to ensure the successful implementation of its newly adopted measure. Such a crucial tactical error would eventually prove catastrophic.

Although widely unrecognized, the most detrimental obstacle in the burners' pursuit of economic progress stemmed from their debtor status. Exploited by their creditors, the burners were attached by debt to the merchants, counting among them some Italian compatriots. Apparently, the burners' concern for the price of charcoal was a secondary hurdle, though the most evident to outside observers—one that could not be adequately dealt with until the debtor-creditor relationship had been radically altered to meet the burners' needs. The iniquitous business relationship between the burners and the merchants was firmly denounced in a letter published by the *Leader* on August 6:

> Is it the fault of the companies if the coal burners do not get their receipts? They say, "we are robbed, plundered, we are slaves and

subject to worse treatment than the negroes were during the rebellion." But let us get at the root of the evil; let me ask the coal burners, what do you pay for overalls, boots, flour, sugar? He answers, "Two hundred per cent more at the stores of my countrymen, who have grown wealthy and opulent, than we would have to pay elsewhere." "Why do we go there? Because we are in debt; we cannot go elsewhere."

The author, writing under the pseudonym "Sincerity," advocated for the rights of the trampled burners by strongly endorsing the thirty-cent resolution. Sincerity implied that the burners viewed an increase in charcoal price as the only way out of the state of bondage in which the usurious merchants held them. He further declared that if the burners were relieved of the oppressive overcharges exacted by the merchants, they could even settle for twenty-six cents a bushel.

A painfully concrete instance of the merchants' usury was provided by a disheartened burner who claimed he had been charged thirty cents for a pound of cheese bought on credit, while the same quantity of cheese would have cost him half that amount had he paid in cash.[36] Another dismayed burner claimed that after toiling for three years manufacturing charcoal, his total earnings amounted to a meager forty dollars.[37] Precluded from establishing alternative lines of credit with fairer-minded dealers, the burners' indebtedness swelled.

As if contending with the avaricious merchants was not enough, the burners, wrote Sincerity, were also swindled by the teamsters and the furnace operators. For those skeptics who doubted his claim, Sincerity urged them to examine the accounting records of the businesses indicted by the victimized burners. Further, the burners complained of being shortchanged by the teamsters on payments for quantities of charcoal delivered to the furnaces; allegedly, the teamsters claimed lower quantities than declared by the burners. To rectify the discrepancy, Sincerity advised the burners to obtain receipts stating the actual amount of charcoal entrusted to the teamsters upon loading, thus compelling them to account for any disparity upon delivery.

Desirous for a prompt and peaceable resolution of the ongoing dispute, Sincerity concluded his statement by endorsing the compromise rate of twenty-eight cents per bushel, deeming it the most advantageous deal for all Eurekans. Sincerity's defense of the vulnerable burners ended with the Latin maxim "Fiat Justitia Ruat Caelum" (Let justice be done, though the heavens fall).

Sincerity brought to light a key point: although on the surface the issue of charcoal price appeared paramount, the real crux of the dispute hinged on the burners' inability to transact reliably with the smelters, having to rely on the teamsters as intermediaries. In the heat of the public debate, the issue of charcoal price overshadowed the burners' aspiration to negotiate directly with the consumers of their commodity for a mutually satisfactory price. Not to allow such a win-win arrangement raised legitimate doubts about the exclusive business pact between the teamsters and the smelters.

Reportedly, some of the town merchants, in addition to operating merchandise establishments, were also engaged in the charcoal hauling business. Among those diversified merchants, three were prominent Italian figures, Joseph Tognini and Joseph Vanina, who operated as a partnership, and Joseph Torre, who operated a charcoal ranch. The fact that the burners, in their direct negotiations with the smelters, did not address the transportation issue suggested that the teamsters' hauling services were nonnegotiable.

A prior arrangement had been worked out between the burners and the teamsters whereby the latter rendered "free" hauling services by coalescing the transportation costs with the burners' preexisting accounts at their merchandise outlets. Such a deal could appear to provide mutual benefits. For one, by resorting to this debt-postponing strategy, the burners would be spared the hardship of paying in cash for the hauling of their charcoal, money they obviously lacked. Conversely, by compounding current hauling costs with previous expenses, the teamsters could substantially increase interest rates on the burners' debt. Although actual proof that such a crafty system of trade binding the indebted burners to the teamsters is lacking, its inferred existence is, however, consistent with what we know about the padrone system. Being illiterate in both Italian and English, most burners could have been easily bilked by unscrupulous dealers.

Given the burners' illiteracy and their inability to examine the merchant-teamsters' account books, concealing a fraudulent transaction would have been easily accomplished. The confounding of the hauling costs with debts incurred at the teamsters' stores presumably blurred the magnitude of the burners' liability while depriving them of any legal redress. The burners became, unwittingly, captives in a fixed game orchestrated by unsympathetic business owners, some of whom were their compatriots.

Meanwhile, speculative reports claimed that negotiations toward a middle-ground solution of twenty-eight cents were still under way. Further, based supposedly "upon undoubted authority," the *Sentinel* reported the imminent closure of the Richmond and Eureka Consolidated, unless the burners yielded to the smelters' terms.[38]

Perhaps emboldened by the internal strife that weakened the CBPA and the general confusion that surrounded the charcoal debate, Eureka Consolidated rescinded its early intention of paying thirty cents per bushel of charcoal. On August 11 Eureka Consolidated stated that it would "brook no dictation from any person or association as to where and whom they shall purchase [charcoal], and if they cannot secure a supply on these terms they will shut down the furnaces until the question regulates itself."[39]

Daunted by the seemingly imminent closure of the smelters, some burners relented to the offer of twenty-eight cents, as a number of their more determined comrades held out for the thirty-cent rate. On August 7 a sizable group of resolute burners sprang into action, determined to stop all charcoal deliveries until the smelters complied with the thirty-cent figure decreed by the association. Equipped with shotguns, grubbing hoes, and pruning knives, the staunch burners left Eureka bound for the outlying charcoal camps.[40]

At this the *Leader* asserted, somewhat prophetically, that the insurgents "will find that the shotgun policy is somewhat expensive before they get through with it." Intending to make its position clear, the *Leader* reiterated the right of every man to hold his goods and sell them at the price of his choice. However, the newspaper warned, "when a party of armed men attempt to destroy another's property or threaten his life because he sees fit to dispose of his own wares at what he pleases to ask for them, it is carrying things a little too far and we hope the Coal-Burners Association will not attempt any such high-handed outrage."[41]

Already contending with a spreading economic depression, Eureka's business class viewed the burners' uprisings crossly. While characterizing Eureka's merchants as "chronic grumblers" and subscribing to the old saying "The more we get the more we want," the *Sentinel* did admit that "times are hard in Eureka."[42] Unwilling to acknowledge the greater economic forces at work, and alarmed at the prospect of furnace shutdowns, Eureka businessmen blamed the rioters for further damaging the local economy by allegedly sending remittances abroad.

Giving expression to these sentiments, the *Sentinel* stated that each month, nearly forty thousand dollars was being withdrawn from the local economy destined for the coffers of foreign lands, with an almost equal amount bound for localities across the American Republic. On August 8, 1879, the *Sentinel* remarked, "Right on the heels of this general stagnation, when a feeling of universal distrust pervades all classes, comes the ill-advised and untimely strike of the coal burners to add to the demoralization that seems to have seized our business men." With more than half of Eureka's 4,207 residents being foreign born in 1880, foreign remittances could have indeed strained Eureka's economy.[43] Nonetheless, considering that the bulk of Eureka's Italians engaged in the unprofitable activity of charcoal burning, it is unlikely that the penniless burners partook in the capital flight spawned by remittances.

Unfortunately, the *Leader*'s premonition was borne out. Alerted by threatening reports foretelling the imminent destruction of private property, on August 8 Sheriff Kyle rode out to Alpha, a small community about thirty miles northwest of Eureka, escorted by a few deputies.[44]

Simultaneously, the CBPA issued a warning to George Lamoureux, a local strong-willed teamster, not to dispatch his team to the charcoal camp owned by Cassani, as no charcoal loading would be allowed. In an editorial comment, the *Leader* recognized Lamoureux's inalienable right to dispose of his teams as he saw fit, adding that the teamster could appeal to the law for protection should anyone prevent him from securing the charcoal he was legally entitled to haul.[45]

However, on August 10, Lamoureux had been served a legally binding notice drafted on August 7 by James Bassetti, Cassani's business representative, which explicitly forewarned the teamster to desist from obtaining charcoal from his employer. Incidentally, Bassetti was also secretary of the CBPA. By acknowledging his CBPA rank after signing the note, Bassetti implied that the association had officially endorsed the note. Further, CBPA president Andrew del Bondio was identified as the bearer of the note, while association vice president Martinoli endorsed it. Thus, the CBPA involvement in the Cassani ranch incident appeared incontrovertible. The note, with an array of grammatical and spelling errors, read, "Youill not send to Cassamis ranch your teams because it shall not be loaded, as Cassamis delegate for its business of coal I remain respectfully yours," and it was signed by James Bassetti.[46]

Bassetti was Cassani's "delegate," or, more accurately, his business agent, and as such he was vested with the legal authority to deliberate on Cassani's business affairs. Indeed, Bassetti's double role as Cassani's agent and as secretary of the CBPA should have substantially increased his leverage in business transactions rather than eliciting blatant disregard from Lamoureux.

Keenly aware of Lamoureux's determination to fulfill his contractual obligations with Eureka's major furnaces, and almost certain that he would attempt to defy the association's injunction, early on the morning of August 9 six burners forced their entry into Lamoureux's home, with the clear intent to intimidate the teamster. The intruders dragged him from his bed and threatened him with bodily harm. Astonishingly, later in the same day, a defiant Lamoureux proceeded to Cassani's ranch, intending to load his team as planned.[47]

Upon arrival at the site, Lamoureux was, once again, overwhelmed by a roving group of armed and ill-disposed Italians. Realizing he was greatly outnumbered, the teamster turned his empty team around and headed back to Eureka, promptly reporting the incident to the authorities. With Sheriff Kyle still away at Alpha and troubled by Lamoureux's account, Deputy Sheriff J. B. Simpson immediately issued arrest warrants for those presumably implicated in the charcoal stoppage and swiftly set out to execute the summons escorting Lamoureux back to Cassani's charcoal camp. Unperturbed that Sheriff Kyle and his patrol had not yet returned from their mission at Alpha, Simpson declared that in the event trouble should ensue, the sheriff and his men would be relied upon.[48]

Peculiarly, not only was Bassetti's legal authority superseded, but his business immunity was also breached by the issuance of a generic arrest warrant, which though void of name and profession strongly alluded to his person.[49] Also known as a "John Doe warrant," a generic arrest warrant is customarily issued to arrest a person who may be known by sight but whose name is unknown. Although applicable only in circumstances in which an unnamed person is sought by authorities, use of such a potentially corruptive legal device has been resorted to throughout the centuries.

Presumably, the trek to the charcoal-loading point, named Higby's Station, near Cassani's ranch, was expected to be an overnight affair. Once in the proximity of the station, Lamoureux and Deputy Simpson set up camp for the night, expecting to carry on their mission the next morning. Lamoureux would proceed with the loading of his contracted charcoal, while Simpson would execute his warrants. However, at daybreak the teamster and the deputy found themselves encircled by a throng of forty burners who had descended upon the two unsuspecting travelers during the night, following a series of signal fires that announced their presence at Higby's Station. The vigilant burners, once again without resorting to force, effectively prevented the loading of the charcoal wagons, thus compelling Lamoureux and Simpson to return to Eureka without any charcoal.[50]

On that same eventful Sunday of August 10, similar incidents were reported in other sections of the charcoal country outside Eureka. The Fish Creek district, an area thirty miles southwest of Eureka, being one of the larger and more productive camps, experienced additional stoppages. Reportedly, throngs of burners besieged the bustling loading station to make sure that no charcoal would be transacted. Among the hauling outfits impacted were those of Henry Kaye, Reinhold Sadler, Thomas Riley, H. B. McKee, and M. L. Causey, who had simultaneously dispatched their teams to pick up their charcoal supplies at Fish Creek.[51]

Anticipating that their slow-moving wagons would be readily intercepted by the burners, the teamsters undertook strong precautionary measures to ensure their precious cargo would be safely delivered to the smelters in Eureka. In fact, a force of sixteen armed guards was enlisted to escort the wagon convoy on its perilous trek. At some undetermined point, the teams crossed paths with twenty armed charcoal burners, determined to see that the wagons would return to town vacant, while a much larger force lingered in the hills, ready to intervene. Wavering before the resolute burners, the armed escort yielded.[52]

The teamsters' contingency plan had failed, and the convoy was steered on its homeward track carrying no supply of charcoal. Although the stoppage had thwarted Lamoureux's headstrong plan to obtain his merchandise, the obstructionists did not resort to either violence or dumping of the coal sacks.⁵³ With only a slight numerical difference between the sixteen-man armed escort attached to the convoy and the twenty-man charcoal burner patrol, the latter prevailed.⁵⁴ Clearly, the burners had been effective in preventing the teamsters from loading their wagons by means of an armed escort.

Meanwhile, another incident occurred at Newark, some ten miles northeast of Eureka, where one of Sadler's team had journeyed to acquire a load of charcoal. Apparently, Sadler's wagon had already been filled to capacity when a contingent of forty armed burners stopped the team, unloaded the charcoal from the wagons, and ordered the teamsters back to Eureka. As was by now customary, no destruction of property or physical violence marked the burners' raid at Newark.⁵⁵

However, the most troublesome occurrence of that day took place at the charcoal ranch belonging to Joseph Tognini, near Alpha.⁵⁶ At this location, according to an early account, presumably seventy-five Italians assembled. After seizing an alleged load of two thousand bushels of charcoal, the rioters proceeded to scatter it throughout the sagebrush, littering an area twenty acres wide. Following the episode, the strikers rewarded themselves by taking possession of a local saloon, where they held a wild revelry. The merrymaking was cut short when rumors reached them that an armed force was headed their way from Eureka. Hurriedly, the burners scattered to the hills.⁵⁷ This account turned out to have been greatly exaggerated. On Monday, August 11, Charley Grimm, one of Tognini's ranch employees, who had witnessed the affair firsthand, stated that only about seven hundred sacks of charcoal had actually been strewn, over a smaller area.⁵⁸

Those townsfolk who harbored magnanimous feelings toward the burners' plight assigned blame for the destructive deeds to a few reckless instigators. However, the acts perpetrated by a few offenders engendered much public enmity toward the collectivity of burners. Giving expression to the frustration shared by the majority of Eurekans, the *Leader*, assuming an increasingly active role as a civic force, advocated that the culprits be "branded as outlaws," while inciting "all good citizens" to assist the official authorities in their efforts to restore public order.⁵⁹

The *Sentinel* echoed a widespread sense of disillusion festering among those townspeople who had been sympathetic to the burners' cause. According to the newspaper, the burners' misconduct was so flagrant that it elicited censure even from the "better class" of their countrymen. Reflecting a keen analysis of the charcoal crisis, the *Sentinel* also pointed an accusatory finger at Eureka's predatory merchants, whose extortionary business practices had precipitated the current strife.[60]

Also suspect were teamsters Sadler and Lamoureux, major challengers in the charcoal dispute. Lamoureux's vehemence against the burners' interference with the charcoal trade was amply revealed in his personal confrontations with the strikers. Sadler, whose commercial interests in the charcoal trade were considerable, ranked among the staunchest opponents to the burners' cause. Their fierce hostility toward the burners' struggle eventually prompted them to appeal to the governor for military intervention. To counter accusations of alleged business fraud by manipulating burner receipts, Sadler and Lamoureux publicly upheld their presumed blamelessness: "In no case have we ever refused to exhibit all coal receipts to any and all parties from whom we have purchased coal, and have never had any disagreements or disputes in regard to the amount of such receipts."[61] Although the details of their business accounts were never disclosed, Sadler's role as the proprietor of a merchandise store and as a charcoal contractor and Lamoureux's known belligerence toward the burners cast doubt as to the purity of their business motives.

Besides being plagued by unsteady leadership, the CBPA never developed a following substantial enough to influence significantly the direction of the charcoal industry. In fact, Grazeola suggests that only about one hundred burners were completely loyal to the association and could be counted upon in the event assertive measures needed to be taken to stir the public's consciousness about the burners' woes.[62] Whatever their numbers, the loyal followers probably sensed the insurmountable odds they faced against the overwhelming power of the status quo. Perhaps in an attempt to overcome their vulnerability, the charcoal burners may have resorted to bravado.

By early August the deepening charcoal crisis was a palpable reality. Indeed, the chilling atmosphere gripping the mining community of Eureka was aptly expounded by the *Leader* with a provocative editorial titled "THE COAL WAR." The grave tone of the article was plain from the start. "The coal troubles have at last come to a crisis, and it is evident to all that the serious aspect assumed is fraught with promises of evil." The article went on to assert that "the lawless element now on the rampage throughout the coal districts seem determined to precipitate a conflict." In condemning those presumed responsible for the escalating crisis, the newspaper asserted, "The instigators and ringleaders of this movement are acting not only very foolishly, but are inviting," added the editor in a not-so-veiled menacing tone, "riot and bloodshed and precipitating a conflict in which they and their deluded followers are very sure to get the worst of the contest."

Hinting at an imminent retaliatory action against the rioters, the newspaper declared that "in stepping outside the boundaries they invite and deserve full and severe punishment." The editors, no longer doubting that the lawbreaking burners "have adopted concerted action to carry out their designs," acknowledged that the burners had crossed the point of no return. Not only had the "deluded" burners violated the law of the land, but they had also impudently ventured beyond the union cause, their last hope for an amenable solution of their desperate grievances. "In stepping outside the boundaries," the burners asserted their faith in the power of collective action to decide one's future, unmediated by well-meaning but misguided advocates whose class interests aligned them with the status quo rather than its disruption. Forging an aura of unanimous condemnation against the rioting burners, the paper stated paternalistically, "This is the sentiment of every citizen, and the authorities will receive the aid and support of the entire community."[63] Whether or not that was true, it did seem that Eureka was on the brink of violence.

NOTES

1. Limerick, *Legacy of Conquest*, 111.
2. *Leader*, July 17, 1879.
3. Ibid.
4. *Sentinel*, July 18, 1879.
5. *Leader*, July 22, 1879.
6. *Sentinel*, August 17, 1879.
7. David M. Emmons, *The Butte Irish: Class and Ethnicity in an American Mining Town, 1875–1925*, 360.
8. *Leader*, July 18, 26, 1879.
9. Ibid.
10. *Sentinel*, July 19, 20, 1879.
11. *Leader*, July 7, 1879.

12. *Sentinel*, July 19, 20, 1879.
13. *Sentinel*, July 20, 1879.
14. Ibid.
15. *Leader*, July 21, 24, 1879.
16. *Leader*, July 24, 1879.
17. *Sentinel*, July 25, 1879.
18. *Leader*, July 21, 1879; *Sentinel*, July 22, 1879.
19. *Leader*, July 21, 1879; *Sentinel*, July 22, 1879.
20. *Leader*, July 23, 1879.
21. *Leader*, July 21, 1879.
22. Ibid.; *Sentinel*, July 22, 1879.
23. *Leader*, September 2, 1879.
24. *Sentinel*, July 23, 1879.
25. Grazeola, "Charcoal Burners War of 1879," 54.
26. *Leader*, August 12, 1879.
27. *Leader*, July 24, 1879.
28. *Leader*, July 25, 1879.
29. *Leader*, August 4, 1879.
30. *Sentinel*, August 5, 1879.
31. *Leader*, August 5, 1879.
32. *Leader*, August 5, 1879; *Sentinel*, August 6, 1879.
33. As attested by the 1880 census, all of the aforementioned officers were coal burners (Strozzi, *Leader*, August 14, 1879; del Bondio and Martinoli, *Leader*, August 11, 1879), except for the secretary of the association, Guido Bassetti. The latter's identity is rather perplexing, since he bears the same surname as other individuals directly linked to the CBPA. In fact, a certain James Bassetti was both secretary of the CBPA and purchasing agent for Cassani, a charcoal rancher. The same James Bassetti was the author of the cautionary notice later sent to George Lamoureux to dissuade the teamster from attempting to load charcoal at Cassani's ranch. One G. (G. could stand either for Guido or Giuseppe) Bassetti had been elected temporary chairman at the first meeting held by the charcoal burners, on July 6, at Celso Tatti's saloon. Finally, there is Louis Bassetti, a member of the coal burners' association who was arrested on July 29 on a warrant sworn out by a Mr. Bonnetti, charging him with threats against his life (*Leader*, July 30, 1879). There is a strong possibility that all of these identically surnamed individuals were members of the same family. However, pondering the great challenge seemingly confronting Eureka's newspaper editors in spelling foreign names at the time, one cannot exclude the prospect that all previous appellations might have referred solely to one individual.
34. *Sentinel*, August 6, 1879.
35. Ibid.; *Leader*, August 5, 1879.
36. *Sentinel*, August 10, 1879.
37. *Sentinel*, September 2, 1879.

38. *Sentinel*, August 7, 1879.
39. *Leader*, August 11, 1879.
40. *Leader*, August 7, 1879; *Sentinel*, August 8, 1879.
41. *Leader*, August 7, 1879.
42. *Sentinel*, August 8, 1879.
43. US Department of the Interior, Census Office, *Statistics of the Population of the United States at the Tenth Census*, table 9, 452.
44. *Leader*, August 8, 1879.
45. *Leader*, August 9, 1879.
46. *Leader*, August 11, 1879.
47. *Sentinel*, August 9, 10, 1879.
48. Ibid.
49. *Leader*, August 11, 1879.
50. Ibid.
51. Ibid.
52. Ibid.
53. Grazeola, "Charcoal Burners War of 1879," 59.
54. *Leader*, August 11, 1879.
55. Ibid.
56. Grazeola, "Charcoal Burners War of 1879," 61.
57. *Leader*, August 11, 1879.
58. *Sentinel*, August 12, 1879.
59. *Sentinel*, August 10, 1879; *Leader*, August 11, 1879.
60. *Sentinel*, August 9, 10, 1879.
61. *Leader*, August 12, 1879.
62. Grazeola, "Charcoal Burners War of 1879," 56.
63. *Leader*, August 11, 1879.

VI

Escalation of the Charcoal Troubles

Determined to dramatize their plight, the burners persisted in staging protests throughout the charcoal territory of Eureka County. On August 11 sixteen burners carried out another charcoal stoppage at Roberts Creek. Teamster Burlingame was at that location to haul Pete Strozzi's coal to the smelters in Eureka when the strikers confronted him.[1] The burners ordered Burlingame not to fill the wagon, but the teamster proceeded to load. Burlingame reminded the burners that he was, after all, hauling Strozzi's property and not theirs, as mandated by his lawful contract.[2]

One of the burners then pushed Burlingame away from the wagon while reiterating the order not to load. As the confrontation waned, Strozzi himself appeared on the scene and promptly attempted to persuade the burners to permit his wagons to be loaded. Hoping to appeal to the burners' sense of fairness, Strozzi pointed out that unless his coal was hauled, he would incur a double financial loss, for his commodity would not be sold, while Burlingame would have to be paid nonetheless for his unutilized services. Despite Strozzi's plea, the burners remained unmoved; Strozzi and Burlingame had no choice but to return to Eureka with their wagon unfilled.[3]

Two days later, on August 13, the burners orchestrated another stoppage, this time at Pete Hansen's ranch, located in the proximity of Pine Station. Left in charge of ranch affairs directly by Hansen, teamster Patterson was making arrangements for loading coal. At that point, the burners burst on the scene under the command of Severino Strozzi, a high-ranking officer of the CBPA. On this occasion, the burners exhibited some willingness to compromise. In fact, the burners informed Patterson that they would allow the loading of those wagons already on the ranch grounds before the burners' arrival. However, all other wagons that reached the loading site afterward would be precluded from loading. Disconcerted by the unusual request, Patterson proceeded to inform Hansen by telegram of the burners' demands.[4]

Although this further incident went unmarked by violence or destruction of private property, local authorities responded swiftly and, the day after the stoppage at Pete Hansen's ranch, Deputy Sheriff J. B. Simpson arrested Severino Strozzi, the treasurer of the CBPA, on a riot charge.[5] Remarking on Strozzi's arrest, the *Sentinel* stated, "Simpson always manages to get away with his man and Strozzi is now lodged in the County Jail."[6] The following day, August 14, elapsed without reports of any significant charcoal disturbances. In fact, several charcoal teams, including Reilly's, Sadler's, Kaye's, and Foley's, were able to load their wagons without any interference from the burners.

While no major mishap occurred, August 14 did not end without a hurdle. The noteworthy incident of the day took place at John Torre's ranch and coincided with the final charcoal stoppage on record prior to the bloody confrontation that was to happen at Fish Creek a few days later. The target of the burners' wrath that day was Torre's young cousin. Confronted by several burners, whose faces were deliberately concealed beneath a mask of charcoal soot to elude identification, the young man was ordered to halt the loading of charcoal under the threat of death. All ranch activities immediately ceased, and any inclination to load even a speck of charcoal was quickly abandoned.[7]

The rationale behind the coal stoppages is hard to determine for certain. Surely, the burners were running out of options. The CBPA had not been effective. Its creation had represented a giant leap forward in the affirmation of the burners' right to a living wage. But the fledgling organization could expect to achieve only modest gains. Beyond being plagued from the onset by a dismally low membership of about 10 percent of the labor force engaged in charcoal production, the CBPA failed to articulate a comprehensive strategy to effectively further the interests of the charcoal burners, thus spawning factionalism within its rank and file.

It may be that by orchestrating systematic stoppages, the disaffected burners hoped to disrupt the distribution of charcoal and, subsequently, cripple the smelting industry of Eureka. If so, they failed: smelting continued throughout the period of the burners' skirmishes. As gleaned from the pages of the *Leader* of August 12, the Richmond Company had nothing out of the ordinary to report and simply stated that shipments had been sent out as customary, without the slightest allusion to any business impediments.

Similarly, H. Donnelly, superintendent of Eureka Consolidated, reported business as usual for the week of August 3 as well as the crucial week of the eighteenth, the time of the Fish Creek tragedy.[8] Further, the burners' implicit hope of harnessing the publicity generated by their activities to boost CBPA membership did not materialize, nor did community approval or solidarity with the burners' plight increase following the stoppages.

Although the burners' David and Goliath–like struggle elicited much popular support, the smelting operations remained the economic bastion of the entire community, from which the common wealth was derived. Clearly, any attempt at destabilizing smelting activities, thus threatening the collective welfare, would have been met with decisive opposition and strong condemnation. Ultimately, the only realistic alternative available to the militant burners was to elicit community sympathy by rendering their plight publicly and reenacting their struggle nonviolently.[9]

Eventually, the distressed burners, aware of that intangible line they dared not cross, opted to stage their passion play to advance their cause. In a balancing act, as deftly rehearsed as by a trapeze artist, the burners' protest assumed all the elements of a valiant, yet risky, contest. The outcome of their uprising had to be carefully regulated to avert a full-blown collision with legal authorities. By channeling their pent-up aggression on a few erratic wagon stoppages, uttering ominous threats, menacingly patrolling the countryside, and dumping charcoal sacks, perhaps the burners hoped to foster the perception of an overwhelming force determined to achieve their crucial objective by all available means, short of blatant warfare.

In examining the gradual unfolding of events, the careful observer will notice that the most aggressive stoppages involved the Italian charcoal producers of Eureka County. This seemingly fortuitous phenomenon was not a mere coincidence; it was symptomatic of a deeper conflict plaguing the relationship between the ostracized burners and their antagonistic conationals. Exploited by the Italian charcoal ranchers, the exasperated burners bitterly resented the open repudiation of ethnic solidarity of their callous countrymen, deeming it a worse betrayal than the antagonism waged by the Anglo charcoal producers. The ethnic conflict was exacerbated further by the existence of a padrone system that bound the riotous burners to the prosperous Italian charcoal merchants.

What seems certain, however, is that the CBPA failed to address the complex interplay of economic forces that loomed in the background and that ultimately determined the burners' miserable working conditions. The CBPA never evolved its outlook and remained narrowly and rigidly fixated on two key concerns, namely, the price of charcoal and the dubious handling of receipts. Although those were definitely the most immediate grievances impacting the burners' welfare at the time the crisis arose, the CBPA seemed oblivious to the deeper and more insidious economic underpinnings that constituted the broader context of the burners' grievances. And even in the sphere of charcoal price and receipt issuance, the association's well-meaning efforts fell considerably short of expectations.

Eventually, the burners must have come to the painful realization that theirs was a futile cause and that the odds were overwhelmingly stacked against them. Cognizant of their numerical weakness, their political impotence, and their ineffective leadership, and with public indifference staring them cruelly in the face, the burners must have felt compelled to take charge of their own disastrous affairs.

However ill-fated, the offensive strategy resorted to by the burners did enable them to succeed in temporarily disrupting the flow of charcoal without being apprehended by the law. Having firsthand knowledge of the territory and organized in bands of varying sizes, in the tradition of guerrilla warfare, the strikers would unleash a series of surprise raids at different loading stations throughout charcoal country and then abscond to the safety of the hills. Through an elaborate clandestine network of informers and messengers spanning the entire district, the rioters, endowed with the foreknowledge of the teamsters' available routes, could orchestrate their attacks with efficient impunity. The intricate scheme devised by the militant burners proved extremely successful in eluding the law enforcers trailing at their heels.[10]

The weekend of August 9–10 had represented another setback for the enforcers of the law. Initially dispatched to the troubled coal camps outside Eureka to seize the respective ringleaders, Eureka's lawmen found themselves greatly outnumbered by the adamant burners. Powerless to arrest the agitators, the lawmen begrudgingly returned to town, frustrated by their failed endeavor.

The spiraling crisis affected Sheriff Matthew Kyle with particular vehemence. The sheriff's temperament flared on Sunday, August 10, when Deputy Sheriff Simpson, who had been dispatched to Diamond Station to serve arrest warrants, turned up without the culprits in custody. Simpson not only reported his inability to find the parties sought but also acknowledged that even if he had found them, it would have been folly for him to attempt their arrest. Dismayed by Simpson's fruitless mission and exasperated by the widespread disturbances caused by the raiders, Sheriff Kyle countered his frustration with verbal resoluteness, announcing his "determination of arresting the parties for whom warrants had been issued at all hazards."[11]

With his personal credibility and that of the entire Eureka law enforcement agency at stake, Sheriff Kyle might have felt compelled to act swiftly and decisively to reassure his constituency that law and order would soon be restored. Perhaps by performing an overzealous deed, he could placate public apprehensions while sending a stern warning to the menacing burners. In retrospect, the acceleration of the charcoal crisis may also explain the "flying visit to Eureka on Saturday" by Sheriff Ed Raum,[12] an experienced lawman from White Pine County.[13] Conceivably, Raum visited Eureka to offer personal counsel to a beleaguered Sheriff Kyle.

In response to the rapid escalation of the saboteurs' activities, Sheriff Kyle held an urgent meeting with his deputies on the afternoon of August 10 to evaluate the gravity of the developments and formulate an appropriate action plan to placate the urgent situation. Subsequently, the lawmen decided to intervene by means of a selected and well-armed one-hundred-man posse to be deployed to the trouble spots in the hills the next morning. Sheriff Kyle entrusted Deputy Sheriff J. F. Mason with the responsibility of raising the posse while authorizing him to carry out all the needed preparations. Impelled by a sense of great urgency, by ten o'clock that night the dutiful deputy had recruited a force of thirty-five volunteers, far short of the desired number. Seemingly unperturbed by the meager lot assembled, Mason proceeded to make the necessary plans to launch the hurried mission in the wee hours of the approaching day.[14]

However, Mason's arrangements were swiftly aborted under pressure from influential Eurekans, including some notable Italians, who effectively argued that such a small force would be unable to enforce the law against the overwhelming force of the insurrectionists and that persisting would be sheer suicide. The wiser course of action pointed out by the judicious denizens was to appeal to the governor for military assistance. This far more prudent, though less heroic, alternative was submitted to an ambivalent Sheriff Kyle, who begrudgingly endorsed it.[15]

While grappling with the mounting crisis, defenders of law and order formulated alternative strategies for how best to handle the militant burners. The *Leader*'s editors advocated the creation of a sizable posse to escort the teams bound for the loading stations, where large quantities of charcoal awaited delivery to the furnaces. Under such a plan, the teamsters would be afforded legal protection to transact their loading activities safely, one loading post at a time.[16] Although seemingly a viable solution, the proposed strategy could not ward off the germ of violence. Indeed, it failed to consider the burners' capacity to muster an even superior force, thus fostering the hazardous conditions for imminent bloodshed.

On August 11 tensions were further heightened when representatives from Eureka Consolidated issued a cautionary statement, advising against the imposition of conditions restricting the company's discretionary power to secure charcoal from sources of its own preference. Further, the company's spokesmen bluntly declared that if their enterprise could not obtain charcoal at the price it requested, the furnaces would be shut down.[17] That same morning, Sheriff Kyle and B. J. Turner, chairman of the Eureka Board of County Commissioners, alerted Governor John Kinkead about the coal troubles in Eureka via telegram (as will be discussed in chapter 7).

Meanwhile, with the hastily assembled posse disbanded, a fragile calmness ensued in the police quarters. However, in the blink of an eye, Kyle, who only a few hours earlier had acquiesced to the intervention of the militia, went back on his pledge. Perhaps not wanting to appear weak or be beholden to the state authorities for the resolution of the local crisis, Kyle suddenly reclaimed the authority of his office. While displaying a more circumspect disposition toward the conflict, Kyle stated, in less confrontational terms, his intention "to make an effort to serve the warrants." In an interview released to the *Sentinel* on Monday evening, the sheriff admitted to "doing all in his power to arrange the present difficulties with the Italian coal burners. [Kyle] is anxious to avoid bloodshed, but is determined to be firm. The law will be enforced at all hazards."

The incongruous statements uttered by an ambivalent Kyle reflected the depth of the quandary the sheriff confronted. Perhaps in an effort to make light of the crisis and uplift the collective spirit, Sheriff Kyle infused his assessment of the crisis with an optimism unwarranted by the fragile circumstances, alluding to "some indications that the whole trouble will be satisfactorily adjusted to-day without the military going to the front." However, such unqualified "indications" might have been a mere strategy to buy time and forestall military intervention. Further, the sheriff's confidence in an imminent resolution of the coal crisis contrasted sharply with an "evenly divided" public opinion. The reporter ended the sheriff's interview on a confident note, stating, "In any event Sheriff Kyle may be relied upon to discharge his duty."[18]

Nevertheless, as suggested by the *Sentinel*'s headline of August 12, "The Coal Burners Strike Assumes a Serious Aspect," the crisis appeared to be precipitating rather than dissipating. After all, the various attempts made over the weekend by law officers to apprehend the instigators among the burners had proved futile, while their encounters with the riotous strikers had been pervaded by an unmistakable hostility. To exacerbate matters, a stern warning had been issued by one of the ringleaders, reiterating the strikers' determination to persevere in their efforts, while reminding the townsfolk of the burners' numerical superiority, so as to dissuade those contemplating retaliation against them. The *Sentinel* reported, "A body of 75 armed burners rode to the hotel, and the leader, in response to a remark that they were getting themselves into a bad box, replied that they fully appreciated the responsibility of the job they had undertaken, and were determined to carry it through. He also said that if any body of men should come from Eureka to check them, it would have to muster sufficient force to overcome not only his own but other bands that could soon be gathered."[19] Thus were the assertive intentions harbored by the strikers unequivocally conveyed to the local authorities. Disregarding such an explicit warning would have defied prudence.

On August 12, Sheriff Kyle abruptly reclaimed the authority he had surrendered to the Nevada Militia the day before by announcing his renewed determination to pursue all available options to resolve the coal crisis peaceably. According to the *Leader*, "Sheriff Kyle's plan...is to take one hundred picked men, well armed and mounted, and by their aid execute the warrants in his possession. [Kyle] is not only anxious to enforce the law, quell the disturbances, and protect those who are peacefully following their business, but to do it as economically as possible, so as not to impose an immense burden upon the taxpayers."[20]

The *Sentinel* confirmed the plan: "Sheriff Kyle is determined not to call upon the militia until he has exhausted all other means at his command." The article went on to say that "should [Kyle] find himself opposed by a force too strong to tackle, he will return to Eureka and call upon the State authorities for aid." Kyle and his posse left Eureka bound for Fish Creek the very same evening of August 12. Notwithstanding Kyle's earlier plan to rely on "a posse strong enough to cope with the largest body of burners yet seen together," the adamant sheriff returned to Eureka on the evening of August 13, accompanied only by H.B. McKee and Hank Storey, after having apprehended four of the ringleaders at Fish Creek.[21]

Despite Sheriff Kyle's avowal to end the charcoal dispute, some crucial elements of his plan remained unspecified in the newspaper's commentary. First, no qualification was provided as to what "at all hazards" might entail. It can be reasonably inferred that it implied enforcement of the law at all costs, including human lives. Second, the extent to which Sheriff Kyle was willing to endeavor before he "exhausted all other means at his command" remained undisclosed. Further, no elaboration was ever given as to what "all other means at his command" might have included. Last, what constituted "a force too strong to tackle" was left undefined.

Inexorably, the conflict deepened, while attitudes grew increasingly polarized between the burners and their adversaries. Indeed, the coal burners' troubles had intensified so dramatically that "the officers of the law felt that they either had to meet the issue squarely or to surrender ignominiously."[22] Such acute ambivalence revealed the severity of the dilemma the local authorities faced, obscuring any realistic hope for a mediated solution of the conflict.

Notes

1. Typically, a charcoal rancher was the owner of a forested tract of land. He hired charcoal burners to cut the trees on the property and dig earthen pits to transform the timber into charcoal. While the vast majority of Eureka's charcoal burners were Italians, only a handful of Italians were charcoal ranchers. Among them were Joseph Tognini, owner of a charcoal ranch at Alpha Station; John Torre, owner of a charcoal ranch near Fish Creek; and Peter Strozzi, owner of a charcoal ranch near Roberts Creek. Pete Strozzi was a charcoal rancher, not to be confused with Severino Strozzi, treasurer of the CBPA.
2. *Leader*, August 12, 1879.
3. Ibid.
4. Ibid.
5. *Leader*, August 14, 1879.
6. *Sentinel*, August 14, 1879.
7. *Leader*, August 15, 1879.
8. *Leader*, August 12, 1879.
9. Grazeola, "Charcoal Burners War of 1879," 65.
10. *Leader*, August 11, 1879.
11. *Sentinel*, August 12, 1879.
12. Ibid.
13. Myron Angel, *History of the State of Nevada*, 651.
14. *Sentinel*, August 12, 1879.
15. Ibid.
16. *Leader*, August 11, 1879.
17. Ibid.
18. *Sentinel*, August 12, 1879.
19. Ibid.
20. *Leader*, August 12, 1879.
21. *Sentinel*, August 13, 14, 1879.
22. *Sentinel*, August 12, 1879.

VII

The Deployment of the Militia

Anxious to secure the intervention of the militia to quell the labor unrest spawned by the charcoal crisis, Eureka's officials overstated the emergency. Keen on informing Governor Kinkead about the difficulties they faced in dealing with the rioters, Sheriff Matthew Kyle and B. J. Turner claimed that a force of two thousand armed burners patrolled the charcoal country, precluding teamsters from loading their charcoal supplies. An apprehensive Turner reported as fact rumored threats by the burners to carry out destruction of private property and even to set Eureka ablaze. The telegram's authors urged the governor to order the immediate deployment of the Second Brigade of the Nevada Militia. A second telegram was wired to the governor by a group of teamsters who had been victimized by the burners' actions, corroborating the first telegram and further pressuring the governor to intervene militarily.[1] Upon further inquiry into the burners' uprisings in Eureka, the governor approved the activation of the militia.

Once news of an impending intervention by the militia spread, the state press tuned in to the clamor from Eureka. Given the remoteness of the camp, most Nevada newspapers gleaned the particulars from the Eureka-based press, namely, the *Daily Sentinel* and the *Daily Leader*. Some journals, undeterred by distance from the troubled scene, ventured their own accounts. On August 12 the *Carson City Morning Appeal* misguidedly asserted that the daring charcoal burners, "the majority of whom are unnaturalized Italians," had seized control of the town of Eureka and were threatening to carry out much destruction unless their demands were satisfactorily met.[2]

Subsequently, the unchallenged notion that the burners actually seized control of the town of Eureka while threatening to raze it entered the annals of American history. Perhaps the most egregious of historical inaccuracies regarding the Italian charcoal burners' actions in Eureka was sanctioned by Hubert Howe Bancroft and James G. Scrugham. In compiling their respective histories of the Silver State, the authors lent credence to the false claim that Governor Kinkead deployed the state militia for the specific purpose of ridding the beleaguered town of Eureka of the assailing charcoal burners. Bancroft stated, "In 1879 the mine superintendents at Eureka rebelled at paying 30 cents a bushel for this indispensable article [charcoal], and fixed the price at 27 cents. The Charcoal Burners' association immediately declared war, refused to permit any to be delivered at the smelters, and took possession of the town of Eureka, threatening destruction to their enemies, the mine managers." In the same vein, Scrugham declared: "The new price schedule [27 cents] provoked the 'war.' The Charcoal Burners Association refused to deliver to the smelters. Not only did the smelters shut down, but for a time the town of Eureka was in possession by the strikers, who bade defiance to the owners and operators."[3]

In contrast to the *Carson City Morning Appeal*'s alarmist distortions, the view on the ground was more optimistic. Indeed, many Eurekans believed that, ultimately, no armed contest would pit the charcoal burners against the local authorities. In all likelihood, the local press predicted, the rioters would scatter to the hills, abandoning any thought of armed resistance once confronted by a resolute force.[4] One proponent of such a view was Pete Hansen, a coal rancher, who had just returned from the coal country the night of August 11. Though admitting that some of the burners had defied the law, Hansen stated that he did "not apprehend any serious trouble when the authorities once put in an appearance in force."[5] Similarly, the editor of the *Sentinel* opined that in calling upon the governor for assistance with the charcoal crisis, the petitioners had succumbed to rashness and that, in the end, military intervention would prove unwarranted.[6] Despite the auspicious predictions voiced by the local press, a disquieting uncertainty about the charcoal crisis persisted among Eureka's citizenry. In a fleeting remark, the *Sentinel* acknowledged that Eurekans held divergent expectations as to the outcome of the charcoal dispute: "People were about evenly divided last night as to whether the present coal troubles would end in a farce or a tragedy."[7]

News of an imminent deployment of the militia to quell the burners' insurgency was received with a blend of apprehension and excitement by many Eurekans. Reportedly, several establishments along Main Street were in ferment, their patrons engrossed in idle speculation about the uncertain outcome of the dispute. So pervasive was the fervor associated with the charcoal affair that the town children themselves were swept away by the social hysteria that engulfed Eureka. The *Leader* remarked that the youngsters of Eureka, no longer thrilled to assume the more conventional roles of Indians and cowboys, now preferred to emulate the far more exciting characters of the heroic militiamen in their pursuit of the lawbreaking burners. Apparently, the children's "battle," like the adults', was currently at a standstill.[8]

The role of the press in shaping public perception about the charcoal crisis was not insignificant. The *Leader* was less than detached in its reporting about the mounting tensions stemming from the disruption of the charcoal trade. In a decision reeking of partiality, the *Leader* of August 12 withheld from public scrutiny "a communication... received from a party signing himself 'Observer,' presenting the coal question from the coal burners' view." The editors apologetically informed readers that they would have been "pleased to publish, had not the writer forgotten an inexorable law of newspaper offices, and neglected to give his real name." While the editors themselves readily admitted that the real name of the presumed "observer" was not a requirement for publication, they pointed out that the signature of the "observer" would have lent "a guarantee of the good faith of the correspondent." As if to coax the "observer" out of anonymity, the journal declared, "If 'Observer' will call at the LEADER office, or send his name, the communication will be inserted."

Such an inflexible attitude toward the anonymous "Observer" contrasts sharply with the paper's relaxed stance with regard to "a letter from a well-posted gentleman in San Francisco," who informed the *Leader*'s editors that the Eureka Consolidated Company was seriously considering shipping all ore to California for reduction. Receipt of such a letter was publicly acknowledged by the journal on July 18 in a column titled "We Hope Not." Despite the destabilizing effect of the anonymously authored missive, the *Leader*'s editors did not seem to waver in presuming "the good faith of the correspondent."

While the charcoal burners struggled to better their meager livelihood out on the fringes of the Nevada frontier, Republican governor John Henry Kinkead steered the political affairs of the Silver State. Elected to office in 1879, Kinkead served his only term through 1882 as the third Nevada governor. Kinkead had previous ties to Eureka County as a bonding agent with the Great Republic Mine, which later became Eureka Consolidated.[9] The fifty-three-year-old governor was the most influential man in Nevada during the charcoal dispute. Possessing extensive business experience coupled with a formal knowledge of the legal system, Kinkead was aware of the legal issues surrounding the charcoal question.

Specifically, the charcoal impasse concerned two particular Nevada laws, namely, conspiracy and riot. At the time, conspiracy was defined as "two or more persons who either planned or instructed someone else to commit acts that injured health, morals, or trade and commerce."[10] The charge of conspiracy could be issued on the grounds of mere intent or planning. Thus, several charcoal burners, irrespective of their affiliation with the CBPA, were charged with conspiracy based on their willful refusal to provide needs for the charcoal market with the intent of prompting a commodity shortage to justify a price hike. Preventing charcoal from reaching the marketplace was thus construed as interference with state commerce.

The second alleged violation was rioting, defined as "an unlawful act of violence, either with or without a common cause or quarrel, or even…a lawful act, in a violent, tumultuous and illegal manner."[11] Intertwined with the conspiracy law, rioting in this case qualified the means by which the conspiracy was to be realized, namely, resorting to violence as a means to achieve the burners' end.

Following a narrow interpretation of the vaguely defined riot law, a charcoal burner could be considered guilty by merely exhibiting what a lawman could interpret as a potentially criminal act. In Grazeola's words, "A charcoal burner who yelled to a teamster 'No!' once and loudly while waving his arms could be arrested."[12] Clearly, Nevada's conspiracy and riot laws lent themselves to prejudicial interpretations that favored the interests of the state and large business owners to the detriment of the individual's rights, and the rights of immigrants in particular.

That Nevada was a state in which the execution of the law was taken quite solemnly, particularly when dealing with violations, actual or presumed, impacting state trade and commerce, was exemplified by an incident involving the Virginia & Truckee Railroad in early August 1879. Involved in a labor dispute, the mechanics' union barred a train with Governor Kinkead aboard from traveling into Storey County. Anticipating serious hostilities, twenty-five special lawmen "armed and ready to fight" were called to the scene by railroad superintendent Henry Yerington. The union men were arrested and charged with conspiring to interfere with trade and commerce. Bail was set at two thousand dollars each.[13]

Whereas harsh laws ensured the smooth functioning of trade and commerce by deterring those who threatened them, laws regulating conflicts between labor and management were virtually nonexistent. Acknowledging such a legalistic void, Limerick stated, "American law was not well prepared for the questions raised by industrial conditions in any form, but it was particularly unprepared for mining.... [T]the early premises of a rudimentary legal system drew attention away from the workplace and the company and toward individual responsibility.... The courts embraced the notion of individual responsibility, and, in the process, set up a perfect climate for corporate irresponsibility."[14]

Notwithstanding the appearance of neutrality, the laws of Nevada and their interpretation during the "bonanza years" clearly favored the interests of big business, branding this period of the state's history as one of extreme political dishonesty. In the words of historian Malcolm J. Rohrbough, "The advantage always accrued to the wealthy man of influence, regardless of what the laws said."[15]

According to the gospel of capitalism, the fruits of America's collective wealth sprouted directly from the industrialists' invested capital, making it seem perfectly natural that the propertied class should be accorded full hegemony of the marketplace, as well as determining the conditions to be accepted by the laboring masses. As Limerick observed, "In the West mine owners held great political power; when mining was a state's major source of income, its legislators had no interest in scaring away investors by seeming to support labor's side of the struggle. The political power of mine owners led to the intervention of the state militia in strikes, ostensibly to maintain order, but frequently to break the strike. Mine owners also had the support of the judges, as the conservative judicial temperament of the times ratified the rights of property."[16]

Indeed, during those turbulent years, out on the mining frontier politics and economics seemed to share a symbiotic relationship, frequently to the detriment of the public good. "The leaders in the mining industry became the state's most influential politicians," wrote Hulse. "There was much corruption, and the money of the wealthy rather than the will of the people decided the outcome of senatorial elections." The political influence of Nevada's powerful mining interests even reached the state's governorship: "In 1877, while serving his second term, Governor [Lewis] Bradley became the enemy of some of the richest mining companies on the Comstock Lode.... [W]hen he tried to win a third term, the mining firms opposed him and he lost the election. The winner was John H. Kinkead, a well-known mining and milling man who was more acceptable to mining interests."[17]

Definitely, Eureka charcoal burners' goals clashed with the decidedly probusiness policies favored by the government of Nevada. Governor Kinkead, with his strong ties to the mining industry, could hardly be expected to act as an impartial arbitrator of the charcoal crisis. The governor's callous view of the burners' revolt was reflected in the *Carson City Morning Appeal:* "His Excellency Governor Kinkead received no advices from Eureka yesterday, relative to the Civil War, from which it is to be inferred that the civil authorities have control of the mob.... [I]t is to be hoped so, and furthermore, it is to be greatly wished that the instigators to the uprising will be harshly dealt with."[18]

That the governor entertained little doubt about the burners' transgressions and the consequent justice meted out by the sheriff's posse would be confirmed in a speech given by Kinkead in 1881. While addressing the state legislature, the governor characterized the charcoal dispute of 1879 as an "impending riot" that "threatened the majesty of the law."[19] As Nevada's foremost authority, it was incumbent upon the governor to act swiftly and decidedly to guarantee the rule of law allegedly threatened by the rebellious burners. Following the chain of command, Kinkead called upon Brigadier General George M. Sabin, head of the Second Brigade of the Nevada Militia, stationed in Eureka, to take the appropriate steps to restore public order.

In carrying out the governor's order, General Sabin (then traveling out of state) issued an emergency call to his troops, urging them to stand ready for active engagement. Evidently, the militiamen were to perform an auxiliary role, lending support to Eureka's authorities as they mobilized to guarantee the safety of Eureka's citizenry and property.[20] Certainly, the somber reverberations of such a dramatic development did not go unnoticed by the thrill-seeking press, which heralded the governor's order in alarming tones, as attested by the following headlines: "A Speck of War: The Coal Burners' Strike Assumes a Serious Aspect; The Militia Ordered to Support the County Officials; Probabilities of a Conflict."[21]

Naturally, the authorization to deploy the state militia issued by Governor Kinkead implied the perception of an imminent peril beyond the power of local authorities to expunge. Lacking direct knowledge of the convoluted circumstances surrounding the charcoal crisis, the governor hinged his decision to mobilize the state militia wholly on the information he received from officials in Eureka, conveyed by means of three crucial telegrams all transmitted on the afternoon of August 11, 1879. The first and most elaborate one was authored by B. J. Turner, chairman of the Eureka County Board of Commissioners, and by Eureka sheriff Kyle.[22]

The second wire was sent by seven wealthy Eureka businessmen: W. W. Bishop, G. W. Baker, M. D. Foley, Tognini & Co. (Joseph Tognini), G. W. Lamoureux, J. Vanina, and Reinhold Sadler. The third telegram was originally addressed to General Sabin. It was a request for arms and ammunition submitted by Major H. T. Headley, ordnance chief of the Second Brigade of the Nevada Militia, regularly stationed in Eureka.[23] Given that Sabin was absent, Major Headley forwarded his appeal to Governor Kinkead.

Taken as a whole, the three telegrams seemed to provide enough evidence to support the governor's decision to intervene militarily. Certainly, the three wires compounded their respective strength into a compelling portrayal of an ominous scenario and ultimately swayed the governor. While all three telegrams reiterated a dire sense of urgency, the first was, undoubtedly, the most comprehensive and inflammatory:

> A large class of the citizens of Eureka county, Nevada, known as "The Coal Burners' Association," numbering some 2,000 persons, are now banded together and with arms in their possession are defying the civil authorities, and refuse to allow any of their number [for whom warrants have been issued] to be arrested. They now hold forcible possession of many coal-pits in the county, and by force have prevented and are now preventing the owners of charcoal from

hauling it to the furnaces, and are threatening to destroy other property and to burn this town.... [R]ioters...are under the command of desperate leaders. We, therefore, respectfully ask your Excellency to order the military of the Second Brigade into active service to quell such insurrection.[24]

The second wire, dispatched by the Eureka businessmen, conveyed an apocalyptic plea, asserting that the deployment of the militia was "absolutely necessary" and that the militiamen should "be called out at once to suppress those now in armed force, resisting the officers of the county."[25]

The third telegram, originally drafted for General Sabin, contained a detailed list of military supplies presumably needed to deal effectively with the state of emergency. Major H.T. Headley and Major C.J.R. Butler, adjutant of the Second Brigade, asked for "100 stands of arms, with full equipments, together with 4,000 rounds of cartridges, caliber 50, and 2,000 caliber 45." Obviously, the request for arms could have been granted only after the governor had deemed Turner and Kyle's petition to be legitimate.[26]

In turn, Governor Kinkead issued two replies. In accordance with formal procedure, Kinkead first wired General Sabin. Reiterating the assertions dispatched to him by Sheriff Kyle and B.J. Turner that "the county authorities are unable to suppress a riot in Eureka County and enforce the laws," the governor ordered General Sabin to "call into active service all force... necessary to aid the law officers in the proper execution of the laws," but only if such an intervention was "warranted by the facts." The governor instructed them to keep him abreast of the latest developments. Given Sabin's absence from Nevada, the governor dispatched a second telegram addressed to Colonel E.M. Robinson, the highest-ranking officer stationed in Eureka. The governor inquired about "the correct condition of affairs, the amount of available arms and ammunition, where the rioters are, etc."[27]

By labeling the burners "rioters," the governor's telegram to Robinson betrayed a thinly veiled prejudice. And the governor's latent misgivings were amply confirmed by Robinson's subsequent responses. In the first reply, Robinson confirmed that "rioters are preventing law-abiding citizens from sending coal to the furnaces and in some cases destroying property." Robinson further stated that, according to the sheriff, "1,000 men at Alpha, Roberts creek, Fish creek and Newark will resist his authority, with 1,000 more at various points who may aid the rioters in case of trouble." Despite the allegedly large number of rioters scattered throughout the charcoal camps and ready to confront the authorities, Robinson reported, "Sheriff says that with 100 men he can enforce the law." The colonel went on to say, "We have 100 stands of arms but no ammunition."

As if to underscore the seriousness of the situation further, Robinson asserted that "immediate action is necessary to prevent furnaces from closing down." Revealing the local authorities' proclivity toward a quick and economical resolution of the crisis, Robinson reassured the governor that "the law will be enforced with expedition at as small an expense to the State as the circumstances will admit." Robinson's second communication merely confirmed the state of readiness assumed by the newly mobilized militia forty-eight hours earlier, as commanded by General Sabin, per Butler. Last, the telegram solicited the governor's urgent instructions.[28]

Issuing forth as it did from such an authoritative source as a high-ranking military officer on the ground in Eureka, the report enhanced the credibility of the previous accounts of the emergency. Thus persuaded of the absolute necessity of authorizing an armed intervention to subdue the rioters, the governor informed Colonel Robinson: "Will send ammunition by express to-night. You can get guns from Elko if required. There are none here at present. Will do everything in my power."[29]

Quite likely, the military intervention urgently requested by Eureka's civil authorities to quell what they viewed as a growing menace hinged upon a critically mistaken number of the actual rioting burners. In their panicky telegram of August 11 to Governor Kinkead, B.J. Turner and Sheriff Kyle put the number of Eureka's charcoal burners at "some 2,000 persons...with arms in their possession." The inflated figure of 2,000 armed burners was reiterated on August 12 when an apprehensive Colonel Robinson, alarmed by rumors of legions of rioting charcoal burners running rampant through the hills of Eureka, sent a report to Governor Kinkead to inform him of "the correct conditions of the affairs" regarding the menacing activities of the burners. In his reply to the governor's request, Robinson affirmed, as previously noted, that 1,000 belligerent burners at Alpha, Roberts Creek, Fish Creek, and Newark were determined to defy the law, while another 1,000 were ready to support their comrades.[30]

Although less disquieting in the assessment of the actual threat posed by the armed strikers, the total number of burners potentially ready to engage the civil authorities cited in Robinson's reply, based upon Sheriff Kyle's earlier estimation, remained unchanged. Perhaps as a result of mere repetition by authoritative sources, the perception of a vast horde of charcoal burners numbering 2,000 was irreversibly established in Eureka's collective mind. While the charcoal crisis was deepening, it is likely that the figure of 2,000 armed burners was deliberately inflated by Eureka's leaders to secure the governor's immediate military intervention and thus permanently quell the charcoal burners' uprisings.[31]

Yet the actual number of ill-disposed charcoal burners actively engaged in charcoal stoppages, as attested by eyewitnesses who encountered the rioters in the Eureka countryside, was minuscule when compared to the titanic figures dispatched to the governor by the local authorities. The largest concentration of hostile burners was reported on August 12 by teamster Charley Grimm, who saw 75 armed Italians gathered at Alpha two days earlier.[32] On Monday, August 11, a teamster named Jose Burlingame was prevented from loading coal for Pete Strozzi from Roberts Creek by a force of 16 burners.[33] Strong corroboration for a considerably lower estimate than the one furnished by the fretful authorities was further provided by a teamster and charcoal rancher named Pete Hansen. Hansen recalled that while following one of his customary rounds of the local ranches, he had seen roughly 50 Italian burners in all during his entire day. Of course, there would be no way to know whether the Italian burners spotted by Hansen were or were not CBPA members or were or were not primed for violent action. The teamster reported that "not over half of these belonged to the Coal Burners' Association or were in sympathy with that organization."[34]

Hansen's estimate of the burners sighted in one day assumes particular relevance when considering his role as a charcoal rancher and teamster. Being adversely affected by the burners' disruption of the charcoal trade, Hansen would have had every incentive to exaggerate the number of burners he had seen along his route. Incidentally, on Wednesday, August 13, the burners carried out a stoppage at Pete Hansen's ranch near Pine Station.[35]

Certainly, the discrepancy between the relatively low cumulative number of roughly 130 cited by direct observers, such as Hansen and Burlingame, and the exorbitantly high figures of 2,000 burners declared by Eureka's authorities was quite vast. Further evidence that the inconsistency was indeed enormous stemmed from the later testimony of Domenico Quadro, a charcoal burner and active CBPA member called to appear before the grand-jury hearing convened to probe the Fish Creek incident. Quadro admitted his active participation in the wagon stoppages on the day of the incident at Fish Creek as a member of a burner band tasked with patrolling the charcoal-hauling routes and stopping any team it intercepted. Quadro's testimony placed the size of the burners' band at 80 or 90.[36]

Given the extreme circumstances, some precautionary measures were certainly warranted, and the appeal for help by Eureka's officials seems quite defensible. In accordance with their civic duty, the city leaders had already taken action to forestall a further deterioration of the crisis. In fact, as previously mentioned, late Sunday evening of August 10, Deputy Mason had issued a bugle call with the intention of assembling a 35-man posse. Presumably, this law-enforcing body was formed to apprehend the instigators of the charcoal uprisings. As recounted by the *Sentinel* of August 12, Deputy Mason "was prevailed from going by prominent citizens including several Italians who argued that such a number would be inadequate to enforce the law, that a conflict would be inevitable if they attempted to do so, and that the result of a fight would only result in the annihilation of the posse. They argued the advisability of calling upon the Governor for men and arms, and this was finally agreed to."

Almost certainly, the impulse not to dispatch the posse, on the evening of August 10, was the same that prompted Turner and Kyle to dispatch the telegram to the governor on August 11. It was, after all, the simple realization by the commissioner and by the sheriff that there were not enough lawmen in Eureka to subdue the belligerent charcoal burners that led them to request the militia's intervention.

Indeed, those who pleaded for the deployment of the militia seemed spurred more by emotion than by reason. Without detracting from the gravity of the mounting crisis, ostensibly Eureka's civic leaders fell prey to hysteria, causing them to inflate greatly the burners' alleged threat, as corroborated by the *Sentinel* of August 15: "Here [civic leaders] make believe by their assumed terrified looks that an army of lawless rebels and revolutionary men (worse than a barbaric invasion) threaten destruction at Alpha one of the teamster stations where charcoal was picked up for shipment to the smelters and all around while people coming here from there know nothing about it, and have to come to Eureka to be informed of that fact."

The *Sentinel*, openly critical of what it saw as an irrational stance assumed by the city leaders, reiterated its skepticism: "The local authorities acted hastily in calling the Governor for aid, we think it extremely doubtful whether the militia will be needed at all."[37]

The premature call for the urgent deployment of the militia loses further legitimacy when one considers Colonel Robinson's erroneous assessment of the impact the burners' actions were having upon Eureka's smelting industry. In his telegram to Governor Kinkead, Colonel Robinson appealed for immediate action in order to prevent the furnaces from closing down. Yet it was public knowledge that the closure of the major furnaces, allegedly occasioned by a severe charcoal shortage, was not as certain as Colonel Robinson implied in his telegram.

According to the *Leader*, Eureka Consolidated held a two-week charcoal supply and had "a considerable amount…coming in by both rail and team." Similarly, at the Richmond, there was "coal enough on hand to run the furnaces about ten days," and small deliveries continued to trickle in.[38] Besides the charcoal supply already in store at the two major smelting sites, "a well-posted gentleman" informed the *Leader* that, as a result of overproduction, there was enough charcoal already burned throughout the coal country and ready for delivery to satisfy the furnaces' needs for fuel for a year.[39] Although the actual amount of coal available in the charcoal camps around Eureka was undetermined, the assertion put forth by the anonymous gentleman was strongly challenged by the coal producers themselves. The *Leader* of August 15 noted, "There is much dispute as to the quantity of coal available in the hills. The coal burners claim that not more than three months' supply is available." In any case, it seems clear that the smelters were not in imminent danger of closing.

Spokesmen for the Richmond, echoing Donnelly's earlier pledge to continue smelting, reiterated that their company would not suspend operations until the supply of available charcoal was exhausted. Because no bleak declarations of an immediate shutdown of smelting operations had been issued by the industry, it was implicitly understood that the smelter operators remained optimistic that a resolution of the charcoal crisis was at hand. In fact, the *Leader* reported a statement allegedly made by Donnelly in predicting that the charcoal dispute would be resolved "shortly."[40]

The sequence and description of events thus far outlined clearly suggest that the perception of the tense circumstances involving the defiant burners, as reported in the string of telegrams sent to Governor Kinkead, was tainted by prejudice. The governor's decision relied upon the information received from the official sources in Eureka, information the governor naturally accepted at face value. After all, there was no sound reason for the governor to doubt the accuracy of the reports provided by Eureka's most prominent citizens and corroborated by the local sheriff. Yet notwithstanding the credibility of the sources, the accounts depicting the state of affairs in Eureka were flawed.

A detached analysis of the unfolding developments reveals a less gloomy reality than that painted by the telegrams addressed to the governor. Indeed, from the very onset of the stoppages, which began on July 17 and continued through August 11, when the telegrams were first issued, law and order within Eureka and surroundings had been only fleetingly breached. Certainly, during this period the burners engaged in acts of defiance against their presumed enemies as a reaction to long-standing conditions of extreme exploitation. Nonetheless, the charcoal stoppages, as frustrating to local commerce as they were, represented moderate acts of protest by which to draw public awareness to the burners' plight rather than a challenge to law and order except for interfering with teamsters and the destruction of property. Indeed, throughout this phase, not a single openly hostile confrontation between the burners and the law took place.

At about this time, things got worse. Within the next forty-eight hours, the charcoal troubles intensified so acutely that the smelter managers felt compelled to reconsider their earlier decisions to remain in operation. Announcing the news to its readers, the *Leader* stated, "It is understood that the Richmond Company has decided to close down for a time, and has given orders to Messrs. Tognini & Vanini [sic] and other contractors to cease delivering coal." The newspaper further declared, "It is also understood that the Eureka Consolidated Company will shortly follow suit." As to the reasons behind such a drastic decision by the two smelting giants, the *Leader* explained: "The managers agree that to continue operations under the present circumstances would be impracticable, and as the coalburners will submit to no arbitration or accept any settlement except absolute dictation of the manner in which coal shall be delivered and the price paid, there is really no other resort."[41]

The newspaper lamented the circumstances leading to the closure of the smelters while also bemoaning the austere effects the suspension of the smelting works would cause. In addition to describing widespread unemployment, the paper further cautioned that "the full force of the suspension will be most grievously felt by the coal burners themselves." The newspaper elaborated: "With no demand for coal, and 2,000 men cut off from their only means of subsistence, this army of producers will be confronted with want and destitution." The *Leader*'s article reproached the burners, whose overproduction of coal had unwittingly wreaked havoc within the local Eureka economy. The burners' unrest came "at a time when capital was seeking investment in the district, and when the prospects of the town were never brighter."[42]

Conceivably, the smelters' decision to shut down their operations was prompted more by expediency than by necessity. As we have seen, it was widely known that the smelting companies' warehouses abounded with charcoal, with a large-enough surplus to see them through the winter. More likely, the move was designed to increase their bargaining power in dealing with the burners' demands.[43]

Though the charcoal dispute comprised several strands, its abrupt deterioration might be linked to one of the burners' antagonists, Italian charcoal contractor Joseph Tognini, one of the signers of the second telegram dispatched to the governor. On August 10 the burners converged on Tognini's ranch with the intent of halting a charcoal shipment. In the process, an undetermined number of sacks filled with charcoal, allegedly ranging from seven hundred to two thousand, were also dumped.[44] Because the affray occurred the day before the telegrams were forwarded to the governor, it seems conceivable that the burners' incursion at Tognini's ranch precipitated a critical aggravation of an already tense state of affairs. Such an inference would be consistent with the internal dynamics of the padrone system previously described.

Eagerly awaiting the delivery of arms and ammunition promised by the state authorities due to arrive in Eureka on the evening train of August 12, the command of the Second Brigade dispatched Lieutenant Budd Reynolds with a six-militiaman escort during the morning hours. Fearing a potential raid by the burners to seize the traveling arsenal, the militia squad carried out a reconnaissance mission along the Eureka and Palisade Railroad line to ensure a safe delivery of the awaited shipment.[45]

This general state of alertness, along with the official mobilization of the state militia, induced a temporary suspension of burners' hostilities, spawning the conditions for an implicit truce. Although the militia was placed on a state of readiness, and remained idle at the local armory, the possibility of its imminent intervention appeared to temper the rebellious spirit of the bolder insurgents. In effect, hostile resistance subsided, enabling law enforcers to execute their outstanding warrants more readily while taking into custody some of the wanted outlaws. Among the presumed lawbreakers figured the president of the burners' association, Angelo del Bondio, who, on the morning of August 13, was escorted before Justice Cromer for a preliminary hearing.

Charged with fomenting unrest and inciting riot, as well as other offenses, del Bondio was held on one thousand dollars' bail, while his trial was set for an unspecified date in September. In an informal interview with a *Sentinel* reporter, del Bondio refuted the charges lodged against him. In fact, he asserted that his goals as president of the association were twofold: first, the promotion of the price of charcoal and, second, the elimination of discriminatory practices waged by certain merchants against the burners. Ultimately, del Bondio denied any responsibility for any of the criminal deeds perpetrated by the burners.[46]

Coincidental with del Bondio's arrest, on August 13 the treasurer of the association, Severino Strozzi, was placed in the county jail. Strozzi had been arrested the day before by Deputy Sheriff J. B. Simpson, at Pine Station, for his leading role in preventing the loading of Patterson's team. According to the *Sentinel*, Strozzi's "career had suddenly been checked, after giving Charlie [sic] Grimm a wild goose chase on Sunday." Meanwhile, the very same day, Sheriff Kyle arrived in town, escorting four ringleaders from the Fish Creek area, whom he had apprehended with the help of teamsters H. B. McKee and Hank Storey. Once the lawbreakers were securely behind bars, the lawmen hastily departed for Roberts Creek, where they intended to carry out additional arrests.[47]

Although the lawmen succeeded in decapitating the leadership of the burners' movement, several small groups of burners remained on the prowl, scouring the hillsides in their relentless pursuit of teamsters. Admittedly, the strikers succeeded in fomenting a climate of fear throughout the charcoal country, intimidating those imprudent teamsters bent on continuing their charcoal trade activities. In an increasingly desperate effort to prevail in spite of the odds, scores of burners preserved their anonymity beneath a mask of coal grime, thus hoping to enhance their chances of going unrecognized by the lawmen.[48]

As if to allay public fears of a rash military intervention, General Sabin stated categorically that the militia would be deployed only as a last resort, in the event the civil authorities proved ineffective in settling the charcoal dispute. Seemingly satisfied with the lawmen's handling of the conflict, General Sabin remained in the background and simply monitored the situation.[49]

Notes

1. *Leader*, August 11, 1879.
2. *Carson City Morning Appeal*, August 12, 1879.
3. Hubert Howe Bancroft, *History of Nevada, California, and Wyoming, 1540–1888*, 284–85; James G. Scrugham, *Nevada: The Narrative of the Conquest of a Frontier Land*, 320.
4. *Sentinel*, August 12, 13, 1879; *Leader*, August 12, 1879.
5. *Sentinel*, August 12, 1879.
6. *Sentinel*, August 12, 1879.
7. *Sentinel*, August 12, 1879.
8. *Leader*, August 12, 1879.
9. Angel, *History of the State of Nevada*, 434.
10. M. S. Bonnifield and T. W. Healy, comps., *The Compiled Laws of the State of Nevada in Force from 1861 to 1900*, no. 2416, sec. 110, 1:478–790.
11. Ibid., no. 2428, sec. 122, 1:580–81.
12. Grazeola, "Charcoal Burners War of 1879," 68.
13. *Daily Nevada State Journal*, August 2, 1879.
14. Limerick, *Legacy of Conquest*, 108–11.
15. Malcolm J. Rohrbough, *The Land Office Business: The Settlement and Administration of American Public Lands, 1789–1837*, 61.
16. Limerick, *Legacy of Conquest*, 117.
17. Hulse, *Silver State*, 105–6, 118, 120.
18. *Carson City Morning Appeal*, August 14, 1879.

19. Nevada State Legislature, *Appendix to the Journals of the Senate and the Assembly, Tenth Session (1881): First Biennial Message of Governor Kinkead, Governor of Nevada, Delivered to the Legislature, January 4, 1881*, 3–4.
20. *Carson City Morning Appeal*, August 12, 1879.
21. *Sentinel*, August 12, 1879.
22. *Leader*, August 11, 1879.
23. Ibid.
24. Ibid.
25. Ibid.
26. Ibid.
27. Ibid.
28. Ibid.
29. Ibid.
30. *Sentinel*, August 13, 1879.
31. *Leader*, August 12, 1879.
32. *Sentinel*, August 12. 1879.
33. *Leader*, August 12, 1879.
34. *Sentinel*, August 12, 1879.
35. *Leader*, August 13, 1879.
36. *Leader*, September 2, 1879.
37. *Sentinel*, August 12, 1879.
38. *Leader*, August 12, 1879.
39. *Leader*, August 13, 1879.
40. *Leader*, August 12, 1879.
41. *Leader*, August 15, 1879.
42. Ibid.
43. *Leader*, August 13, 1879.
44. *Sentinel*, August 12, 1879.
45. *Leader*, August 13, 1879.
46. *Sentinel*, August 13, 1879.
47. *Sentinel*, August 14, 1879.
48. *Leader*, August 15, 1879.
49. *Leader*, August 16, 1879.

VIII

Veritas's Denunciations

In the absence of mitigating forces such as the Eureka Catholic Church headed by Father Montiverde or the Società Italiana di Mutua Beneficenza, the Italian Mutual Benefit Society, founded in San Francisco in 1858[1] to help Italian immigrants in need of assistance and replicated in other major centers with a large Italian presence, class antagonism between the Italian charcoal burners and Italian entrepreneurs intensified. Class strife among the Italians had already been exposed in an August 6 letter to the press by a social critic with the pen name "Sincerity." In a dispatch to the *Leader*, the self-appointed advocate for the charcoal burners' cause denounced the prominent Italian merchants of Eureka for exploiting their poor countrymen.[2]

On August 15, 1879, the *Eureka Sentinel* published "a statement of facts, in justification of the Coal Burners' Association," authored this time under the pseudonym "Veritas," Latin for "Bearer of Truth." Lamenting the fact that the "coal question" had been treated one-sidedly by the press, favoring the "corporations" and the "contracting middlemen," the crusader for the burners' struggle wished to rectify the bias.

In this author's view, the bold exposé drafted by Veritas could be dubbed an "Emancipation Proclamation" for the oppressed Italian charcoal burners, who found in the mysterious orator their truest defender. Veritas displayed an erudite upbringing and an eloquence that was incisive and disarming. Well versed in nineteenth-century political discourse, his article reads like a populist manifesto, a sharp critique of laissez-faire capitalism. "Veritas" wrote: "Rumors have been circulated to the effect that the furnaces would shut down, through the cause of this coal burners' strike, to prejudice the people against the most sacred right of the American people, the right of free labor, free speech, freedom of public meetings, unions, orders or societies, but with great care hushing the real motives that may justify a temporary suspension of our furnaces."

As if anticipating a cynical response from the contemptuous teamsters, who allegedly cheated the charcoal manufacturers, the foresighted writer urged the doubtful reader to draw a comparison between the contractors' wealth, derived from easy work, and the abject poverty endured by the toilers of the forest. Veritas asserted boldly:

> Not even the slightest hint has been thrown to the...wrong treatment these poor coal burners have been subjected to through their contractors, who have grown fat and opulent, generally at the expense of the poor producers, while these latter are left in the most dire destitution, and driven to despair...to starve to death, or to rise against monopoly, their oppressor...by a natural instinct of nature and law of preservation.... [T]his strike has been going on for a month, yet no lives have been taken or threatened, nor any property destroyed.

Veritas further declared that, in reality, the rate of thirty cents per bushel of charcoal was an incidental issue for the rioting burners. The insurgents' real aspiration was the dissolution of all exploitative contractual bonds with the grasping charcoal dealers. Ultimately, the burners' goal, wrote Veritas, was the establishment of a straightforward business arrangement with the smelters, thus enabling charcoal producers and consumers to deal directly with each other, bypassing the middlemen. Echoing the burners' grievances, Veritas reiterated that the intermediary agents swindled the charcoal manufacturers, hence ensnaring them into perpetual indebtedness.

In his vigorous denunciations, Veritas exposed what he perceived as a crafty scheme, presumably orchestrated by those responsible for the burners' plight. The writer claimed that the wagon-stoppage incident at Alpha had been exaggerated to ignite the indignation of the community, providing a compelling pretext for the deployment of a repressive force to the troubled district. In fact, the inconsistency of the critics' claim regarding the events at Alpha was swiftly laid bare by the accuser. Apparently, the residents of Alpha were utterly unaware of the imminent destruction about to be unleashed by an army of lawless rebels upon their community. The oblivious townsfolk learned about such a diabolical plot from their fellow citizens in Eureka.

Veritas concluded the strikers' defense by soliciting an altruistic gesture from the dealers: "Enough, gentlemen; throw down your mask, be fair and just, and in atonement for the past be at least humane in time to come. And since you have been made rich by these poor workers, don't try to raise prejudices or talk of sending an army with guns, bullets, etc." Perhaps in an attempt to ease tensions, Veritas ended his intercession on a lighthearted note: "But it better becomes your duty to send an army of cheese and macaroni to quench the hunger of these poor, famished, desperate wretches, who are really more hungry than ill-disposed" (see appendix A).

Predictably, Veritas's diatribe did not go unchallenged by his critics. The next day, August 16, the *Eureka Sentinel* published a caustic rebuttal articulated by Joseph Tognini and Joe Vanina, two of the most influential Italian charcoal dealers in Eureka County (see appendix B). Tognini and Vanina endeavored to attract the sympathy of the general citizenry by opening their scathing attack on Veritas's denunciations with a categorical condemnation of strikes. They stated: "Strikes don't pay. Take the railroad strikers and the glass-blowers at Pittsburgh, Pa. What have they accomplished?"

Careful to defuse Veritas's powerful humanitarian message, the two *prominenti* craftily framed the debate in the impersonal terms of "labor and capital," revealing a deeper objectification of workers as mere commodities deferential to capital. By dehumanizing their poorer countrymen, the two Italian entrepreneurs seemingly reflected the materialistic spirit of America during the waning years of the nineteenth century. Seemingly aligned with capital, the local press had previously reported on the negative effects of strikes nationwide such as the Fall River strike in Massachussets.[3]

Clearly resentful of the personal insinuations voiced by Veritas, the vilified contractors challenged their accuser to reveal the presumed identities of the contracting middlemen, reworded as "bloodless monopolies" by the accused Italian merchants. Undaunted by the accusations hurled by the burners' crusader, the two Italian contractors demanded precise information pertaining to names, dates, facts, and other details while bluntly rejecting the sweeping generalities stated by Veritas. Candidly challenging the veracity of their accuser's claims, Tognini and Vanina urged Veritas to reveal the names of those "poor devils" who supposedly had been starved to death.

Consistent with their entrepreneurial interests, the contractors invoked the supremacy of the law of supply and demand as the incontrovertible determinant of human conduct in the realm of commerce. Implying the primacy of the business impulse, the contractors surmised that the state of local affairs was virtually inalterable. As beneficiaries of a free-market economic system at the time of the Eureka charcoal crisis, Tognini and Vanina's unshakable faith in the marketplace is quite comprehensible. However, in their ardent desire to submit all business transactions to the rigid law of supply and demand, Tognini and Vanina seemed to have forgotten the controversy that arose two years earlier when the smelters, in an attempt to curb their transportation costs for charcoal, articulated a plan to contract with the railroad for the delivery of a substantial amount of fuel and ore directly to the smelting sites at much cheaper rates than the teamsters could offer.[4] Plainly, on that significant occasion, the venerated "law of supply and demand" was altered to favor the interests of the broader economy, which benefited more by protecting the greater freighting industry's labor force than the railroad's fewer workers.

Expanding further upon the intrinsic virtues of the marketplace, the charcoal dealers reminded Veritas that Eureka Consolidated and the Richmond Company were to be viewed as the community's vital benefactors, upon whose successful operations the financial well-being of every Eurekan depended. Accordingly, no interference with their smelting activities should be permitted.

In their barbed retort, the Italian merchants distanced themselves further from their ethnic cohorts, the charcoal burners, whom they defined as "a lawless band calling itself a union" and "an organized mob." In an effort to neutralize their accuser's harsh depiction of them as "bloodless monopolies," the contractors declared that they "are doing everything in the world for the benefit and welfare of the camp." Presumably, in the eyes of Tognini and Vanina, the charcoal burners were not viewed as legitimate members of the "camp," but were summarily dismissed as an unruly lot whose seditious acts threatened the camp's prosperity.

While denying personal responsibility for the creation of the exploitative conditions under which the oppressed burners toiled, Tognini and Vanina seemed to imply that the general welfare of the camp depended, in no small degree, upon the relentless exploitation of the charcoal burners. Indeed, nowhere in their indignant rejoinder is a hint of compassion toward the suffering of their conationals to be found, nor is the burners' ill treatment by the contractors ever acknowledged. Yet in their categorical and overstated denial of any culpability toward the downtrodden burners, the two Italian contractors seemed to, inadvertently, admit some measure of responsibility.

Further, from the contractors' perspective, events at Alpha had hardly been exaggerated. Tognini and Vanina asserted that private property consisting of two thousand bushels of charcoal had, in fact, been disseminated over a twenty-acre surface, while armed rioters threatened the lives of those teamsters and burners legally permitted to load and transport the contracted charcoal.

In their vehemence to silence their vocal critic, the merchants admitted the existence of a hierarchical order within Eureka's Italian enclave. Notably, the merchants' final assertion perhaps revealed in earnest the true dimension of their ambivalent ethnic allegiance. Bluntly dismissing Veritas's true intent in suggesting the delivery of "cheese and macaroni" rather than sending "an army with guns, bullets, etc." to the destitute burners, the incensed merchants chose to react to the ethnic slur they presumed lied concealed within the critic's exhortation. In an incongruous display of ethnic solidarity, the shrewd merchants attempted to discredit their challenger by seizing upon his unwitting prejudice.

Unaware of Veritas's true identity, the two prominent detractors went on the offensive by stating, "Veritas is exceedingly funny in his conclusions, when he speaks of cheese and macaroni as opposed to guns, bullets, &c., but we imagine his levity will not be appreciated by the better class of Italians, who thoroughly understand the meaning of this slur against their countrymen. 'Cheese and macaroni!' 'Veritas,' you have put your foot in it. Your sympathy is not wanted."

Acknowledging only obliquely their shared ethnicity with the burners, the merchants, convinced that Veritas was some non-Italian humanitarian, and perhaps even a charcoal burner himself, though ignorant of the peculiar traits of the Italian immigrants, warned their litigant, "Your sympathy is not wanted by the better class of Italians." Indeed, the prosperous Italian dealers, who vehemently opposed the burners' quest for economic emancipation, seemed ideologically and pragmatically aligned with the preservation of the capitalistic system and its class-based design.

In a final verbal clash, reported by the *Eureka Daily Sentinel* on August 17, Veritas eloquently addressed the Italian contractors' rebuttal (see appendix C). Undaunted by the merchants' unyielding refutation, Veritas proceeded to address, methodically, each contention raised by his detractors. Once again, he reiterated the parasitic and opportunistic conduct exhibited by the predatory charcoal brokers. In answering the crucial question "Who has grown fat?" Veritas indicted "those who but a few years ago were burning coal for a living, then willing to enhance the prices, but now leading an easier life, and some other following other business."

Veritas's revelation that the prominent Italian merchants, now intent on exploiting their countrymen, had been, only four years earlier, "as poor as the average coal burner" adds a subtler dimension to the class-conflict dynamics confronting Eureka's Italians. Having acquired a privileged status only recently, and partly at the expenses of their laboring countrymen, the newly successful Italian entrepreneurs had reason to feel anxious about their latest financial achievements.

With their newly attained position still fragile and vulnerable to potential upheavals within the social order, the emerging Italian elite may have resolved to solidify their social rank. Determined to preserve their hegemony in the face of increasing pressures arising from the lowest stratum of the Italian labor force, Eureka's Italian elite might have assumed an intransigent posture toward the clamoring burners. Increasingly, the burners fought to end those deprivations bred by the merchants' exploitation. With tensions mounting, Eureka's privileged Italians reacted by intensifying their hostility toward their laboring counterparts, in the hope of preserving a firm foothold on their social standing while simultaneously amassing ever-increasing wealth.

Although the foregoing line of reasoning is wholly conjectural, it does find a hint of support within the hazy realm of Italian folklore. Following millennia of thorny history on their soil, Italians seem to have noticed certain human tendencies, regular enough to become embodied in their belief system. Accordingly, the popular proverb "Dio ci liberi dai poveri arricchiti" (May God keep us from the poor who have become rich) has gained much currency over the centuries. The dynamics exhibited by the new Italian bourgeoisie in Eureka, Nevada, at the close of the 1870s seem to have confirmed the forewarning embedded in the old Italian adage.

Last, Veritas, sensing that the end of his mission was near, decried the penury of those he sided with, lamenting the burners' helplessness to hire skilled lawyers in their quest for justice. Then, in the following line, Veritas prepared to remove the mask of anonymity under which he assiduously advocated for the charcoal burners' just cause, revealing that the charcoal burners' loyal friend "is not a professional knight of the quill, but a knight of the camera.... [He] has volunteered his services to the cause in as far as things are kept within the limits of the law...having been chosen by these burners, to fairly submit to the public their grievances, their wrongs and their reasons." Declaring that the burners' aim had been attained, Veritas asserted, "The other side of the medal has been exposed.... To the people belong the sentence. This is our ultimatum." For those still baffled by Veritas's true identity, the halo of mystery in which the champion of the burners' cause shrouded himself was dispelled when his pseudonym was cast off to reveal "Louis Monaco, Alias Veritas, for the Coal Burners."

Although Monaco was not himself a burner but a Swiss Italian photographer and owner of a successful studio in Eureka, he articulated the burners' cause most poignantly.[5] The crusading photographer argued passionately in favor of the Italian charcoal burners' strike in the summer of 1879. Monaco's condemnation of the exploitation and abject destitution imposed upon his countrymen by "the better class of Italians" demonstrated that class allegiance can trump ethnic loyalty, but, on rare occasions, the converse may also prevail. In defiance of intransigent class boundaries, Monaco exhibited an enduring spirit of compassion in the face of human suffering, an empathy for the oppressed that transcended space, time, and the prejudice of class.

In his earnest condemnation of the maltreatment endured by his countrymen at the hand of a coercive economic system, Monaco demonstrated singular intellectual sophistication as well as a masterful use of the English language, a rare attainment for any immigrant in any age. Endowed with remarkable knowledge and political insight disproportionate to his age, the Swiss Italian effectively drew subtle analogies and inferences regarding the plight of the impoverished burners and their offenders. Monaco advocated for the abolition of the unfair contracts that held the burners in bondage, "where one side reaped all the benefits, and the other the toilsome labor."[6]

Exposing with clinical dexterity the ideological contradiction in which the Eureka contractors lay entangled, Monaco compared their one-sided logic to that espoused by Anglo workers to justify the mistreatment of Chinese laborers. Indeed, if in order to protect the economic interests of the Anglo labor force and other non-Chinese workers in a depressed economy the "coolies" could be removed from the marketplace, then the same logic could be conversely applied. Thus, it would become equally legitimate to demand the abolition of those exploitative contracts that undermined the economic interests of the Italian charcoal burners, a segment of the American labor force.

The persuasive power of Monaco's oratory on behalf of the downtrodden burners was greatly enhanced by the author's thorough knowledge of American history. In a sympathetic attempt to further legitimize the burners' grievances, Monaco drew a direct parallel between the struggling burners and the beleaguered American colonists of early days, when they too were oppressed by the exploitative yoke of their English masters. Mining the wisdom of America's glorious past, embodied by the US Constitution, Monaco boldly stated, "We claim it by the very right our fathers declared, 'When in the course of human event [sic], it becomes,' etc. By the identical law this country has freed itself from tyranny, injustice and imposition."[7]

In his unflagging endeavor to legitimize the burners' uprisings, Monaco implied that the "coal strike" was just and quintessentially American. Deftly, Monaco employed the rhetoric of American independence invoked by the Republic's founding fathers in their fervent struggle to rid the colonies of their British oppressors at the dawn of the Revolutionary War of 1776 to justify the equally universal aspirations adopted by the forsaken charcoal burners.

Monaco's bold parallel reveals a powerful allusion. His reference to the pre-Revolutionary liberation creed implies that if the American colonists were utterly justified in their military insurrection against their British rulers to attain liberty and justice, by the same righteous principles the oppressed charcoal burners were equally entitled to rebel against their subjugators who also deprived them of liberty and justice. In Monaco's view, the impoverished charcoal burners of Eureka in the year 1879 wielded legitimate grievances toward their oppressors, not unlike the Boston rope makers who boldly provoked the British militia and sparked the notorious Boston Massacre of 1770.

Contrary to the founding fathers' resolve to engage in a bloody struggle in order to attain their democratic ideals, Monaco endorsed a strategy of civil disobedience to appeal to the community's conscience and spur the citizenry to the aid of the oppressed burners. With astuteness and wit, Monaco attempted to humanize the burners' plight without fueling the perpetrators' antipathy. In executing such an elaborate maneuver, Monaco created a framework conducive to peaceful negotiations wherein the attainment of a compromise could have defused the charcoal dispute before it erupted.

Regrettably, the fragile opportunity for peaceful conciliation was missed while the opposing factions grew increasingly polarized. Monaco's resolute reproach of Eureka's Italian bourgeoisie laid bare the convoluted relationship between class and ethnicity that vexed Eureka's Italians. Had Monaco's counsel been promptly heeded, perhaps the tragedy at Fish Creek might have been averted.

Certainly, Monaco emerged as the leading proburner voice of reason amid the charcoal crisis, advocating not only for the cause of the beleaguered charcoal burners but also for the collective welfare. Although operating initially under the veil of anonymity, Monaco transcended his class interests in a remarkable expression of ethnic solidarity toward his destitute countrymen. Impelled by an enlightened fortitude and by an indomitable yearning for social justice, Monaco carried out a one-man crusade against the excesses exhibited by the Italian bourgeoisie, of which he was, after all, a bona fide member.

Unlike a few other prominent Italians who came to the early rescue of the troubled burners but soon dropped out of the struggle once union activities threatened their social status and class interests, Monaco never surrendered his ethnic allegiance to the burners. Indeed, the Swiss crusader stuck with his countrymen before the tragedy at Fish Creek, which he desperately tried to prevent, and afterward, when he provided his services as a court interpreter for some of the accused burners.

Deeply steeped in the burners' struggle, Monaco eventually dropped his expedient pseudonym and revealed his true identity, seemingly unconcerned with the potentially damaging repercussions upon his reputation. Certainly, Monaco's public alliance with the oppressed burners could have been interpreted as a repudiation of his social status, thus inviting ostracism from his class cohorts. However, no evidence of such dire consequences ever surfaced in the historical record.

In fact, judging by the advertisements published in the local press, following the Fish Creek trial, Monaco's photography business grew as the enterprising artist introduced technical innovations in his South Main Street studio. Attesting to Monaco's excellent reputation as a photographer, the *Eureka Daily Leader* announced: "If any one desires to see some real excellent photographs, they should examine those taken by Monaco since the completion of his new skylight." In its rave review, the newspaper declared that the photographs "will bear comparison with the work of any photographer in the country, and are far superior to Brady's, whose galleries in Washington and New York, it has been claimed, are the best in the country."[8]

Further evidence that Monaco's professional reputation remained intact in the aftermath of Fish Creek surfaced in early December 1879 in the local press. Lauding Monaco's exceptional artistic talents, the *Leader* declared, "Louis Monaco has just finished a sample life-sized portrait of R. Rickard, in crayon." The paper concluded that "in point of art it cannot be excelled anywhere."[9]

Monaco's business transaction with the superintendent of the Richmond Mining Company, a major antagonist in the charcoal dispute, demonstrated that Monaco's professional ties with Eureka's elite had not been damaged by the photographer's zealous involvement in the burners' struggle. On the contrary, Monaco experienced a surge of business activity, suggesting that, perhaps, his active involvement with the burners' cause might have even enhanced his status as a photographer.

Monaco's reputation as a social critic was already well established even before the charcoal crisis erupted, and it extended beyond Eureka. In a sarcastic attempt at divulging the identity of an anonymous detractor, a special correspondent of the *Leader* based in Pioche, Lincoln County, Nevada, notorious as the state's most lawless community,[10] wrote:

> The quiet and serenity of our far-away town in the sagebrush has been greatly disturbed of late, especially the "Literati" thereof, as to the author of those spicy effusions which have appeared in your valuable paper over the sobriquet "Veritas." I wonder if the author's latin [sic] is not at fault? It seems so to me. He (?) has certainly

the faculty of making much out of little, and has surely, at some period of his life kissed the blarney stone. But who is he? Some think they recognize the pen of our learned and scholarly townsman, Andrew O.D. Others find the ring of our worthy District Attorney; but 'tis still an open question. Can't you give us a hint? We all wish to become acquainted with the great men in our midst.... But I encroach. Trusting that "Veritas" will not deem me an intruder, but favor me once again, when we may, perhaps, discover his *in cog*.

         —Viator [Latin for "Traveler"][11]

Given the fact that Monaco was Swiss Italian, his camaraderie with the predominantly Italian charcoal burners becomes even more striking when considering the nationalistic sentiments that distinguished Swiss Italians from their neighbors to the south. While the census of 1880 listed them separately, 840 Italians and 243 Swiss Italians, mostly from the Canton Ticino region bordering northern Italy, it is unclear to what extent the two groups diverged.[12] Though culturally similar, the two groups differed in terms of citizenship and language, thus precluding a homogenous classification in the census records.

That the Swiss Italians viewed themselves as distinct from their Italian neighbors was evidenced in the summer of 1878. Following a shooting affray on a coal ranch west of Eureka, the *Sentinel* inaccurately reported the presumed involvement of some Swiss Italians in the incident. Promptly, a number of Swiss residents informed the newspaper's editor that "there were no natives of Switzerland concerned in the affair."[13] While recognizing the inadvertent mistake on the part of the reporter, the offended parties considered it, nonetheless, a grave injustice to the Swiss community and urged the paper to rectify its mistake.

A year later, a brief entry published in the *Sentinel* once again suggested that the two groups did not perceive themselves entirely as members of the same community. The newspaper sarcastically reported, "O. Yergi and R. Bianchi, a Swiss and Italian respectively, managed to kick up a devil of a row on Main Street on the Fourth [of July]." Persisting in its derisive tone, the paper elaborated on the cause of the squabble: "Each wanted the flag of their respective nations to be run up before a certain saloon, and being unable to agree upon the matter amicably, both endeavored to settle the disputed point by punching each other's heads."[14]

However, the differences between the two immigrant populations were more than compensated for by their shared history. While the Congress of Vienna of 1815 granted Switzerland its inviolable neutrality, it also surrendered the fiercely independent region of Lombardy to the despised Austrian Empire. In the following decades, Italians' resolve to break free from Austria's tyrannical rule spawned a series of bloody insurrections. Among the most loyal supporters of Italian independence were the people of Ticino.

During the nineteenth century, Canton Ticino also witnessed repeated struggles between conservatives and liberals. By 1830 the liberals had triumphed and a constitution was adopted. The liberal government then proceeded to secularize Ticinese society. However, the staunch support provided by Ticino liberals to the cause of Italian unification provoked the wrath of the Austrian regime. Acting on intelligence that strongly implicated the people of Ticino with the northern Italian nationalists, to whom the Ticinesi offered a safe haven from which to carry on their war for independence, along with financial aid, in 1853 Marshal Joseph Radetsky, the Austrian ruler of Lombardy, sealed off the Ticino-Lombardy border. Immediately, some sixty-five hundred Ticinese men were summarily expelled from northern Italy and repatriated to their already economically depressed communities.[15]

Overwhelmed by such a massive wave of deportees, the economy of Canton Ticino became hopelessly strained. Ticino's liberal government, held responsible for the hardships endured by the Ticinesi, was ousted, and the conservatives reestablished their dominance. This single historical event, borne out of political solidarity with a territorial neighbor, marked the onset of a calamitous exodus of the Ticinese people to distant lands of emigration, first to Australia and later to the United States. In 1856 Austria removed its blockade, and economic activity in the region rebounded, stemming the immigration tide. However, the heartening economic recovery was short-lived. In 1868 a series of devastating floods struck the shores of Lake Maggiore, ruining crops and killing livestock, thus setting the inauspicious stage for another mass exodus.[16]

Conceivably, the dire economic conditions and reactionary political shift that pervaded his native Ticino induced Louis Monaco to emigrate. Hailing from Verscio, in Canton Ticino, the young Swiss entrepreneur arrived in California in 1860, seven years after Austria had sealed off the Italian-Swiss border and expelled thousands of Ticinesi from neighboring Lombardy.

After engaging in several business ventures in Virginia City and Gold Hill, Nevada, Monaco turned to photography. His first studio opened in Virginia City in February 1871. Six months later he moved to the booming silver-mining city of Eureka, Nevada, where he became owner of the City Photographic Gallery. Besides bringing with him vast intellectual capital, Monaco brought to the New World a fervent humanistic spirit and an indomitable social conscience indelibly impressed upon him by the historical vicissitudes of his homeland, which for most of the nineteenth century had been a safe haven for political exiles, socialists, and revolutionary unionists.[17]

His personal correspondence with relatives and friends overseas in Canton Ticino reveals that young Monaco was an ardent liberal-republican and a passionate supporter of the Italian unification movement.[18] A great admirer of Mazzini and Garibaldi, the architects of the Italian Republic, Monaco brought with him from his turbulent native land, where Austria's tyrannical rule reigned for decades, a fierce opposition to oppressive institutions and a fervent longing for social justice. It is in light of his political background, devoted to the fulfillment of the ideals of the Italian Risorgimento, that Monaco's ethnic loyalty to the oppressed charcoal burners of Eureka can be fully appreciated.

Whereas Monaco's bond of solidarity toward the burners can be explained in terms of a shared history of foreign oppression, the conflict between the prosperous Swiss merchants of Eureka and the disenfranchised burners can be understood as an expression of class discord. Hailing from a country that enjoyed a precious neutrality since 1815, many early Swiss Italian immigrants to the American West were literate and financially advantaged. Some were industrious tradesmen and astute merchants who, for generations, had plied their trade within and without the border region, according to the economic tenor of the seasons. Unanchored to either side, the loyalty of these roving entrepreneurs was frequently suspect, giving rise to the Italian adage "Genti di confini, o ladri o assassini" (Border people, either thieves or assassins).

With the closure of the Swiss-Italian border, a dearth of work resulted and emigration beckoned. Already accustomed to cyclical migration, these wayfaring folks probably joined the earlier waves of immigrants to America, carrying with them greater financial and human capital than the multitudes of common laborers from either side of the Swiss-Italian border soon to follow. US immigration records of the latter nineteenth century indicate that "even though most arrivals from Switzerland could only afford third-class ship passage, they had more cash to kick-start their new lives."[19]

Consistent with the above-cited trend, Eureka's Swiss Italians stood out markedly as some of the most prominent citizens of Eureka. Incidentally, two of the wealthiest merchants implicated with the charcoal dispute, namely, Tognini and Vanina, were Swiss Italians. So was Maginni, businessman and the first president of the CBPA. Celso Tatti, the saloon keeper who made his locale available to the charcoal burners in their early organizing attempts, also hailed from Italian Switzerland. "To service the immigrants," stated historian Rolle, "there came to America a small army of merchants who had been tradesmen in Italy."[20] Besides supplying their countrymen with imported home-style fare, frequently at exorbitant prices, these ethnic merchants or padrones sought to perpetuate the economic dominance they once exerted in the old country upon their newly transplanted customers.

Having examined Eureka tax rolls, Frehner surmises that Vanina and Tognini attained great wealth with remarkable speed. "Becoming the wealthiest Italians in such a short time," declares Frehner, "must have been a struggle and, as a result, they would not to the ideals of ethnic solidarity surrender the class advantages they had fought so hard to win."[21] Indeed, a portion of the fortune amassed by the two Italian Swiss moguls between 1875 and 1880 could have derived from the exorbitant prices charged to the burners for basic supplies.

While the prosperous Italian merchants and contractors attempted to replicate the rigidly stratified society of the Old World, when feudal lords reigned over their vassals, the social flexibility afforded by the western frontier militated strongly against the cultural vestiges of inherited privilege. Whereas those Italian immigrants who had "made good" at the expense of their compatriots became conservative forces in the preservation of Eureka's established capitalistic order, the dominated charcoal burners, believing themselves entitled to a fair and equitable share of the prosperity that surrounded them, wittingly banded together to oppose the exploitative practices of the capitalists and their henchmen, who, like the oppressive landlords of old, strove to hold them in perpetual servitude.

Nonetheless, Monaco was not a one-dimensional Italian Swiss expatriate wedded to the liberal ideals proclaimed by the Italian Risorgimento but a versatile pragmatist firmly anchored in the fabric of nineteenth-century industrial society. Rather than opposed to the tenets of a capitalistic society, Monaco advocated a broader distribution of the economic opportunities promised by the American system of free enterprise. That Monaco did not disdain material wealth is amply attested by the public records. According to the Deed Index of Eureka County, between 1875 and 1880 Monaco carried out several lucrative business transactions. The Italian Swiss entrepreneur purchased numerous buildings and real estate right in the heart of Eureka's business district. The record shows five purchases and two sales of property.[22]

Monaco could be not only quick-witted but also cantankerous. Perhaps indicative of an overly grasping proclivity, Monaco became embroiled in a dispute with Dr. A.C. Bishop, another prominent Eurekan, over a strip of real estate. Allegedly, Monaco had obtained legal consent to fence in a vacant lot next to the Episcopal church and adjacent to his residence, "to prevent any one from jumping the land, and thus causing trouble." Six months after the fence had been erected, Dr. Bishop attempted to tear it down, claiming that both parties had previously agreed that the enclosure would be temporary. Upon finding out that Monaco had acquired title to the land by subterfuge, Dr. Bishop became infuriated and proceeded to remove the barrier that hindered his carriage way. However, Dr. Bishop was prevented from putting his destructive plan into action by a resolute Monaco, who guarded the fence "with the aid of a shotgun." The confrontation fell short of bloodshed. Dr. Bishop was arrested but promptly released on his own recognizance.[23] A short time later, the dispute was settled according to law. Monaco deeded the contentious property to Dr. Bishop, who allowed the land strip to be used as a street.[24]

Perhaps inspired by Monaco's determination to assert his alleged claim, or perhaps aroused by a newfound sense of empowerment rooted in the American belief that men created their own destiny, the desperate charcoal burners of Eureka resolved to take a radical stand. Undaunted by the colossal odds stacked against them and with nothing left to lose, the burners decided that this time they would not flee in the face of adversity, as they had done by emigrating from their homeland to the Nevada frontier. This time they would stand the new ground upon which they had staked their hopes for a life better than the one left behind. This time they would not retreat before the officers of the law sent to assert the orders of the court.

Notes

1. Nicola Larco to the Sardinian minister of foreign affairs in Turin, San Francisco, May 3, 1857, ASDMAE, Rappresentanza Diplomatica Italiana a Washington (1861–1901), Piazzale della Farnesina 1 1-00135, as cited in Salvetti, *Corda e sapone*.
2. *Leader*, August 6, 1879.
3. *Sentinel*, July 23, 1879.
4. *Sentinel*, January 14, 1877.
5. Nevada State Legislature, *Appendix to the Journals of the Senate and Assembly, Eighth Session (1877): Census of the Inhabitants of the State of Nevada*, 259.
6. *Sentinel*, August 17, 1879.
7. Ibid.
8. *Leader*, November 14, 1879.
9. *Leader*, December 7, 1879.
10. Paher, *Nevada Ghost Towns and Mining Camps*, 291.
11. *Leader*, September 5, 1878.
12. US Department of the Interior, Census Office, *Statistics of the Population of the United States*, 520, quoted in Frehner, "Ethnicity and Class," 48.
13. *Sentinel*, July 2, 1878.
14. *Sentinel*, July 8, 1879.
15. Ernesto R. Milani, "Genoa, Wisconsin and the Civil War: The Guscetti Brothers Fight for Their New Country."
16. David Rolland, "Switzerland to West Marin (Part 2 of 10)."
17. *Willy Gianinazzi, in Bianchi et al., Ragioni Critiche* (Critical reasons), year 5, 3rd ser., no. 7, October 8, 1990.
18. Louis Monaco's personal correspondence was provided to the author by his great-nephew Richard Monaco, San Francisco.
19. Dale Bechtel, "When the Swiss Made America," 12:45.
20. Rolle, *Immigrant Upraised*, 154.
21. Frehner, "Ethnicity and Class," 54.
22. Eureka County Recorder's Office, Deed Index, 7:390.
23. *Sentinel*, March 22, 1879.
24. *Sentinel*, April 10, 1879.

IX

The Fish Creek Shooting

Eventually, the seeds of discontent, sown over many days by the desperate burners, bore their gruesome fruit. On a Monday evening, August 18, 1879, around six o'clock, the lives of five charcoal burners were violently extinguished. By all accounts, the slain burners met their end in a canyon on the western slope of Dave Keane Mountain, at the southern end of the Fish Creek mountain range. The site of the carnage lay about thirty miles from Eureka and could be reached via a wagon trail from the southwest.[1]

Although the incident could not have been foreseen, the foreboding signs of an imminent upheaval were apparent. In fact, for almost a month—that is, from July 19, when the burners' first act of protest occurred, to August 11—the charcoal crisis smoldered. This period was punctuated by sporadic yet conspicuous outbreaks of charcoal stoppages, deliberately staged by the discontented burners. The charcoal conflict festered until the distraught community of Eureka reacted.

Realizing their inability to contain the deepening crisis, local authorities resented the unruly charcoal burners, while the beleaguered citizenry clamored for an end to the social tensions the coal affair had spawned. Sheriff Matthew Kyle and B.J. Turner sent a telegram to Governor Kinkead on August 11, requesting the immediate deployment of the Nevada Militia.[2] The branch of the Nevada Militia with jurisdiction in Eureka County was the Second Brigade, a military unit composed of local residents well acquainted with the territory and, by now, thoroughly aware of the charcoal crisis. As historian Phillip I. Earl correctly points out, calling out the Second Brigade would not have been problematic.[3] The placing of the Second Brigade on a state of readiness conveyed unequivocally the seriousness with which the community viewed the burners' disturbance, thus laying another stone on the road leading to the trouble spot at Fish Creek.

August 12 marked the onset of a new, retaliatory phase of the escalating crisis. As if awakened from a protracted state of stupor, the local authorities swiftly took the offensive. The first development of this new campaign occurred on August 12, when the newly elected president of the CBPA, Angelo del Bondio, was apprehended on the charge of "fermenting disturbances and inciting riot and other lawless acts." Although del Bondio "disavowed all responsibility for, or sympathy with any lawless acts," he was held on one thousand dollars' bond while awaiting trial.[4]

The CBPA president's arrest was followed the next day, August 13, by that of the association's treasurer, Severino Strozzi. The treasurer was apprehended by Deputy J. B. Simpson for his alleged involvement in preventing the loading of charcoal at Pete Hansen's ranch, near Pine Station. Two telegrams dispatched from Patterson at Pine Station to Hansen on August 13 describe the situation: "Italians are here, and say they will not allow your teams to load tomorrow. Will send two car loads to-day," followed by "Team will leave in the morning, but Strozzi says he will not allow them to load."[5]

A flurry of additional arrests quickly ensued, and several charcoal burners, most of them from Fish Creek, landed in the county jail the same day. Among those apprehended on the Fish Creek road on August 13 were burners D. Corichino, L. Pinoli, G. B. Cordano, and G. Cesanoli. Taken before Judge Cromer, they were held on one thousand dollars' bond on charges of conspiracy. Predictably, the four burners were unable to pay for their release and remained detained.[6] At this time the jail housed twelve inmates, with several more expected to swell their ranks soon. Meanwhile, the rounding up of the alleged "ringleaders" proceeded vigorously. On Thursday evening, August 14, Constable Fred Gorman arrived in Eureka, escorting five more burners from Fish Creek, while four more trailed right behind. Concurrently, Sheriff Kyle delivered another burner from Alpha Station and was planning to travel to Roberts Creek to serve additional warrants at that location the next day.[7] This wave of arrests was unprecedented in Eureka history and put a strain on the housing capacity of the local jail, which proved grossly inadequate for a throng of twenty-two energetic prisoners.

On August 15, in an effort to relieve overcrowding, some prisoners were removed, under the authorization of Sheriff Kyle, to the Eureka State Militia Armory, where they remained confined under close military guard. Although warranted by legitimate considerations, the transfer of prisoners had been effected without the knowledge or the approval of the ultimate military authority in Eureka, namely, General George M. Sabin, who was temporarily absent from the scene. The transfer also committed transgression of jurisdiction by placing civilian prisoners in a military facility under military surveillance.

Upon his return to Eureka, on Friday evening, August 15, the general was duly informed of the transfer of prisoners earlier that day. Instantly aware of the illegality of such a procedure, a perturbed Sabin disavowed the ill-conceived action. In order to mend the broken legal boundaries, General Sabin had the prisoners relocated to a room located above Tommy Douglas's saloon, which was promptly and sarcastically dubbed "Camp Douglas."[8] Far from being mistreated, the prisoners at Camp Douglas were provided more than adequate accommodations at this unconventional place of detention. The unusual circumstances were humorously portrayed in the local press: "Eighteen strikers are now confined in the room over Tommy Douglas' saloon. The prisoners are a well-behaved, orderly set of men, who take their confinement philosophically, and spend their time in singing and playing several musical instruments. They are well fed; have all the comforts possible under the circumstances, and unanimously assert that Sheriff Kyle is a devilish good fellow. Should nothing worse befall them now, they will probably hereafter occasionally get up a rebellion in order to obtain a little relaxation at the county's expense."[9]

By contrast, Sheriff Kyle, burdened with the responsibility of maintaining the public order and ensuring the obedience of the law, did not take a light view of the chaotic circumstances and the festive atmosphere hailing from Camp Douglas. Indeed, the entire charcoal affair weighed most heavily on the sheriff's shoulders, taxing his time and resources while also demanding perhaps the most critical decision of his career as a lawman. After all, crucial developments in the community hinged on his ability to defuse the burners' uprisings and, in the process, restore calm. If Sheriff Kyle's peacekeeping mission failed, then the intervention of the militia would have been inevitable.

Notwithstanding the exasperating tactics perpetrated for weeks by the burners and causing slight disruptions to the teamsters' charcoal-hauling activities and schedules, no intimation of any bellicose confrontation was sensed by Sheriff Kyle as he prepared to execute the remainder of the arrest warrants already issued. Although Kyle did admit to the possibility of encountering a potential opposition "by a force too strong to tackle," presumably the sheriff equated "force" with a numerical entity large enough to impede the actual serving of the warrants rather than an organized armed presence eager for fighting. After all, the previous arrests had been carried out successfully, and in no instance had he encountered violent opposition.[10]

Further, the expectation of nonviolent conduct on the part of the burners was also corroborated by an analysis published in the *Eureka Daily Leader*: "It is evident that the policy of the obstructionists is simply to embarrass the loading teams wherever they have an opportunity to overawe the drivers, but not precipitate any conflict with the authorities."[11]

In the grand scheme of things, the burners' guerrilla-style skirmishes were intended to disrupt the charcoal trade rather than challenge the established order and its power brokers. The burners were not unlike a pack of forsaken wolf cubs, trying to fend for themselves by sheer instinct in the hostile wilderness; their growl was more a deed of self-preservation than a display of aggression. Paradoxically, the burners' dramatic actions succeeded in convincing some of the more susceptible spectators that their threatening overtures were indeed dangerous, instilling in their hearts a disproportionate amount of fear.

On the afternoon of August 18, the day of the bloodshed, Deputy Simpson, accompanied by an eight-man posse placed under his leadership, set out for Fish Creek with the intention of arresting six strikers at that charcoal camp. The peacekeeping force included Joseph Toomey, William Martin, Robert Brown, Jim Porter, G. H. Smith, Marshall Rich, Hank Storey, and Thomas Arrivey. It should be noted that one of their number, Marshall Rich, was a foreman with the hauling outfit owned by George Lamoureux. The posse reached Fish Creek, on the western slope of Dave Keane Mountain, at the southern end of the Fish Creek mountain range, in the late-afternoon hours.

On August 19, in its early appraisal of the shooting at Fish Creek, the *Leader* fostered the mistaken impression that those members of the posse who were not official lawmen had been duly deputized by Sheriff Kyle before being dispatched to the troubled charcoal camp at Fish Creek. The paper stated: "Sheriff Kyle sent the following deputies to protect the teams, Joseph Toomey, Wm. Martin, Robert Brown, Hank Storey, Jim Porter, G. H. Smith and one whose name we could not learn, specials, and Officer Simpson, regular deputy. Marshal Rich, foreman for George Lamoureux, was also deputized and accompanied the team." Perhaps in haste to provide its readers with a straightforward account of the tragic occurrence at Fish Creek the day before, the paper omitted a salient detail. Given the fact that those members of the party who were not official lawmen, namely, Rich, Brown, Martin, and Porter, were teamsters already in the vicinity of Fish Creek attempting to transact charcoal, when Kyle dispatched the deputies "to protect the teams," the sheriff could not have deputized them. However, given the mounting tensions, Kyle might have authorized Simpson to deputize any civilian qualified to aide in the execution of the warrants. Firmly questioning the presumed legal authority of those four teamsters who as posse members participated in the Fish Creek shooting, Earl laments, "In all the reports of the incident, there was no indication that any of [the teamsters] had been deputized by Simpson or that he even had such power."[12]

In light of the fragile circumstances that pervaded the charcoal camps, the sudden arrival of the lawmen might have produced a destabilizing effect upon the angst-ridden burners. Certainly, fuel was added to the smoldering conflict when these few, but determined, lawmen appeared on the burners' turf to serve arrest warrants.

Sheriff Kyle, committed to squelching the growing unrest once and for all, had disregarded the previous warning of the leader of the seventy-five strikers at Alpha on August 11 who cautioned, "If any body of men should come from Eureka to check [the burners], it would have to muster sufficient force to overcome not only his own but other bands that could soon be gathered."[13] Nonetheless, Sheriff Kyle proceeded with his plan to arrest the "obstructionists." He continued to rely on the execution of arrest warrants to purge the charcoal camps of their seedy elements, believing that such a strategy would permanently resolve the charcoal crisis. However, it was becoming clear that serving the arrest warrants was going to be a nebulous and awkward process, likely to arouse confusion and resentments among the burners.

Part of the problem was that the warrants were imprecise and ill-conceived, for they failed to bear the specific names of the individual burners to be arrested. Inscribed with the anonyms "John Doe" and "Richard Roe,"[14] the warrants were expedient but intrinsically flawed tools, lending themselves naturally to unsound outcomes. Clearly, the generic warrants granted the officers vast latitude in linking the unspecified identity implied by the warrant with a real person. By such a faulty device, almost anyone could have been arrested on a whim.

Law enforcement officials justified the issuance of the anonymous warrants by arguing that it was impossible to establish with a reliable degree of certainty the burners' respective identities. Concealed beneath a semipermanent mask of black coal soot and belonging to an ethnically homogenous people, the burners could thus appear indistinguishable from one another to the eye of the outsider, unfamiliar with the unique nuances of each burner. Given such obstacles, the fictitiously named arrest warrants granted the officers the flexibility necessary to execute their task expediently. Nonetheless, the possibility of misidentification persisted.

The arrest warrant in question thus provided the crucial spark that ignited the Fish Creek conflagration. Though Simpson's forthcoming mission to arrest six or seven strikers at Fish Creek was fully authorized by the law, it is difficult to establish with certainty whether Simpson discharged his legal duty by executing the arrest warrants properly.

Of all the mutinous charcoal camps in Eureka County, the one at Fish Creek emerged as a bastion of the burners' uprisings. In reference to this locality, the *Leader* remarked: "There seems to be a more determined resistance at this place than anywhere else."[15] The camp's prominence was likely due to its larger share of charcoal manufacturing, which, in turn, translated into a greater number of discontented burners, as evidenced by the larger percentage of arrests at that point. In retrospect, these thorny antecedents paved the way for what this distant coal camp was about to endure.

During the early-morning hours of August 19, news of a shooting at Fish Creek the evening before resonated throughout the town of Eureka. Despite a pervasive frustration over the burners' repeated skirmishes, the community met the dreadful news of the Fish Creek Massacre, as the violent confrontation came to be known, with disbelief, grief, and consternation. Although the burners' grievances were widely known and tensions surrounding the charcoal dispute had been intensifying, hardly anyone would have predicted such a tragic turn of events.

Following the carnage, various accounts of the events at Fish Creek were reported in the local press. Some of the early journalistic commentaries were personal testimonials recounted by eyewitnesses at the scene.

An early, though fragmentary, sketch of the incident appeared in the *Eureka Daily Leader* the afternoon of August 19. The report relied almost exclusively on the personal account provided by Special Deputy Hank Storey, who, after witnessing the violent outbreak, was sent back to Eureka in the middle of the night to alert the sheriff about the tragedy that had just occurred. Immediately after hearing from Storey, Sheriff Kyle, J. W. Smith (the coroner), and Dr. G. H. Thoma left for the scene of the bloodshed.

Reportedly, the shooting broke out at the twilight hour of August 18 and resulted in the death of five Italian charcoal burners and six wounded. Storey acknowledged being a deputized member of an eight-man posse placed by Sheriff Kyle under the leadership of Deputy Simpson and dispatched to the Fish Creek district to prevent a party of menacing burners from interfering with the loading of charcoal at that camp. Presumably, the posse's plan had been to take into custody the instigators of the mayhem, for whom Deputy Simpson carried generic warrants. The strategy seemed to depend on the hope that once the agitators were arrested, the trouble would subside.

As recounted by Special Deputy Storey and reported by the *Leader*, upon reaching the charcoal loading station, about seven miles south of Fenstermaker's ranch, on Fish Creek, the posse encountered a large crowd of Italians, numbering approximately one hundred burners. Although Storey did not report the burners being armed, later reports alleged that some strikers wielded weapons.

Storey reported that some of the bolder burners reiterated their firm intention of preventing the charcoal teams from loading until the dispute had been settled satisfactorily to the strikers. A contest of wills rapidly ensued, whereby each side strove to prevail over the other. In open defiance of the burners' order not to attempt loading, Marshall Rich reminded the burners that they had no legal claim to the coal to be transacted. Then he signaled to the legitimate owners of the coal, those who had actually burned the charcoal, to commence loading. Caught right in the middle of a tug-of-war, the coal suppliers were immediately pushed back by the insistent burners.

Unwilling to desist, an exasperated Rich darted forward toward one of the vacant wagons and, with the help of Smith, began loading the charcoal sacks. Infuriated by such a bold display of bravado, the leader of the strikers commanded the deputies to stop. In the blink of an eye, a group of burners descended upon the deputies and pushed them away from the wagon. When Smith and Rich attempted to resume loading, the leader of the rioters drew his pistol and fired at Rich, the ball grazing the deputy's scalp. From Storey's account, it appears that one single shot was fired by the ringleader, rather than two, as recounted later by Thomas Arrivey, a deputy and member of the posse who participated in the Fish Creek clash. Simultaneously, another striker rushed toward Smith with a long knife. Reportedly, at that very instant the lawmen opened fire on the burners with their "latest improved arms," which they had held in readiness.

Storey related that "at the first fire eleven of the Italians dropped. Five of them were instantly killed and six wounded." Special Deputy Storey then described how the demoralized burners "scattered and ran like sheep, shooting wildly at the officers," who remained unharmed. According to Storey's account, "The officers did not attempt to follow the retreating strikers, but stayed by the wagons, expecting that they would gather their forces and renew the attack." This claim would later be contradicted by Arrivey's report, in which the opposite was alleged.

Later in the afternoon of August 19, Officer Arrivey made his entrance into town with three prisoners in his custody, rioters who had participated in the fight at Fish Creek the day before. Although Arrivey's account of the shooting at Fish Creek, as reported by the *Leader* in the same issue, seemed generally consistent with Storey's report, it also provided additional particulars that widened the scope of the incident.

Arrivey declared that Simpson did indeed serve a warrant to one of the burners' leaders, who allegedly tore up the writ and threw it in Simpson's face while uttering an insulting remark. The striker's indignant display toward Simpson was swiftly followed by another burner's bellicose outbreak. Indeed, Arrivey said that the same burner who had impeded Rich's earlier attempt to load his team now sprang into action and, drawing his pistol, fired two shots at Rich (rather than one, as reported by Storey). Arrivey identified the initial spark of the conflict as the two shots fired by the recalcitrant burner.

Arrivey recounted that up to the time the shots were fired at Rich, about half of the Italian force was visible. Presumably, up to that crucial moment, the other half had remained concealed behind the trees and the underbrush, from which they emerged immediately following the two shots. Allegedly, the second Italian contingent hurled itself upon the armed posse, shooting and yelling in the hopes of startling the small band of lawmen into retreat. However, to the rioters' dismay, their orchestrated pandemonium failed to intimidate the outnumbered officers, who promptly opened fire upon the cantankerous crowd with their unforgiving Henry rifles and six-shooters. Further, in Arrivey's view, the posse's firing-line stance, held before the shooting began, suddenly shifted, with the officers separating before commencing to fire their guns. According to Arrivey, the band of burners numbered 117, or 17 more than reported by Storey.

Disheartened by the gunfire of the posse, the rioters dropped their weapons and fled to the hills, apparently without "shooting wildly at the officers," as had been claimed by Storey. The officers, in Arrivey's account, set out in pursuit of the escapees. This is another departure from Storey's report. The chase resulted in the capture of 17 burners. As night wore on, all the fugitives were released except 3; they were escorted to town by Arrivey the next day and subsequently jailed. In the meantime, the burners who had been turned loose rushed to gather the bodies of their slain companions. The grieving immigrants retrieved their fallen comrades and took them to McKennan's ranch, in the vicinity of the shooting. There the bodies were placed in a wagon bound for Eureka. In Arrivey's story, the exact number of rioters wounded in the fight remained undetermined, and among the lawmen only Marshall Rich received a slight wound, from the first shots fired.

Following the news of the fight at Fish Creek, contradictory rumors spread throughout Eureka. Even Storey's account appeared muddled. In an effort to sift through the perplexity, and striving to arrive at an accurate interpretation of what happened at Fish Creek the fateful evening of August 18, the *Sentinel* laid claim to the truth by publishing a "clearly explained" and detailed account of the incident as was reported up to that time. The article was titled "The First Blood."[16]

Reportedly, on Monday afternoon, August 18, 1879, Deputy Simpson left Eureka in the company of Special Deputy Joe Toomey. Traveling in a buggy, the two lawmen headed for Fish Creek. Simpson's mission was to apprehend the 6 strikers who were allegedly responsible for impeding the loading of charcoal onto George Lamoureux's wagon teams earlier. In the proximity of Page's upper ranch, Simpson and Toomey crossed paths with Special Deputy Billy Martin, who immediately informed them of the latest developments. Martin reported that a throng of burners, numbering between 75 and 100, had just prevented the loading of Lamoureux's teams, despite the presence of newly deputized Marshall Rich, Lamoureux's foreman. The loading site was located about seven miles south of Fenstermaker's ranch, on Fish Creek territory.

After acknowledging his lack of interest in the loading of teams, Simpson alerted Martin that the sole purpose of his trek was the execution of arrest warrants of specific burners. In a rather boisterous display of self-confidence, Simpson declared that he "did not think that there would be any trouble when they saw me." After that brief clarification, the 3 lawmen proceeded toward the Page Ranch. There, the 3 itinerant officers met up with the following special deputies: Robert Brown (a team owner), Marshall Rich, Hank Storey, James Porter, G. H. Smith, and Thomas Arrivey. Brown relayed to the assemblage that a band of burners had emptied about 750 sacks of his charcoal. At this point, Simpson and the rest of the party, 9 men in all, pressed on to the south in pursuit of the burners who had perpetrated the deed.

Along the road, at a spot about eight miles distant from the Page ranch, Simpson, following the posse in a buggy, supposedly caught sight of 3 men intent on crossing the road about 150 yards to his right. Convinced they were the advance guard of a larger force, Simpson called out to his forward-riding fellows, urging them to follow the suspects. Meanwhile, Simpson made a sudden detour and was now forging ahead of the posse, speeding toward the point where the figures had crossed. Upon reaching the crucial spot, which lay beyond the next ridge, Simpson hastily maneuvered the buggy to seal off the exit of the ravine in which the 3 men had absconded, thus precluding their escape. By now the rest of the posse had caught up with Simpson. As if prey to some illusionist act, the lawmen were now confronting not 3 men but a vastly greater force of approximately 125 burners, 50 of whom, as reported by Simpson, were armed with revolvers, with several others on horseback. Thus, the editorial recounts an even larger number of burners present at the site than stated in the previous accounts.

After recovering from seeing the larger group, Simpson inquired about the identity of the presumed leader of the strikers, whom he had recognized from a previous encounter at Brown's ranch and for whom he carried a generic warrant. Meanwhile, the members of the posse dismounted, aligning themselves about 20 feet in the rear while forming an almost straight line 20 to 30 feet long. Simpson stood at the right of the formation, while Billy Martin stood at the opposite end. Simpson squarely faced the bulk of the burners, who huddled together, occupying a space scarcely larger than the posse's. The strikers' lead party seemed to be a half-dozen, mostly mounted, burners. Some yards in the rear stood more than a dozen burners surrounding Simpson's buggy.

The sequence of events thus far chronicled, with particular emphasis on the confrontational stance assumed by the dismounted posse, indicates plainly that Deputy Simpson, the commanding officer in charge of the posse, had thrown caution to the wind, thus seriously compromising the legitimate purpose of his mission. Dispatched by his superior with explicit instructions regarding the manner in which the arrest warrants were to be executed, Simpson overstepped his legal authority by forging ahead with his overzealous approach. Clearly, Simpson disregarded Sheriff Kyle's stated cautionary mandate, as reported in the same editorial: "Should [Simpson] find himself opposed by a force too strong to tackle, he will return to Eureka and call upon the State authorities for aid." Simpson's disobedience of his superior's directive, besides constituting insubordination, engendered catastrophic consequences.

Conciliation between the two vehemently opposing parties would have required the shrewdest diplomatic discretion rather than the quarrelsome tactic exhibited by the posse. Yet the signs of an impending altercation were palpable. The strikers' thinly suppressed aggression became overtly manifest when Toomey, who stood on Simpson's inside left, took a few steps forward, moving menacingly close to the strikers. A burner swiftly barred Toomey's advance with the muzzle of his rifle. Undaunted by the burner, Toomey grasped the muzzle and threw it to one side. At this juncture, another burner, perhaps angered by Toomey's display of bravado, advanced toward the officer, brandishing a huge knife. Sensing imminent danger, Simpson issued a warning to the armed aggressor to desist from assaulting an officer of the law, while simultaneously displaying his own badge.

With violence scarcely averted, Simpson engaged the leader of the party in a conciliatory dialogue. As the conversation unfolded, the deputy, in an ironic twist of fate, pointed out to the leader the "folly of opposing the law," advising him to cooperate peacefully and return to Eureka, when on August 10 the lawman himself had acknowledged the "folly" of his own mission to arrest a large number of rioters at Diamond Station. The leader of the strikers, seemingly impervious to the deputy's counsel, merely asked for "the officer's authority," to which Simpson readily complied by reading him the warrant.

At this stage, a subtle shift occurred, exacerbating the latent antagonism underlying the fragile negotiation process. Another burner, who "spoke excellent English," approached, asking permission to examine the warrant. Simpson readily complied with the request and handed him the warrant. Then, seemingly without cause, perhaps in an attempt to reassert his influence over the mediation, which seemed to be slipping from his grasp, the leader of the strikers abruptly uttered, "You can't arrest anybody here; you haven't men enough and can't bring enough." Simpson, obviously aware of his precarious position, cautiously retraced his steps, asking for the warrant to be returned. Then, as recounted by Simpson, the inquisitive burner who had been verifying the warrant, perhaps troubled by the document's content, bluntly refused to return it, stating that "he could take care of it."

With tensions mounting, teamster and now special deputy Marshall Rich accosted Simpson and requested that the deputy arrest a burner who was standing next to the buggy. Rich claimed that the unnamed burner had threatened his life with a revolver the day before, Sunday, August 17, thus preventing him from loading coal. In response to Rich's accusation, the mounted leader, presumably outraged by Rich's claim, hurled an insulting remark at the accuser—"You're a God-damned-lying-son-of-a-bitch, no one ever drew a revolver on you"—to which Rich promptly retorted: "You are a God-damned-cowardly one, and think you can scare us because you are ten to one." Rich's emotionally charged, and equally insulting, outburst must have had the predictable effect of breathing fresh oxygen into a nascent blaze, thus accelerating the combustibility of the conflict.

Although impelled by equally legitimate emotions, officers of the law, in light of their heavier burden of public responsibility proportionate to the superior authority conferred to them by the badge, would have been expected to exhibit greater self-restraint than the common man. Simpson, a full-fledged lawman, and his deputized posse would have been naturally held to a higher standard of moral conduct, particularly when confronted by circumstances in which their personal pride would be challenged and their courage dared. However, in contrast to the poised conduct expected of lawmen, particularly under extremely volatile circumstances in which even the slightest irritation could spell disaster, Special Deputy Rich yielded to imprudence. Instead of defusing the counteraccusation launched by the leader of the strikers, the obstinate teamster indulged in a perilous verbal counterattack, squandering a precious opportunity for appeasement and ultimately heightening tensions to a boiling point. In retrospect, one is left to wonder why a man as impulsive as Rich was enlisted as a deputy for such a treacherous mission.

Almost immediately after Rich delivered his audacious remark to the mounted leader, the latter drew a revolver and, after taking deliberate aim at Rich, fired his gun. As the shot rang out, the shooter's horse, startled by the bang, reared violently, fatefully altering the bullet's course, perhaps sparing its target's life. But the tumult of Fish Creek had been set in dreadful motion. The first shot was instantly echoed by a deluge of lead, and in the blink of an eye "a perfect fusillade" had violently erupted.

The volley of lead discharged by the posse's weapons sowed instant death. Five of the burners immediately in front—thus caught directly in the crossfire, three mounted and two on foot—collapsed before the officers' deadly fire. The three mounted burners were killed instantly, while the other two were fatally wounded and died hours later, both at around three in the morning. Remarkably, only one member of the posse was wounded in the "fusillade." Marshall was the only officer engaged in the shooting who was slightly injured.

While most of the reportedly unarmed strikers fled to the hills to take cover as soon as the shooting began, others lingered. Among them, fourteen were seized by the lawmen. The posse escorted three of them, deemed important witnesses by Deputy Simpson, back to Page's ranch and then to jail in Eureka. The others remained on the scene of the killing to attend to the dead and to care for the six wounded. Anxious to send a report of the fight that had just occurred to Sheriff Kyle, Simpson dispatched Storey back to Eureka, where he arrived in the early morning of Tuesday, August 19.

The next day, the *Virginia City Chronicle* carried a letter presumably authored by a Eureka Italian and addressed to a fellow immigrant residing on the Comstock. The writer, a witness of the Fish Creek incident, described what happened in a light that contrasted notably with the versions rendered by Storey and Arrivey. In fact, the witness claimed that about one hundred burners had assembled at Fish Creek on the fateful day, among which approximately twenty men wielded arms. The author of the letter recounted that the lawmen, led by Deputy Simpson, had traveled to Fish Creek to arrest a number of burners, presumably ringleaders, for whom warrants had been issued.[17] The burners argued with the officers, contending they were being unfairly treated and that they merely sought redress for the wrongs suffered.

The lawmen, nevertheless, renewed their request for the surrender of certain leaders. However, after conferring with one another in their native language, the burners refused to yield to the lawmen's demands. While admitting that three or four burners subsequently displayed revolvers, the writer asserted that no overtly hostile gesture to resort to arms was made by the burners. According to the writer, it was the officers who suddenly drew their weapons and opened fire on the unsuspecting burners, who instinctively ran for cover in all directions.

The foregoing account of the incident at Fish Creek parallels the testimonial given to a *Sentinel* reporter by another Italian who allegedly witnessed the bloody affray. Again, the contrasting version of the fight rendered by the anonymous Italian eyewitness further diminished the alleged veracity of the officers' testimony.

The informer, an Italian who did not belong to the party of strikers but lived in the proximity of the battle site, provided what the *Sentinel* headlined "An Italian Version of the Fight." Attracted to the scene by the brewing racket, the unwitting witness recounted:

> There were…about 90 Italians and Swiss present at the time of the fight, about 30 of whom had had arms, only four or five being armed with shotguns.… They were on the hillside when two men drove up in a buggy and the crowd came off the hill, apparently from motives of curiosity, and [the informer] followed. His boss, who owned a pit, and who is one of the killed, also went from curiosity,

and was unarmed. When the buggy stopped, one of the officers handed a paper to an Italian, and just then the balance of the posse drove up, and after dismounting, ranged themselves in front of the burners. He heard an officer say "fire," when a single shot was heard, and the Italian leader tumbled from his horse. There was a dead silence for an instant, when the officers opened a regular fusillade, and the Italians took to their heels. No shots were fired by the latter and no weapons were displayed.[18]

This version differs from previous accounts in significant ways. According to the Italian, Deputy Simpson had already served the warrant to a burner before the remainder of the posse arrived on the scene, thus making it difficult for the posse members to corroborate Simpson's version of how he executed the writ. In addition, no instance of the warrant in question being shredded was mentioned by the unswerving witness.

According to the Italian eyewitness, the first shot was supposedly preceded by a distinct incitement to violence. Allegedly, the exhortation "Fire!" was uttered by an unidentified officer, immediately followed by the collapse of the Italian leader from his horse. The Italian also asserted that the burners did not return fire, nor did they display their weapons, but hastily took to their heels. However prejudiced the informer's report might have been, it would not be accorded the legitimate and equal opportunity of being heard by the coroner's jury (see chapter 10), thus compounding the partiality of the examination and undermining the integrity of the entire inquest.

Predictably, the Italian press also put forth a contrasting version of the confrontation that took place at Fish Creek. A prominent Italian-language newspaper, *La Voce del Popolo*, based in San Francisco, where a large Italian community thrived, published an informative letter authored by "Veritas," most likely Louis Monaco, the burners' advocate whose sharp commentaries in support of the burners' cause were previously published in the *Sentinel* under the same pseudonym. The content of Veritas's letter ultimately provided the grist for an article published in the San Francisco–based newspaper the *Daily Alta California*.

In his missive, Veritas declared that the encounter between Deputy Simpson and the burners at Fish Creek had started amicably, with the Italians submitting to the deputy's demand for the warrant-cited burners.

Then abruptly, in a bewildering pendulum swing, Deputy Simpson cast a furtive glance around and retreated swiftly into the background as he yelled "Fire!"—a cry with which the posse readily complied. Five burners were instantly killed, while their startled comrades fled in the flanking vegetation in a desperate attempt to eschew the lawmen, who hounded them over a two-mile run. According to the pseudonymous reporter, only a handful of burners carried weapons, while most of them were unarmed spectators to the unfolding tragedy. The writer also disclosed having personally inspected the bodies of the slain burners. His summary examination revealed conspicuous traces of gunpowder in the chests of the victims, thus demonstrating that the burners had been shot at close range.[19]

On August 19, the day following the bloodshed at Fish Creek, General Sabin wired a terse report of the incident to Colonel George Lyon, military adviser to Governor Kinkead. The dispatch, published in the *Carson City Tribune*, cast the riotous burners in the unbecoming role of aggressors. In fact, while the sequence of the somber events was just beginning to be sorted out through the coroner's inquest to determine the dynamics of the fight, General Sabin's statement prematurely portrayed the burners as the assailants of the posse: "Yesterday at 6:00 PM about 100 burners attacked Sheriff Kyle's posse at Fish Creek, about 30 miles from here, when firing ensued. Five coal burners were killed and eight or ten wounded. None of the sheriff's force were hurt. The coal burners opened fire on the sheriff's men. The city is quiet."[20]

Given his role as the highest-ranking military officer in Eureka, General Sabin's allegation that "the coal burners opened fire on the sheriff's men" unduly influenced the public's assessment of the shooting, while prejudicing those who would eventually be called to investigate the incident. Interestingly, in a candid "Report to the State," issued two years after the fact, in 1881, General Sabin admitted his apprehension to what seemed at the time a probable escalation of the charcoal troubles ignited by the violent outburst at Fish Creek. Indeed, on the afternoon of August 19, the day following the shooting, General Sabin, anticipating further violence, had placed the local militia on an indefinite state of readiness. Not until three days later, on August 22, after no manifestations of hostility from the rioters were registered, was the state of emergency called off by a relieved General Sabin.[21]

As mining activity in Eureka County intensified, scores of miners took up residence in New Town Ruby Hill, two miles west of Eureka. The photo shows residents assembled on Main Street, ca. 1870s. Courtesy Special Collections, University of Nevada-Reno Library.

Buildings on Main Street Eureka, with the Bureau Hotel in the background, ca. 1870s. In its early days, Eureka was a desolate mining camp far removed from civilization. Courtesy Special Collections, University of Nevada-Reno Library.

A team of mules pulling a freight wagon loaded with ore from the local mines to Eureka smelters, ca. 1878. Courtesy Special Collections, University of Nevada-Reno Library.

The Richmond Consolidated spewing dense clouds of smoke into the frontier sky, ca. 1870s. Poisonous fumes sullied Eureka's pristine surroundings. Courtesy Special Collections, University of Nevada-Reno Library.

Millwork was seasonal and highly dependent on the availability of charcoal to fuel the furnaces. Ca. 1870s. Courtesy Special Collections, University of Nevada-Reno Library.

By 1878 Eureka had become the foremost smelting district in the entire West. Ca. 1870s. Courtesy Special Collections, University of Nevada-Reno Library.

Eureka Consolidated together with its archrival, the Richmond, opposed the charcoal burners' struggle for a higher charcoal price. Ca. 1878. Courtesy Special Collections, University of Nevada-Reno Library.

Miners in Eureka were predominantly English-speaking immigrants from Ireland and Cornwall. They dug much of the ore in Eureka County and earned an average of twenty-five dollars a week, more than double the average Italian charcoal burner's wage. Ca. 1870s. Courtesy Special Collections, University of Nevada-Reno Library.

Construction of the Eureka and Palisade Railroad in 1875 enabled Eureka to ship its mineral wealth to distant destinations. Linked to the standard-gauge Central Pacific rail system, Eureka became the major hub of wagon and stage transportation for eastern Nevada. Ca. 1870s. Courtesy Richard Monaco Collection.

Dubbed the "old reliable pioneer photographer," Louis Monaco was born in Verscio, Canton Ticino. Monaco opened his first studio in Virginia City in 1871. Six months later he moved to Eureka, Nevada, where he became owner of the City Photographic Gallery. Operating under the pseudonym "Veritas," Monaco became the champion of the charcoal burners' cause. Ca. 1870s. Courtesy Richard Monaco Collection.

Italian charcoal burners atop a charcoal pit outside Eureka, ca. 1870s. Courtesy of JB Monaco Collection, San Francisco History Center, San Francisco Public Library.

However, the general's report omitted an event that did take place on the evening of August 19, only twenty-four hours after the tragedy at Fish Creek. The jubilant general, obviously calmed and reassured by the outcome of the confrontation, turned the armory into a festive hall and treated his charges to a sumptuous party, enlivened by a keg of fresh lager and aromatic Havana cigars.[22]

The *Eureka Daily Leader* reported that "the Italians in town are anxiously watching for the appearance of the wagon containing the dead, and are congregated in crowds about the streets discussing the killing. Some of them indulge in threats of revenge on those implicated in the slaughter, but the most of them appear to regret the affair, and express the hope that there will be no more fighting."[23]

On Tuesday afternoon, August 19, the day after the shooting, Eurekans learned from the driver of the Tybo stage that the wagon transporting the five dead bodies was due to arrive at about six o'clock that evening, accompanied by the coroner and by some of the officers involved in the shooting. Supposedly, the bodies would then be taken to S. P. Haskell, an undertaker on Buel Street. Sometime later, the identities of the five slain burners were made public. They were Pompeo Pattini, a native of Giornici, Switzerland, age thirty-five; Marcelino Locatelli, native of Mozzio, Italy, age twenty-five; Giovanni Pedroni, native of Villa di Chiavenna, Italy, age twenty-two; Antonio Canonica, native of Corte Cissca, Switzerland, age twenty-five, and Theo Zerli, native of San Filippo, Italy, age twenty-eight.[24]

The only reported account describing the general mood that pervaded the charcoal camps immediately following the bloodshed at Fish Creek was provided by Dr. A. C. Bishop, a Eureka physician who visited the troubled area the day after the shooting. Dr. Bishop's observations were reported in the *Eureka Daily Leader* of August 20 under the heading "From the Battle Field":

> Dr. Bishop came in from Maginni Bros. ranch this morning.... From him it is learned that everything is very quiet in that section. The coal burners are at their pits, attending to their regular business. They are very reticent, and have but little to say about the difficulty, beyond unanimously protesting that they did not want any bloodshed, and wished to avoid further trouble. The Doctor did not hear

of any wounded, and it is probable that there are none. There is one man missing, and it is possible that he fell off his horse in the sage brush, a belief strengthened by the fact that a stray horse was seen in the valley, but it is all mere supposition. Doctor Bishop is also of the opinion that no further opposition will be made to the loading of charcoal.

Indeed, Doctor Bishop's prediction that charcoal loading would resume unimpeded, presumably as an effect of the fatal shooting, was readily confirmed in the "Local Lines" section of the same issue of the *Leader*: "A number of teams loaded with charcoal came in to-day from Spring Valley and Diamond Valley, and unloaded at the Richmond and Consolidated."

Reflecting divided public opinion about the blame for the killings at Fish Creek, the *Leader* and the *Sentinel* assumed contrasting positions. An editorial of the *Leader* the day after the killings scarcely disguised its laudatory tone toward the local authorities. While regretting that the conflict had escalated into open warfare, the *Leader* reminded the community about "the absolute necessity of enforcing the law and protecting property rights." After that, the *Leader* condemned the rioters for adopting "the shotgun policy" to remedy their ill treatment. Further, the editor did not deny his apprehension that the killings might "inflame the passions, and intensify the resistance" of the strikers.[25]

The proestablishment *Leader* renewed its antilabor attack in the editorial of August 20. The article's opening sentence carried the unequivocal verdict of guilt for the strikers, who, according to "all the evidence" examined by the newspaper's editor, had been the "aggressors." Casting himself as apologist for the lawmen, the editor declared that "much as it may be deplored that the agitation has resulted in bloodshed, surely no one can blame the officers for so promptly and effectually quelling the outbreak." The *Leader* justified the officers' decision to intervene as they deemed appropriate, for, after all, they were upholding "the dearest of all rights to an American citizen, the peaceful pursuit of his daily labor."

The *Leader* bluntly criticized the rioters for operating under the flawed assumption that their sheer economic destitution entitled them to demand special treatment within the marketplace. Although convinced that the burners' plight could have been remedied through the legal process, the *Leader* argued that the burners, just like any other workers whose labor went unappreciated or inadequately rewarded, still had the option of seeking a more remunerative occupation besides charcoal burning.

By contrast, the editors of the *Sentinel* on the same day assumed a more magnanimous view toward the rioters while adopting a more critical stance toward the authorities. While characterizing the "conflict" as a one-sided affair, evidenced by the glaring disparity of casualties between the two opposing parties, the *Sentinel* cautioned against rash judgments while appealing for a thorough judicial investigation. In an effort to avoid fueling the public hysteria that gave rise to myriad conflicting reports about the incident at Fish Creek, the *Sentinel* abstained from any conclusions while awaiting the emergence of the basic facts.

Nonetheless, the editors of the *Sentinel* did acknowledge the ethical dualism to be confronted in any judicious inquest that was to follow. While concurring with the established numerical dominance of the Italians present at the scene of the killings, the *Sentinel* rejected the inherent implication that the assembled multitude was equally disposed toward violent resistance. In advocating the supremacy of the law, the *Sentinel* asserted that while "the law does not require an officer to be shot without making an effort to defend himself, neither does it contemplate or justify a needless sacrifice of human life on a mere pretext of resistance."

Far removed from the physical reality of the bloody incident, the bulk of the Nevada press echoed the contents gleaned from the Eureka's dailies, the *Sentinel* and the *Leader*. Reflective of a pervasive proestablishment outlook, the editorial commentaries issued by most Nevada newspapers leaned heavily in favor of the lawmen's actions. However, a few dissenting voices could also be faintly heard. Shunning the general consensus, the *Gold Hill Daily News* challenged the soundness of the lawmen's conduct. Disconcerted by the glaring evidence that the lawmen emerged from the violent confrontation virtually unscathed, the editors assigned culpability for the horrid carnage to the officers, whom they viewed as the likely aggressors.

Based upon the one-sided outcome, the editors of the paper concluded that the Italian burners were either unarmed or poorly equipped. Had the Italian rioters been adequately armed and disposed toward violence, the outcome of the conflict would certainly have been different. The dissenting editors surmised that a carnage of such brutality could have resulted only from either shooting directly into a defenseless crowd or staging an ambush. "This sanguinary bit of news has a very curious sound, to say the least, and, if true, simply shows the officers to have fired upon an unarmed crowd, and killed and wounded more than there was in their own number without even getting a scratch themselves, the opposite party evidently having no weapons or not desiring to use any." [26]

Another declaration predominantly sympathetic toward the burners was made by the *Carson City Morning Appeal* of August 21: "Whoever is in the right, this infraction and defiance of law cannot be permitted in this State. There is scarcely a question but that the coal burners have been imposed upon. They furnish coal to contractors, who deliver it at the furnaces from their own teams, and insist that the burners shall take their returns without being furnished with certified measurements from their receivers. It is easily seen how great wrong can be done through the collusion of dishonest parties."

The *Carson City Morning Appeal* also informed the public that during the violent outbreak, Governor John H. Kinkead was in Bodie, California, while Lieutenant Governor Jewett W. Adams was in San Francisco. Consequently, the helm of Nevada's state government was assumed by Senator W.R. King, president pro tempore of the state senate. Cast in the role of provisional governor and confronted by a crisis, Senator King deferred any decision regarding the Fish Creek incident.

Subsequently, Governor Kinkead did not issue any official statements to allay public fears and aid in the fulfillment of justice. Had the governor interceded in the early stages of the conflict, his involvement might have produced a salutary effect on the perturbed community and, perhaps, even prevented the tragedy. The eruption of violence at Fish Creek ultimately demonstrated that the governor had underestimated the volatility of Eureka's charcoal troubles.

That the governor deemed the Fish Creek tragedy inconsequential was confirmed in 1881 when, on the occasion of his address to the state legislature, Kinkead made a tangential reference to the Fish Creek shooting. The governor characterized the emergency as "slight troubles" without acknowledging the loss of five burners' lives and the wounding of another dozen. Nevertheless, Governor Kinkead showered the militia with accolades, praising it for its readiness to cooperate with the civil authorities to maintain the peace. As his congratulatory discourse waxed, the governor paid homage to General Sabin for his instrumental role in the resolution of Eureka's coal troubles:

> Peace and quiet have reigned within our borders during the past two years, with the exception of slight troubles in Eureka County, in August, 1879. There a formidable organization threatened the majesty of the law. The county authorities appealed to me for assistance; the Second Brigade was ordered to hold itself in readiness to assist the civil authorities; some trouble ensued, but was quelled by the civil officials, the fact that the military were ready to cooperate with them doubtless contributing materially to the prevention of the impending riot. In this connection I desire to commend the promptness and earnestness with which Brigadier General George M. Sabin, and the officers and men under his command, responded to...the call of the Executive.[27]

While minimizing the gravity of the incident, Kinkead attributed the "slight troubles" to "a formidable organization [that] threatened the majesty of the law," namely, the Eureka Charcoal Burners Protective Association. Being "a well-known mining and milling man," Governor Kinkead viewed Eureka's disruptive coal burners unsympathetically.[28]

The approbation bestowed by Kinkead upon Sabin for the effectiveness demonstrated in responding to the charcoal crisis was well warranted because, in actuality, Sabin had played a greater role in quelling "the impending riot" than most Eurekans suspected. In a subsequent report addressed to Colonel George Lyon in Carson City, dated August 24, 1879 (see appendix D), Sabin shed light upon Sheriff Kyle's circumspect task in dealing with the emergency. In his letter Sabin stated: "I was of the opinion however that the Sheriff could control the whole matter and insisted that he should do so," reinforced by yet another reiteration: "While I have been aware that the Shff. greatly wanted me to order out my men and take charge I have refused to do so until the disturbance should pass beyond his power to control."

As intimated by Sabin's admission, initially Sheriff Kyle, probably daunted by the numerical superiority of the rioting burners and by their fierce determination to carry on the coal stoppages, was reluctant to confront the adamant strikers. However, compelled by an insistent General Sabin, Sheriff Kyle grudgingly confronted his nemeses. Thus challenged to demonstrate his ability to "control the whole matter," Sheriff Kyle's crucial decision to halt the burners' disturbance despite the odds had become more a matter of personal honor than a question of justice.

In the aftermath, despite Kyle's early reluctance to take assertive action against the burners, Sabin paid Sheriff Kyle an implicit compliment. In his letter General Sabin concurred with "the solid sentiment of all of the best men in the City,... that the Sheriffs men did their duty and no more." In a display of unconditional approval for resorting to force to quell the charcoal uprisings, while also admitting to the possibility of further troubles, General Sabin promised even greater resolve in the future: "One thing is certain...if a like emergency again arises...the action of the Sheriff will be repeated, only perhaps to a greater extent." Eager to reassure the state authorities in Carson City that the Charcoal Burners' War had been won and that the crisis was totally contained, Sabin added: "But I feel confident, there will be no more armed interference by any of the coal burners, or others, and should there be I am confident it will be quelled."

By insisting that the "whole matter" be controlled by the civil authorities, Sabin seemed anxious to spare the governor the trouble of having to deal with the trivial concerns of a mob of destitute charcoal burners hundreds of miles away in the Nevada wilderness. Presumably, the burners' troubles did not merit the attention of the governor. That General Sabin attempted to diminish the seriousness of Eureka's charcoal crisis is evidenced by yet another remark: "I was a little solicitous [with Kyle] lest the Governor should deem the matter more serious than it really was and return from Bodie sooner than he otherwise would." Indeed, to interrupt the governor's travels would have drawn unwelcome attention to the charcoal crisis, exposing Eureka civil authorities' ineptitude, thus necessitating the governor's intervention. In turn, such a precarious state of affairs could have engendered detrimental effects upon the institutions of the state, casting the political leadership of Governor Kinkead in an unfavorable light.

Ultimately, Sabin spawned the conditions that culminated with the Fish Creek Massacre. Arguably, through coercion, the commander tasked a reluctant sheriff with settling the charcoal troubles "at all hazards." Motivated by political ambition of his own, Sabin sought to maintain outstanding relations with Nevada's political elite. Sabin's instrumental part in squelching Eureka's charcoal uprisings enhanced his reputation as a defender of law and order. In 1882 General Sabin attained the position of US district court judge for the District of Nevada. As one of Eureka's most prominent citizens, Sabin also owned interests in some of the local mines, thus providing him with a further incentive to see the charcoal crisis swiftly resolved.[29]

Notes

1. Myron, *History of the State Nevada*, 438; Gent Martiletti, Eureka, NV, April 2, 1968, interviewed by Franklin Grazeola.
2. *Leader*, August 11, 1879.
3. Earl, "Nevada's Italian War," 66.
4. *Sentinel*, August 13, 1879.
5. *Sentinel*, August 14, 1879.
6. Ibid.
7. *Sentinel*, August 15, 1879.
8. *Leader*, August 15, 16, 1879.
9. *Sentinel*, August 19, 1879.
10. *Sentinel*, August 13, 1879.
11. *Leader*, August 13, 1879.
12. *Leader*, August 19, 1879; Earl, "Nevada's Italian War," 76.
13. *Sentinel*, August 12, 1879.
14. *Leader*, August 21, 1879.
15. *Leader*, August 16, 1879.
16. *Sentinel*, August 20, 1879.
17. *Virginia City Chronicle*, August 21, 1879.
18. *Sentinel*, August 21, 1879.
19. *Daily Alta Californian*, August 31, 1879. Hereafter cited as *Californian*.
20. *Sentinel*, August 21, 1879.
21. Nevada State Legislature, *Appendix to the Journals of the Senate and Assembly, Tenth Session (1881): First Biennial Message of the Adjutant General of the State of Nevada; Report of the Brigade Commandant*, 23–24.
22. *Leader*, August 20, 1879.
23. *Leader*, August 19, 1879.
24. *Leader*, August 19, 20, 22, 1879.
25. *Leader*, August 19, 20, 1879.
26. *Gold Hill Daily News*, August 20, 1879.
27. Nevada State Legislature, *Appendix to the Journals of the Senate and Assembly, Tenth Session (1881): First Biennial Message of John H. Kinkead, Governor of Nevada, Delivered to the Legislature, January 4, 1881*, 2:3.
28. Hulse, *Silver State*, 101.
29. *Leader*, February 4, 1879.

X

The Coroner's Inquest

The coroner's inquest into the cause of death of the five charcoal burners commenced at eleven on the morning of August 20, 1879, before coroner Dr. J. W. Smith and ended the next day. The inquiry into the circumstances surrounding the charcoal burners' deaths at Fish Creek would be aided by a coroner's jury.[1]

The first witness called to testify was Marshall Rich, a member of the sheriff's posse and a teamster in the service of Lamoureux. Rich stated that on the morning of August 18, the day of the shooting, he was heading to Fish Creek to load one of Lamoureux's teams. Rich started his trek from Cornforth's ranch, in Antelope Valley, where he was told that about sixty Italians had sworn that no team would be permitted to load at Fish Creek. Despite the warning, Rich proceeded forward and reached Fish Creek at about eleven. As Rich drew nearer to the loading site, he met up with McDonald, another teamster who at that moment was intent on watering his team. McDonald alerted Rich that he had been driven back by the Italians, who were doggedly determined to prevent any charcoal loading.

Realizing the futility of venturing farther, Rich returned to Eureka with the intent of assembling a labor party and subsequently returning to Fish Creek to load. As Rich started down the canyon to turn his team around, he was stopped by a crew of mounted burners. While Rich engaged in negotiations with the obstructionists, one of them secured the team's reins, triggering an impulsive reaction by Rich, who lashed out at the burner with his whip.

During his testimony, Rich admitted that his horses reared and collided with the burner's horse, which in turn tossed the rider to the ground. Alarmed by the commotion, some of the burners hurled threats at Rich, while, suddenly, eighty to a hundred burners rushed down from the hills and encircled the lone teamster. Rich went on to testify that the irate burners threatened to kill him, tauntingly pointing their guns at him. A burner in a white jumper, claimed Rich, boasted particular vehemence by menacingly drawing a gun on him. However, despite the overwhelming odds stacked against him, Rich unleashed a few threats of his own. "I told them to let me out and I would go down and get some men and give them all they wanted, if they were on that," related Rich. "I told them they were all cowards, and did not dare to shoot, and to keep quiet."

One of the burners told Rich he would be held hostage, to be exchanged for some of their fellow burners who had been jailed the day before. Undaunted by the tense situation, Rich cautioned the burners that their actions would incur the wrath of the law. The burners, in turn, replied, almost in unison, that there were not enough men in Eureka to come there and take them, that they could clean out any crowd that could be brought from Eureka, and that after that they would come into Eureka and take their men out of jail. Eventually, the Italians relented and allowed Rich to go free.

On his way back to Eureka, shortly after his release, Rich met with William Martin, Bob Brown, Jim Porter, and two other teamsters, to whom Rich related what had just occurred. Rich, outraged by the burners' audacity, impulsively blurted out his wish to even the score with the daring burners, but, admitting to the burners' superior strength, the impetuous teamster refrained from confronting the offenders right away. "I had nothing but a six-shooter with me, and neither had Martin." Agreeing they were no match for the prevailing burners, the outnumbered teamsters resolved to send Martin to Eureka to recruit four or five men and obtain more arms. Starting out for town from McKerman's ranch, Martin had scarcely traveled five miles when he crossed paths with Joe Toomey and Officers J. B. Simpson and G. H. Smith, hot on the heels of the ringleaders. The four men then headed back toward McKerman's ranch, where Rich and the other companions had taken respite. From there the newly formed squad continued toward Fish Creek to the place where Bob Brown was scheduled to load his team.

Rich testified that at this time he had provided a thorough report of his earlier confrontation to Deputy Simpson, including the number of Italians involved in the squabble. Eventually, the teamsters and the lawmen reached the loading station where Brown's charcoal sacks had been filled, only to find their contents spilled. At this point, according to Rich, Simpson decided to push on in pursuit of the ringleaders presumed responsible for the mayhem. After traveling for a few miles out on the trail, a member of the posse spotted two or three Italians on a ridge. The posse immediately gave chase. Simpson and Toomey, who were traveling in a buggy, headed toward the spot where the Italians were first sighted, while the horsemen rode to the top of the ridge. Just as Simpson maneuvered the buggy to entrap the fugitives, the latter let out a dreadful yell, and, instantly, scores of Italians dashed out of the cedars, running in all directions; some burners attempted to surround the posse but failed.

Simpson jumped out of the buggy and, perhaps hoping to restore calm, yelled for those burners who could speak English to come down from the ridge so they could talk. Simpson introduced himself as a law officer and displayed his badge. Shortly after, three burners on horseback rode down to meet with him. Rich explained that because he was up on the summit helping to keep the Italians in check, he had no knowledge of the exchange between the deputy sheriff and the mounted burners. Following the talk, Simpson, escorted by Brown, started hiking to the top of the hill to join Rich. As the two climbed, Simpson asked Brown if there were any burners there he wanted arrested. With no hesitation, Brown replied, "Yes, I want all these men that are on horseback."

Meanwhile, Rich had recognized one of the burners who had supposedly drawn a pistol on him in the forenoon. He now stood a few feet away, next to the burner who, during the row, had grabbed the reins of Rich's horse. At once, Rich asked Simpson to arrest the fellow who had threatened him at gunpoint. Rich's request prompted the intercession of the man accused of allegedly seizing the teamster's steed. Riding up to Rich, the mediating burner inquired, "What do you want to arrest this man for?" Rich reiterated that the fellow in question had drawn a pistol on him earlier. Rebuking the teamster's accusation, the horseman retorted, "You are a liar," and reached for a six-shooter that hung at his side. In an instinctive reaction to the burner's menacing gesture, an impulsive Rich raised his cocked shotgun. Sensing imminent danger, Simpson pleaded, "For Christ's sake hold on."

Undaunted, Rich vehemently restated his accusation, as if to pressure Simpson to carry out the arrest. Meanwhile, the accused fiercely denied Rich's allegation, branding the teamster "a damned liar." Rich admitted feeling a grave sense of inexorability closing in at this time, stating, "It was perfectly plain to be seen then that there was going to be trouble, there was no way to avoid it." Whether Rich's perception of the impending doom arose from a clear assessment of the escalating circumstances as they unfolded or whether it was a retrospective reflection after the fact could not be ascertained. The teamster went on to testify that no sooner had the burner's imprecation faded than a shot rang out. While denying any knowledge of the shooter, Rich stated confidently that the shot "came from a bunch of cedar trees a short distance off."

Resolutely, Rich spurned any responsibility by the posse for firing the first shot that ignited the event at Fish Creek. Rich reported that after the first shot was fired, "shooting commenced all around." The teamster further stated, "Everybody was prepared, and had their guns all ready," dispelling by such a recollection the intimation that the posse was caught off guard. The readiness of the posse for a gun battle seems confirmed by yet another assertion made by Rich: "The moment the shot was fired Simpson shouted 'Give it to them, boys'; or words to that effect." Indeed, such a bellicose stance shortly after the posse leader called for both sides to be calm is perplexing, symptomatic of a premeditative mind-set.

Moreover, Rich reported that at first, both sides were shooting but that the Italians fled after the first volley. By Rich's own account, "The fire lasted but just a moment," and he had no idea how many shots the Italians fired. Rich went on to provide the particulars of the aftermath pertaining to the chase and apprehension of the fleeing burners. In Rich's estimate, about two-thirds of the burners were armed with shotguns, pistols, or rifles, while others brandished cleavers or knives and clubs. Before concluding his testimony, Rich reiterated once more the dreary premonition he sensed before the shooting: "It was plain to be seen that there was no chance of avoiding a fight; we had no chance of getting out of it; I think if we had weakened in the least particular they would have surrounded us and shot us down; I do not think there was a man there that would have hesitated to shoot us."

The logic transpiring Rich's thinking and shared by his partners was imbued with a cynicism verging on paranoia. While the nerve-racking circumstances faced by the lawmen at Fish Creek warranted a defensive stance, an overinflated fear of an imminent attack incited the posse toward a preemptive strike against the menacing burners. Because none of the lawmen were seriously injured during the lethal confrontation, Rich's fear of inevitable annihilation appeared tenuous. The riotous burners were posturing, in the hope that their defiant and daunting intimations would ultimately deter the lawmen from their pursuit.

Given the decisive role played by Deputy Sheriff Simpson, who led the posse to Fish Creek, the officer's account is crucial in grasping the dynamics that led to the bloody conflict. The officer's testimony was provided over two court sessions. The first part was reported by the *Eureka Daily Leader* on August 20. Simpson's testimony is too extensive and convoluted to report in its entirety. What follows are the salient points of the officer's deposition.

J. B. Simpson stated he was at Fish Creek on August 18 to arrest some Italians for whom warrants had been issued. Simpson said: "I hallooed to one of the men...on horseback to come down to where I was; I told him I was an officer, and that Toomey was too.... [O]ne fellow ran up to Toomey with a shotgun in his hand.... [A]nother ran up to him with a big knife.... I hallooed to him to stay back or I would shoot him."

Simpson testified that he had produced the warrants, but his request was rudely met by one of the camp leaders, who bluntly retorted: "You can't have them, you can't have any man here." Allegedly, a battle of words ensued, and suddenly a shot rang out. Simpson recounted: "I cannot tell exactly where the shot came from, but it came from the cedars, quartering from where I stood." Then, according to the officer, the fusillade commenced in earnest, resulting in the death of five burners and the wounding of seven others. Retracing his steps prior to the shooting, Simpson recalled pleading with the strikers not to shoot: "For God's sake, hold on, don't commence shooting[;]...we could settle it."

The second phase of Simpson's testimony, reported in the *Leader* issue of August 21, amounted to a litany of inconclusive statements. Speaking about the warrant, Simpson stated: "I do not know where it is.... I do not know upon whose complaint it was issued.... I did not notify that man that I wanted to arrest him until after the row was over.... I do not know whether it was the proposition I made to serve the warrant that caused the trouble or not; I do not know what you call attempting to serve a warrant; I did not have hold of any one." Inevitably, the patently uninformed accounts declared by the self-doubting deputy cast serious doubts about Simpson's competence in the implementation of basic law enforcement.

Simpson then proceeded to describe the weaponry wielded by the members of the posse as well as the manner in which it was used. The officer remarked:

> I guess the weapons were all loaded, I do not know it.... Some of the weapons are now in the Sheriff's office.... I do not know where the others are; I did not examine the weapons of my men after the fight; I do not know whether all of my crowd shot or not; I shot; am not positive how many times; I do not know how many times I did shoot.... [I] do not know how many cartridges were in my rifle; do not know whether it was full or not.... [I] don't know of any order by any one in my party for all hands to fire.... I cannot say how many of my party fired; cannot be positive of any one firing except myself, think, though, that they all fired.

In reference to the conduct of the Italian strikers during the row, Simpson asserted: "[I] do not know how many shots were fired by the Italians.... I cannot tell how many Italians were there armed.... I do not know how many shots I fired before they turned to run; I do not know how many fell at the first fire; I do not think any Italians were shot after they fell."

Admitting the arduousness of describing accurately a catastrophic event after narrowly escaping a threat to one's own life, Deputy Simpson's account of the confrontation with the strikers warrants further probing. A lingering perplexity relates to the manner in which Simpson attempted to serve the arrest warrant. Simpson stated, "I did not notify that man that I wanted to arrest him until after the row was over." By Simpson's own admission, the writ he carried never reached the hand of the burner he intended to arrest, whom, though unnamed, the lawman allegedly knew well. Apparently, the path traveled by the warrant was tortuous and fruitless, indicative of the ineptitude of the officer who wielded it unconvincingly. Simpson's failure to effectively serve the crucial warrant might have spawned an atmosphere of uncertainty, further heightening tensions. That

Simpson might have failed to correctly assess the potential risks stemming from his intransigent determination to carry out the arrests despite the dire circumstances seems evidenced by the following dubious statement: "I do not know whether it was the proposition I made to serve the warrant that caused the trouble or not."

Because the arrest warrant bore fictitious names, the only way it could have been executed was through Simpson's personal identification of the wanted strikers. However, the size of the assemblage and the fortuitous arrangement of the strikers did not permit recognition at a glance. Simpson's strategy to serve the warrant seemed haphazard and lacking forethought. Indeed, Simpson's professional competence is called into serious question by his candid admission: "I do not know what you call attempting to serve a warrant; I did not have hold of any one; I told them what the warrant contained, and that is what I call serving a warrant."

In retrospect, had Deputy Simpson clearly communicated the purpose of his mission at Fish Creek, coherently explaining the intent and content of the warrant, antagonism would have been curbed. As Grazeola points out, "It does seem strange that Simpson, outnumbered ten to one, would spend time 'pointing out the folly of resistance' rather than going beyond displaying his badge so as to fully explain the nature of the warrant, its claims, the burner rights, and actually place the warrant in someone's hands."[2] Indeed, had the deputy clarified the reasons for the use of the anonymous warrant, while assuring the burners that they would be treated justly should one of them be arrested, tensions would have been eased. By adopting a less quarrelsome stance in dealing with the desperate strikers, Simpson might have defused the volatile circumstances sufficiently to prevent bloodshed.

The deputy sheriff's testimony, in the August 21 *Leader* report, further revealed a confusing recollection of the crucial moments when he fired his weapons. Confronted by a large armed force, Simpson declared, "I shot; am not positive how many times; I do not know how many times I did shoot; I shot more than once;...do not know how many cartridges were in my rifle; do not know whether it was full or not." Then, a few moments later, the seemingly perplexed Simpson stated, "All the chambers of my six-shooter were loaded when I went there, and I think my rifle was full, with the exception of one or two cartridges."

Simpson went on to deny having issued any rallying call after the first shot was fired, as claimed by Rich. "Don't know of any orders by any one in my party for all hands to fire; I never heard such an order; I did not give any order to fire; do not think I said 'give it to them boys' after they commenced firing, but said 'stand in boys' or something to that effect." Although Simpson's inability to recall whether he gave orders to shoot under the distressing circumstances that suddenly arose is quite justifiable, his scrappy reconstruction of the shooting contrasts sharply with Rich's testimony. After all, Rich stood in close proximity to Simpson, and his ostensibly disinterested account is also credible. Simpson was also of the opinion that all of the men of his party had fired and added, "Each shot I fired I shot at an Italian; do not know how many different Italians I shot at; I shot at the bunch; did not take much aim; did not aim at any particular man."

Undoubtedly, the angst generated by the escalating contest inflamed passions on both sides, impairing in particular the deputy's judgment. In fact, toward the end of his testimony, Simpson acknowledged falling prey to anxiety while straining to cope with the troubling circumstances. "I suppose I was excited some," admitted the deputy.

After close examination of Simpson's testimony, one is left with the overriding impression that the officer who led the posse on such a volatile mission to the troubled coal camp at Fish Creek was an ineffective lawman, one who exercised poor judgment in the execution of his mandate. Simpson's shortcomings might have ultimately exacerbated the conflict, steering the dispute toward armed confrontation.

A further incongruity in Simpson's account pertained to the catalyst that presumably precipitated the dispute. Simpson asserted that the fight was sparked when the mounted leader of the strikers fired his revolver with the intent to shoot Marshall Rich. Thus, according to Simpson, the ensuing retaliatory action unleashed by the posse against the menacing mob constituted a fully legitimate defensive reaction.

However, Simpson's claim that the mounted leader of the strikers triggered the conflict diverged from testimonies rendered by other officers. In fact, Marshall Rich provided the following contrasting account: "[The mounted burner] had a six-shooter on his side and reached for it; I had a shotgun cocked, and I raised it." Simpson said, "For Christ's sake hold on...."

I cannot say who fired the first shot, but I am confident that it came from a bunch of cedar trees a short distance off. It could not have been fired by any of our party. The moment the shot was fired, shooting commenced all around. Everybody was prepared, and had their guns all ready."

Although, according to Rich's version of the incident, the blame for provoking the armed conflict remained with the strikers, the culprit's identity had now shifted. Apparently, the crucial shot was fired not by the mounted leader, who stood conspicuously in the foreground, but rather from a nearby cedar grove. Rich's account of the violent outburst underscores the posse's inclination to resort to arms, as the following statement implies: "Everybody was prepared, and had their guns all ready." Such eagerness on the part of the ranged posse intimates an aggressive disposition and, perhaps, even a measure of deliberation. The likelihood that the sheriff's posse had contemplated resorting to violence in dealing with the rebellious burners before reaching the distant charcoal camp is substantiated by Grazeola's analysis of the Fish Creek shooting. After prefacing that it was unlikely that the burners had anticipated a gun battle at Fish Creek on the evening of August 18, 1879, Grazeola asserts, "The firing stance taken by the posse immediately after it reached the scene suggests that the tactic had been earlier agreed upon. That is to say, premeditated."[3]

Of all the posse members called to testify in the Fish Creek aftermath, Robert Brown proved the most reticent witness. Initially, after being questioned by Thomas Wren, attorney for Sheriff Matthew Kyle and the officers of the posse, and District Attorney George W. Merrill, representing the State of Nevada, Brown corroborated the testimonies given by the posse members who preceded him. His initial description of the shooting revealed little, adding only a few salient particulars not yet heard. At different points in his testimony, while recounting the occurrence of the first shot, Brown stated, "A shot was fired from the brush; ... I saw the smoke of the gun in the brush when the first shot was fired; ... the place where I saw the smoke of the first shot fired was about 30 feet from me."[4] Brown did not recall hearing any command to shoot due to the deafening noise from the gunfire.

The inquest took a remarkable turn when Brown was cross-examined by A. M. Hillhouse, defense attorney for the burners. When questioned whether he had fired his weapon during the fight, a diffident Brown invoked the Fifth Amendment and "declined to answer on the ground that he might incriminate himself, Mr. Wren having said he could adopt such a course."[5] Uncooperative in his demeanor, Brown denied most of the potentially implicating queries posed to him. "I do not know who shot [the burners]," intoned the reticent teamster. "[I] cannot tell who shot at them." Then, as if having suddenly recovered a glimpse of unbroken memory, Brown asserted, "I do not know but that they were shot by their own men."[6]

Brown's audacious allegation that the five burners had perished at the hand of their own comrades' gunfire was certainly his most elusive assertion, an egregious contention to exonerate the posse of any responsibility for the actual carnage. Nonetheless, Brown's enterprising effort at shifting the burden of guilt onto the burners themselves was thoroughly demolished by Simpson's own admission of having fired repeatedly into the Italian crowd.[7] As reported by the *Eureka Daily Sentinel* on August 21, Brown seemed utterly oblivious of the facts as they had occurred on that fatal evening. Indeed, he appeared certain about only two things: a fight had taken place at Fish Creek, and he had been physically present on the scene. The *Sentinel* went on to speculate that Brown's unwillingness to provide informative testimony was rooted in his fear that whatever evidence he might have given would have been distorted to strengthen the prosecution's case.

In other words, Brown sought to avoid "putting his foot in it." According to the article in the *Sentinel*, Brown's striking standoffishness "really injured the officers' cause." Convinced that Brown's faltering demeanor had inflicted a damaging blow to the posse's hopes of acquittal, the *Sentinel* declared, "We should be surprised to know that Mr. Brown's position did not have a bad effect on the jury, and are confident it will prove hurtful to himself and associates."

For the most part, Joseph Toomey's testimony echoed the accounts previously heard from the other witnesses.[8] But Toomey's deposition added one minor but perhaps significant detail. Toomey testified that during the clash with the burners, when suddenly confronted by a reckless striker brandishing a large knife, he had swiftly drawn his revolver in an act of self-defense. He then ordered his assailant to drop the knife, informing him that he was an officer of the law. Although Toomey held the bellicose burner at bay with his revolver, he heard Simpson shout, "Don't cut him, or I will kill you."[9]

Simpson's stern warning to the assailant aimed at extinguishing a nascent spark of violence. However, rather than producing a dousing effect, the warning uttered by the deputy incited the strikers further. Whatever its intended effect, the threat hurled at the attacker alerted unequivocally the burners to Simpson's readiness to fight, ultimately compromising the deputy's reliability as a judicious mediator of the conflict. In enforcing the law, Simpson was known to be adept enough to give rise to the general belief that he "always manages to get away with his man." Perhaps at Fish Creek, Simpson could not prevail, as was his custom.

On August 21 the second phase of the inquest into the death of the five charcoal burners began. A large number of townsfolk were in attendance, eagerly awaiting Judge Hillhouse's much-anticipated cross-examination of the witnesses. Called to represent the burners implicated in the Fish Creek affair by the burners' association, Hillhouse was expected by many to subject the officers to a rigorous interrogation, designed to exploit the glaring inconsistencies of their earlier depositions. However, to the incredulity of most bystanders, Hillhouse employed a startlingly tamer strategy and limited his questioning to Simpson only.[10]

In an attempt to establish a correspondence between the arms fired and the lethal wounds inflicted on the slain burners, Hillhouse grilled the deputy about the specific weapons wielded by the posse at the time of the shooting. The bodies of the dead men had been thoroughly examined by Dr. G. H. Thoma and Dr. James Williams at S. P. Haskell's undertaking establishment, on Buel Street, where the remains were housed. The medical analysis clearly determined the nature as well as the number of wounds meted out by the posse's weaponry. The results were as follows:

- Pompeo Pattini—age 35; Gornici, Switzerland. Shot twice; one shot entered the right breast below the nipple; the other entered the back, on the left side.
- Giovani [sic] Pedroni—age 22; Villa de Chiavina [sic], Italy. One load of buck-shot in left breast, just below nipple.
- Antonio Canonica—age 28; Corte Cissca, Switzerland. One shot entered the breast on the left of the right nipple, and one on the left side, just below the navel.
- Marcellius [sic] Locatelli—age 25; Mozzio, Italy. One shot entered to the left of the right nipple.
- Teodora Zesti [sic]—age 28; San Fellippo [sic], Italy. One load of buck-shot in the breast.[11]

The gruesome evidence gathered by the medical examiners determined that two of the five Italian charcoal burners, Giovanni Pedroni and Theo Zerli, were killed by a load of buckshot each. The other three victims were hit with rifle balls. Because the posse carried only two shotguns, it followed that those who wielded them were responsible for the deaths of the two burners gunned down by buckshot. The common denominator shared by all of the death wounds was the point of entry into the body, that is, the upper-chest area, in the proximity of the breast. The clinical precision with which such wounds were wreaked in such a particularly vulnerable part of the body amounts to a deliberate intent by those who pulled the trigger to unleash a deadly blow. Indeed, the accuracy with which the shots fired by the posse found their marks challenges the notion of an accidental strike, while strengthening the contention of a disciplined and willful act, one entailing foresight. Again, Grazeola maintains, "Correlation of the burners' death wounds and the weaponry used by the posse revealed that what was considered beforehand had been discharged with professional fidelity."[12]

Indeed, the element of deliberation among men engaged in armed confrontations can hardly be emphasized. William Barclay "Bat" Masterson, a US marshal and army scout and one of frontier America's leading lawmen, persuasively stated, "I have known men in the West whose courage could not be questioned and whose expertness with the pistol was simply marvelous, who fell easy victims before men who added deliberation to the other two qualities."[13]

While the regular deputies engaged in the battle at Fish Creek were professional gun wielders with above-average skills in handling guns, it was unlikely that the remainder of the posse, made up of teamsters temporarily deputized, were individuals with superior dexterity with firearms. Presumably, Marshall Rich, Robert Brown, William Martin, Thomas Arrivey, and James Porter were all nonprofessional gunmen who had a personal stake in the speedy resolution of the charcoal crisis. The degree of accuracy exhibited during the Fish Creek clash by such untrained gunmen seems remarkably unerring.

Further, when considering the daunting and fear-provoking circumstances confronting the horde of angry charcoal burners and the minuscule posse, the precision with which the lawmen discharged their weapons becomes even more outstanding. However, if taking dead aim through the scope of premeditation, the gunman's hand is far less likely to quiver. In this regard historian Joseph G. Rosa has stated, "As in any battle condition, the element of surprise counted a lot with the gun fighting elite."[14]

The enigmatic behavior exhibited by the sheriff's posse at Fish Creek may be understood in terms of the "fight-or-flight" response to a life-threatening situation. Confronted with a dangerous event, people are often enabled to react quickly either by fighting the threat or by fleeing to safety. The fight-or-flight reaction is so instinctive that people in danger act even before they think about the action.[15] Sensing the threatening intentions of the strikers and prepared to fight rather than to flee, the lawmen acted before thinking through what they were about to do. The swiftness of the shooting at Fish Creek is also consistent with the behavior commonly exhibited by armed contenders determined to prevail over their challenger, summed up as "Shoot first and ask questions later." In recounting the exploits of the legendary Wild Bill Hickok, Rosa states, "Hickok displayed the true gunfighter's reaction to danger—he shot first and considered the outcome later."[16]

Aided by the crucial element of deliberation, the clinical precision with which the sheriff's posse delivered the deadly blows was facilitated further by the lawmen's proximity to the strikers. Given the short distance that separated the feuding factions, even the lesser shooters of the posse would have been able to attain accurate shot placement. Corroboration that the late burners stood within easy reach of their would-be assailants came from Veritas's commentary, published in the *Daily Alta California* about two weeks after the shooting. Veritas also disclosed having personally inspected the bodies of the slain burners. His summary examination revealed conspicuous traces of gunpowder in the chests of the victims, thus demonstrating that the burners had been shot at very close range.[17]

The cause-and-effect link thus established between the posse's weaponry and the burners' wounds was indeed a critical element in the development of the inquest. However, after posing a few inconsequential questions to Deputy Simpson, Hillhouse made a startling announcement. The jurist deemed it futile to proceed with the inquiry because he expected the case to be tried by another court at a later time. Surprisingly, Hillhouse agreed to submit the case to the jury as it stood, on the sole evidence provided by the members of the posse. In the absence of any dissenting opinion, the jury thus received the case as it had developed up to that point. What prompted

Hillhouse to adopt such a drastic tactical change in his defense of the slain burners remains unfathomable.[18]

Although Hillhouse recognized the public's expectation of hearing the burners' side of the incident, he brought the inquiry to an abrupt end, believing that its scope would exceed the bounds of an inquest. Immediately following final testimony, given by Louis Monaco, who provided the names, ages, and birthplaces of the dead burners, the courtroom was vacated for the jury to begin deliberating. After conferring briefly with one another, the coroner's jury returned the following verdict: "[The five slain burners] came to their death on the 18th day of August, AD, 1879, in this county, from gunshot wounds, received at the hands of a Sheriff's posse of Eureka County, Nevada, while said posse was in discharge of its duty."[19]

Attesting to the shallow and hasty manner in which the verdict was rendered, the *Sentinel* of August 22 reported that the members of the coroner's jury had spent a long time reaching an agreement on how the verdict should be worded.[20] Presumably, less time was invested in the actual analysis of the contents of the meager evidence submitted for their thoughtful consideration. Although a gruesome portrait of the Fish Creek Massacre was vividly painted by the detailed description of the lethal wounds sustained by the slain burners and the deadly weapons that wrought them, amply published in the local press, the coroner's jury seemed to have turned a blind eye to the particulars of the horrific tale.

Hillhouse's ostensibly inconsistent legal defense of the charcoal burners may be partly explained in terms of his strong ideological conflict with the clients called to represent. In fact, gleaning from General George M. Sabin's correspondence with Colonel George Lyon, Governor Kinkead's private secretary, one is inclined to conclude that Hillhouse perhaps never intended to get to the bottom of the truth, as widely believed. Bringing the coroner's proceedings to an abrupt end on the pretense that the inquiry was taking too wide a range might have been an expedient to suppress the truth rather than reveal it. According to Sabin, Hillhouse belonged to that class of "conservative men all of them, good men too, Hillhouse, Cole (Cole Judge) and all of that political stripe who are wonderfully exercised over Constitutional Law" (see appendix D). Characterized as a man of a conservative bent and "of that political stripe," the attorney for the burners could have been counted on for ensuring that the outcome of the inquest favored the status quo. Further,

Hillhouse was included on the list of bondsmen who posted sureties for the sheriff's posse in the amount of two thousand dollars.[21] Like many other influential Eurekans, Hillhouse had personal investments in the local mining industry,[22] giving him additional inducement toward a speedy resolution of the charcoal crisis.

Predictably, the verdict pronounced by the coroner's jury was met with consternation by most Italians in Eureka.[23] Asserting that no explicit transgressions were committed by the burners to warrant the brutal killings, the majority of Eureka Italians strongly felt that a grievous miscarriage of justice had occurred, first at Fish Creek and subsequently in the courtroom. As if partaking in the discontent felt by the Italian community, the *Leader* stated: "It was expected that the other side of the story would be heard, but it being found that the inquiry was taking too wide a range, it was brought to an abrupt end." Then, as if to kindle the hopes of those dismayed by the verdict, the *Leader* added: "It is probable that an examination of the officers and the posse will take place at an early day, at which time the matter will be judiciously investigated, and all the facts from both sides will be learned."[24]

Nonetheless, a sense of finality about the incomplete inquiry seemed to emanate from the newspaper: "The testimony given at the Coroner's inquest has been published in full, and our readers can draw their own conclusions." Reflecting the widespread bewilderment surrounding the abruptness with which the coroner's inquest was brought to an end, the *Sentinel* concluded its editorial on a hopeful note: "The case will undoubtedly be brought before the District Court, when a change of venue will probably be had, and it will be tried in some other county. No jury of twelve men could possibly be found here who have not formed and expressed an opinion on the affair."[25]

As later developments eventually demonstrated, the change of venue predicted by the *Sentinel* never materialized, while the case of the five slain burners was never brought before the district court. Further, in an article titled "An Italian Version of the Fight," reported in the *Sentinel* on August 21, many Italians accused the *Leader* of having published a "biased account." Although most Italians in Eureka were skeptical of the prejudicial accounts published in the local press, they remained "mum as oysters." As legitimate of an inquiry as the coroner's inquest might have been, to many observers it appeared glaringly one-sided. Whereas the officers involved in the Fish

Creek shooting were provided an amenable forum to air their individual accounts, the burners were denied the opportunity to plead their case.

The friends and compatriots of the slain burners were not the only skeptics. In a surprising journalistic effusion, the *Sentinel* echoed the disparagers' doubts the day before the funeral: "As we view it, there is only one question involved in the whole case. Did the officers act with due prudence and discretion? Was the killing absolutely necessary?" The *Winnemucca Silver State*, as quoted in the *Sentinel*, later declared: "There is a strong suspicion that the posse unnecessarily took the lives of five men at Fish Creek." Similarly, the *Gold Hill Daily News* candidly expressed its own qualms: "This sanguinary bit of news...simply shows the officers to have fired upon an unarmed crowd, and killed and wounded more than there was in their own number without even getting a scratch themselves, the opposite party evidently having no weapons or not desiring to use any."[26]

Predictably, not all newspapers questioned the alleged veracity of the coroner's inquest or the soundness of the ensuing verdict. Some even assumed an openly disparaging stance toward the charcoal burners' cause, as attested by an articled issued by the *Stock Report* on August 19, reprinted by the *Sentinel*:

> The bloodletting at Eureka yesterday will doubtless have a wholesome effect, and has probably convinced the Italian coal burners that there is a law of the land that is superior to the rule of the mob. The matter had to come to bloodshed sooner or later, and it is better that it shall be settled now by the arbitrament of the deputy Sheriff's pistol than that it should have been temporized and trifled with until the interests and industries of a great mining region were paralyzed. The best way to meet brute force is with brute force. The Italians took the law into their own hands, banded together to prevent by force American citizens from pursuing their legitimate business, and the law has stepped in and taught them a bloody lesson. We take it that the battle of yesterday ends the so-called charcoal war. The sight of their dead and wounded comrades is enough to deter men of the temper of the Italian coal burners from further hostilities, and as they gaze on the corpses they will feel a respect for American laws and American equal rights which before they were incapable of.[27]

Likewise, a dithering *Sentinel* upheld the posse's conduct in a column titled "What Is Said on the Street": "There are not a few who blame the Sheriff for sending what they are pleased to term 'a fighting posse.' Such men as Simpson, Martin and Toomey, they say, would be quick to resent an insult which more moderate men would overlook in order to avoid trouble. The argument is a poor one, however, for the Sheriff who would send any but men of recognized courage upon such an expedition would only be equaled in jackassical stupidity by the faint-hearted volunteer who would consent to go." In its adamant defense of the posse, the journal boldly portrayed the extemporized law enforcers as follows: "While the entire posse, with perhaps one or two exceptions, are men whose courage or fighting qualities have never been disputed, not one of them has ever been accused of being quarrelsome, or of engaging on broils of any description."[28]

In haste to shield the posse from controversy, the journal seemed to overlook the unlawful misconduct exhibited by some of the posse men both prior to and after Fish Creek. A year earlier, William Martin had been involved in a violent brawl with a local Italian. The incident was reported by the *Leader*: "In an affray in Marion Farrell's saloon last evening, an Italian by the name of Bianca, was stabbed by William Martin, receiving three cuts, one penetrating the left lung. The cutting was done with a pocket knife, and Martin was considered to be justified in his action. The wounded man is quite easy to day, and no fatal results are anticipated." Martin was arrested and charged with assault to kill Bianca, and his bail was fixed at fifteen hundred dollars. About a week before the shooting at Fish Creek, a recalcitrant Martin became embroiled in yet another public disturbance: "Officer Gorman attempted to take a knife and pistol from Wm. Martin, who was on a bit of a spree on South Main street this afternoon. In the scuffle Martin accidentally cut himself in the groin, causing a profuse flow of blood. Dr. Bishop was called and dressed the wound which was not serious."[29]

Another member of the posse notorious for his belligerent temperament was Marshall Rich, a teamster and foreman for George Lamoureux. In dealing with the desperate charcoal burners in the days prior to the Fish Creek shooting, an exasperated Rich had frequently and openly defied the strikers. Shortly before the shooting, Rich demanded the arrest of a burner who had allegedly threatened him the day before. In his defense the accused first denied Rich's allegations, then retorted with profanities of his own. A cacophony of insults followed, with Rich uttering the final slur.[30]

Rich's outburst typified the frontiersman's oversensitivity about personal honor, which had to be defended at all costs, particularly when threatened in front of one's comrades. On the American frontier, a man's reputation was measured by how he dealt with conflict. "To fail to respond to a challenge or insult," asserts historian David T. Courtwright, "is to lose face and therefore to surrender self-esteem." However, retorting with mere verbal insults or threats was not sufficient to defend one's personal honor. Frontiersmen were pragmatic individuals who respected deeds more than words. According to Courtwright, "The approved response is direct action...that displays physical courage, such as dueling." Fittingly, Rich's defense of his manly reputation was manifested in deeds as well. When one of the strikers at Fish Creek grasped the reins of Rich's team, the irate teamster lashed out at the challenger with his whip. Courtwright further asserts that "violent defense of personal honor was reinforced by a legal system that made it unusually easy to justify killing an opponent," and even easier if the killer wore a badge.[31] In his misguided effort to even the score with the insolent burner, the irate Rich exploited the showdown to redeem his injured manly pride.

Another lawman present at the Fish Creek shooting with a propensity toward violent behavior was Deputy Constable Thomas Arrivey. Reportedly, less than a year before the Fish Creek incident occurred, Arrivey was involved in an affray with John Henry King. In the scuffle the constable suffered a minor wound when his opponent's blade, destined for Arrivey's heart, glanced off a rib instead. According to witnesses, the fight was sparked by an argument over the ownership of some checks at a faro table. By all accounts, Arrivey was declared the aggressor.[32]

Lumped together with Simpson and Martin as examples of short-tempered lawmen was Joseph Toomey. Despite Toomey's reputation as a man "quick to resent an insult," this author has found only one corroborating instance in which Toomey clearly exhibited a confrontational stance in dealing with the wrathful burners, shortly before the shooting at Fish Creek erupted. Confronted by the muzzle of a rifle wielded by an adamant burner, a resolute Toomey grasped the menacing muzzle and pushed it aside. As if to disgrace the daring lawman, a second burner flourished a huge knife, but his imminent attack was thwarted by the appearance of Toomey's revolver, drawn in self-defense.

Of all the posse members, teamster Bob Brown had been the most provocative opponent of the burners since the onset of the charcoal crisis. It was Brown who filed a charge of malicious mischief against five strikers who prevented him from loading at Willow Station on July 20. A few days before the shooting at Fish Creek, Brown defied nine strikers who confronted him at Torre's ranch. In the only known physical fight between strikers and teamsters prior to Fish Creek, Brown and his ranch hands overtook the burners and placed them under arrest. However, in Brown's case, debarment from posse membership could be invoked only retrospectively.

In fact, about three months after the bloodshed at Fish Creek, Brown's character revealed a violent streak that in the end cost him his life. Embroiled in a heated dispute with John Chamberlain regarding the ownership and possession of a wood ranch east of Pine Station, about ten miles outside Eureka, Brown engaged his adversary in a shooting scrape, with fatal results for both men. Reportedly, "Brown left Eureka...telling parties he was going down to take possession of the timber land in controversy." In an attempt at making sense of the tragedy at Shipley's ranch, the *Sentinel* stated, "Both Brown and Chamberlain are said to have been men who were not afraid to use a six-shooter, and...when they met they went at each other with a determination that the work should complete." Elaborating further upon the victims' personal histories, the newspaper declared, "Bob Brown had been a teamster in this section for several years. He was regarded as a game man, rather inclined to court than to shun danger."[33]

Yet first among the ill-suited lawmen involved in the shooting of the charcoal burners at Fish Creek was Deputy Sheriff J. B. Simpson, leader of the "fighting posse." Despite his well-meaning final attempts at defusing the conflict, the deputy sheriff, reputed by many as an impulsive man, failed inordinately in the delicate mission he was called to command. Besides his apparent professional ineptitude, Simpson might have harbored a strong ethnic prejudice against the Italian burners, predisposing him toward a violent confrontation. In fact, a few months earlier Simpson had participated in a deadly fight with a rowdy patron in a hurdy house. In the clash Simpson shot and fatally wounded an Italian named Billy Joseph. Simpson surrendered himself, alleging self-defense, and was subsequently released on two thousand dollars' bond by Justice Cromer.[34]

The irascible lawmen just described, placed under the leadership of a heedless Deputy Sheriff Simpson, also known as a quick-tempered officer, constituted a numerical majority within the nine-member sheriff's posse.

Unable or perhaps disinclined to tame the turbulent spirits under his command, Simpson allowed whatever neutral ground still existed between the lawmen and the strikers to be hopelessly erased. Their aggressive temperaments bolstered by the defiant burners, the fighting spirits of the posse most certainly prevailed over their more moderate associates.

Although often rationalized by the unstable and isolated circumstances of frontier society, the latitude bequeathed upon the officers of the law could itself degenerate into lawlessness. In recognition of the latent duplicity of frontier justice, historian Eugene W. Hollon states, "Throughout the last half of the nineteenth century, parts of the Western frontier were ruled by mobs of gunmen who were called outlaws or posses—depending upon one's point of view." Further exposing the ambivalence of frontier justice, Hollon reiterates what was an accepted aphorism of those days: "There is more law in a Colt Six Gun than in all the law books."[35] Conceivably, seeking a pretext for fighting in a highly combustible confrontation with the strikers, the officers of the sheriff's posse acted as extralegal enforcers or, in the lexicon of the American frontier, vigilantes.

With darkness spreading over a remote mountain canyon, far removed from the scrutiny of civilized society, the prospect of carrying out summary justice by the sheriff's heavily armed posse, thus squelching once and for all the protracted conflict, must have been compelling. Further light upon the lawmen's murky conduct at Fish Creek is shed by historian Frank R. Prassel, who states, "A key element to interpreting county law enforcement in the West, and one which cannot be underestimated...[is] politics." Prassel cautions, "Despite misleading appearances, peace officers seldom embody true social power; instead, they normally represent the interests of community wealth and authority."[36]

Persisting in its sympathetic treatment of the "fighting posse," the *Sentinel* buttressed Simpson's position, asserting that public suspicions about the deputy's conduct in the line of duty only added insult to injury: "Simpson seems to feel his position keenly and although he is reticent in everything appertaining to the affair doubtless thinks there is little to induce an officer to risk his life in defense of the interest of others when such a step only results in his actions being questioned by a large portion of our people."[37]

There were also Eurekans who resented the insinuation of partiality hurled at the judicial process by scores of disenchanted Italians. In the

Leader of August 21, under the heading "Fault Finders," these defenders of the status quo voiced their unconditional approval for the manner in which the coroner's inquest had been carried out:

> Considerable comment has been made upon the action of Coroner Smith in allowing the inquest upon the deceased Italians to take so wide a range, and in countenancing the appearance of Counselor Hillhouse. Mr. Smith understood his duty probably better than his critics, and acted very judiciously. Mr. Hillhouse was retained as the representative of the deceased, and it was conceded as much the best course under the circumstances, and one calculated to allay the feeling among the coal burners, that the inquest would be a one-sided affair. Coroner Smith acted under legal advice, and the carpers would have found just as much fault had he choked off all evidence in the beginning.

The coroner's inquest, being concluded so abruptly, left behind a trail of lingering doubts and unanswered questions. Of paramount relevance was the issue of authority under which the posse had presumably acted at Fish Creek. Officially, only Simpson, Toomey, Storey, and Smith were bona fide officers of the law. By contrast, the other posse members, Rich, Brown, Martin, Arrivey, and Porter were teamsters directly embroiled in the coal troubles who happened to join the officers in the pursuit of the presumed ringleaders.[38]

In all official accounts of the brutal affair, there is only one brief mention of the deputation of the teamsters, in the *Leader* of August 19. Definitely, the question of the posse's legal authority represented one of the most controversial elements in the coroner's investigation, one that Hillhouse was expected to vigorously contest but one that went unchallenged as a result of the inquest's sudden cessation.

Besides the inconsistencies of the coroner's inquest, the composition of the jury revealed a conspicuous bias along socioeconomic lines. Far from being constituted by a representative sample of Eureka's population, the thirteen-member panel was largely constituted of prominent Eurekans. In fact, M. H. Clark, Frank Doutrick, M. A. Montgomery, and Pete Steler, or one-third of the jury, belonged to Eureka's upper echelon, potentially exerting disproportionate dominance over the lesser jurors.[39] Yet the composition of the coroner's jury had been greeted with much adulation by the press, extolling the alleged virtues possessed by its members. Brimming with optimism, the *Sentinel* confidently stated, "The Coroner's jury is one of the best and most intelligent that could have been selected in Eureka, and their verdict will be received by the people at large as a just and correct one."[40]

The overly deferential accolades bestowed upon the coroner's jury were bound to unduly influence public opinion, perhaps fostering an unconscious conviction that the jurors were eminently qualified for the difficult task and thoroughly disinterested in its outcome. With prejudicial expectations sown in the public mind, even before the inquest began, an anxious community became predisposed to anticipate the sound verdict of an impartial jury.

Whether fortuitously or by design, the coroner's jury issued its official verdict on August 21, the day the funeral of the five slain burners was held.[41] While the burial of the Fish Creek victims could not wait, the verdict could have been put off to a more deferential time, as a gesture of respect toward the grieving Italian community. Following the massacre at Fish Creek, the bodies of the five slain burners had been taken to S. P. Haskell's mortuary establishment, where they awaited examination by the coroner's jury.[42] Subsequent to the jury's postmortem examination, dubbed by the *Sentinel* as "the farce of viewing the bodies," the burners' remains were prepared for interment. On the day of the funeral, the bodies were transported to Schwamb's Funeral Home, and at three o'clock in the afternoon the hallowed rite commenced. The funeral ceremonies lasted about an hour, and at four o'clock the cortege began its doleful pilgrimage toward the final place of rest. The memorial service was one of the largest and most memorable assemblages of people ever witnessed in Eureka.[43]

The entourage comprised 230 somberly attired mourners proceeding on foot and in double file, stretching more than a half mile. Virtually all participants were countrymen of the deceased. Right behind the multitude trailed a hearse carrying one single body. A wagon dolefully decorated in black, laden with three coffins and pulled by four black horses, followed somberly. A second hearse, also transporting the body of a single burner, trailed behind. The rear of the cortege was filled by a long string of carriages and wagons crowded with friends of the departed.[44]

The funeral procession was a veritable expression of communal grief, which, for one memorable afternoon, gripped the gloomy town in its mournful embrace. Issuing forth from Robbins Street, on the town's north end, the multitude meandered unwearyingly through the town's principal intersections, thronged with hundreds of spectators in reverent silence on both sides, and eventually it reached the south end of town at Bateman Street. Upon arriving at the intersection of Bateman and Main, in prominent view of the renowned Eureka Courthouse, the procession lingered briefly. As if in an ephemerally symbolic gesture of silent recrimination, the core of the procession stood solemnly before the temple of justice. Thenceforth, the cortege commenced the tortuous ascension of Bateman Street, passing in front of Schwamb's Funeral Home one last time, on the way to the Catholic cemetery, on the southwest edge of Eureka.[45]

The grandeur with which the deceased burners were honored was poignant. Indeed, with fervent reverence the funeral service appeared imbued with a sublimated purpose. Grieving the unjust death of their slain fellow immigrants, Eureka's mournful Italians attempted to give expression to their suppressed hatred by turning the funeral into a tacit but mighty act of protest. At least for the few hours that the funeral ceremonies lasted, a huddled and forlorn Italian collectivity on the Nevada mining frontier cried out against injustice, perhaps shaming the verdict announced by the coroner's jury into insignificance.

Notwithstanding the *Leader*'s defense of the coroner, J. W. Smith, most Italians, along with many Eurekans, still felt that the inquest had been indeed a one-sided affair. With the coroner's investigation concluded and the slain burners laid to rest, an atmosphere of order seemed to have been restored to the beleaguered community. Such a perception had been distinctly voiced by the *Leader* of August 21: "All excitement in reference to the coal troubles seems to be allayed." Yet as a belligerent faction of the defeated burners soon demonstrated, the coal troubles still smoldered. Perhaps desperately seeking to avenge their fallen comrades, whose number was presumed higher still by those who had lived through the Fish Creek shooting, the feud lingered. In fact, twenty of the burners engaged at Fish Creek were reported still missing, with three of them rumored to have died from wounds sustained during the affray.[46]

That the coal dispute was still blazing was confirmed by teamster Tom Reilly upon his August 22 return to Eureka, after having failed to load charcoal near Fish Creek. Prevented from sacking and loading his teams by the striking burners, not far from the scene of the recent shooting, Reilly duly reported the persisting trouble to Sheriff Kyle. Apparently, a band of coal burners had taken up position near the charcoal pits and threatened Reilly's men with death should they attempt to sack even a single piece of charcoal. Learning of Reilly's encounter with the resisting burners, the editors of the *Leader* swiftly condemned the belligerent strikers for pursuing the same bulldozing tactics as before, fearing the likelihood of further bloodshed.

Assuming the role of defender of private property, the newspaper's editors sternly reminded the strikers that they had no right to interfere with the material goods of others. They also alerted their readers to the imminent financial burdens about to be imposed upon the county coffers in defraying the damages incurred by the local teamsters and charcoal owners, all stemming from the destructive acts of the burners. Further, the newspapermen indulged in a satirical diatribe aimed at those citizens who had withdrawn their endorsement of what they deemed irresponsible conduct by the sheriff's posse at Fish Creek. With little self-restraint, the editors stated:

> The officers have done the best they could to stop the proceedings of the strikers, and being censored by so many of our citizens, after risking their lives in the performance of their duty, is not calculated to inspire them with any considerable amount of zeal in their efforts to arrest the offenders. There is now an opportunity for those of the law and order loving portion of the community, who are so ready to denounce the officers and to proclaim that the recent killing was uncalled for and unnecessary, to show what they can do in settling the question and arresting the mob that is today interfering with the rights of property and the vocation of peaceful citizens. The Sheriff will no doubt be most happy to deputize them. But he will not attempt to lead them, if he has any regard for his head.[47]

Although it is impracticable to assess accurately the effects spawned by the *Leader*'s stirring rhetoric, the suspicion that the newspaper's one-sided opinion hardened public attitudes toward the upcoming burners' trial seems plausible. Considering the power of the press in molding public opinion, the excessively partisan commentaries voiced by the *Leader*'s editors in their unwavering support of the officers' conduct at Fish Creek undermined the conviction of those inclined to denounce the officers for having killed futilely.

By appealing to the universally venerated individual rights to property, the editors eviscerated criticism of the bloody affair, thus fanning the flames of prejudice against the mob that threatened such noble rights.

Notes

1. *Leader*, August 20, 1879.
2. Grazeola, "Charcoal Burners War of 1879," 96.
3. Ibid., 114.
4. *Leader*, August 21, 1879.
5. *Sentinel*, August 21, 1879.
6. *Leader*, August 21, 1879.
7. *Leader*, August 21, 1879; *Sentinel*, August 21, 1879.
8. *Leader*, August 21, 1879.
9. *Leader*, August 21, 1879; *Sentinel*, August 21, 1879.
10. *Leader*, August 22, 1879.
11. *Sentinel*, August 21, 1879.
12. Grazeola, "Charcoal Burners War of 1879," 114.
13. W.B. (Bat) Masterson, "Famous Gun Fighters of the Western Frontier," 9.
14. Joseph G. Rosa, *The Gunfighter: Man or Myth?*, 124.
15. "Understanding the Stress Response."
16. Rosa, *Gunfighter*, 146.
17. *Daily Alta California*, August 31, 1879.
18. *Leader*, August 22, 1879.
19. *Leader*, August 21, 1879.
20. *Sentinel*, August 22, 1879.
21. *Leader*, September 2, 1879.
22. *Leader*, February 4, 1879.
23. Earl, "Nevada's Italian War," 77.
24. *Leader*, August 21, 1879.
25. Ibid.; *Sentinel*, August 22, 1879.
26. *Sentinel*, August 20, 30, 1879; *Gold Hill Daily News*, August 20, 1879.
27. *Sentinel*, August 24, 1879.
28. *Sentinel*, August 21, 1879.
29. *Leader*, July 13, 1878, August 9, 1879.
30. *Sentinel*, August 20, 1879.
31. David T. Courtwright, *Violent Land: Single Men and Social Disorder from the Frontier to the Inner City*, 28, 29.
32. *Leader*, December 18, 1878.
33. *Sentinel*, November 25, 1879.
34. *Sentinel*, February 6, 1879.
35. Hollon, *Frontier Violence: Another Look*, 106.

36. Frank R. Prassel, *The Western Peace Officer: A Legacy of Law and Order*, 111.
37. *Sentinel*, August 22, 1879.
38. Earl, "Nevada's Italian War," 77.
39. Grazeola, "Charcoal Burners War of 1879," 98–99.
40. *Sentinel*, August 21, 1879.
41. *Leader*, August 21, 1879.
42. *Leader*, August 19, 1879.
43. *Sentinel*, August 21, 1879.
44. *Leader*, August 21, 1879.
45. Ibid.
46. Ibid.
47. *Leader*, August 22, 1879.

XI

The Trial of the Charcoal Burners

Absolved from any wrongdoing by the coroner's jury, the members of the sheriff's posse emerged unscathed from the investigation, just as they had risen unharmed from the fight at Fish Creek. Their conduct, though marred by glaring inconsistencies that surfaced during the inquest, was ultimately deemed blameless. The verdict rendered by the coroner's jury on August 21 asserted that the sheriff's posse killed the five Italian burners while "in discharge of its duty."[1] Dissatisfaction with the superficiality of the coroner's inquest and the abruptness of its conclusion was widespread, particularly among Eureka's Italians.

Perplexed by the trail of unanswered questions left behind by the coroner's inquiry, the *Eureka Daily Leader* declared, "It was expected that the other side of the story [the Italians'] would be heard, but it being found that the inquiry was taking too wide a range, it was brought to an abrupt end." As if to nurture a glimmer of hope that the legal proceedings would eventually be resumed, the newspaper went on to state, "It is probable that an examination of the officers and posse will take place at an early day, at which time the matter will be judiciously investigated, and all the facts from both standpoints will be learned."[2] Lamentably, the hope expressed by the *Leader* would remain unrealized. What did follow "at an early day," on August 22, was a preliminary hearing for twenty burners accused of malicious mischief, riot, and conspiracy, followed the next day by murder charges filed against the members of the sheriff's posse.

The charge of malicious mischief was filed by teamster Robert Brown on July 20, whereas the heavier charges of riot and conspiracy were presented by Reinhold Sadler on an unspecified date sometime between mid-July and mid-August. Confronting the accused burners were powerful businessmen who fiercely opposed the burners' efforts to obtain a higher price for their charcoal. Among them stood Sadler, a prominent citizen described as an "active and go-ahead businessman," who was directly embroiled in the charcoal crisis. German by birth, Sadler came to Eureka in 1875 and opened up an extensive wholesale and retail establishment. In January 1879 Sadler had been appointed county commissioner.[3] On August 11, as the charcoal crisis intensified, Sadler was among those who signed the telegram dispatched to Governor John Kinkead requesting the intervention of the state militia to quell the uprisings.[4] In early September, just a few days after the Fish Creek shooting, Sadler became the chairman of the Eureka Mining District, with the authority to appoint the inspector, the two judges, and the two clerks of the organization.[5] Early in 1880 the German entrepreneur was elected treasurer of Eureka County.[6]

Evidently, Sadler possessed strong business instincts and political ambitions, for he eventually attained the office of lieutenant governor of Nevada. In 1896, after only a year in that capacity, Sadler suddenly rose to the governorship when Governor John E. Jones died in office. After winning election to a term of his own, Sadler served his tenure effectively but declined to run for reelection, preferring to resume his business pursuits instead.[7] Considering Sadler's successful political and entrepreneurial career, the Eureka mogul was well placed to hold great sway upon the legal system that confronted the charcoal burners.

Another likely adversary of the burners was Thomas Wren, Republican congressman and leading prosecutor at the charcoal burners' trial. Judging by the frequency with which Wren's name appeared in the local press in conjunction with his personal mining affairs, one would be inclined to conclude that, practically speaking, Wren appeared to be as much a mine owner as a jurist. An excerpt from the *Leader* reinforced that suggestion: "Hon. Thomas Wren has received some rich samples of ore found in the Odger mine, White Pine mountain, of which he is owner. The prospects are very flattering." Another reference to Wren's prosperous mining activities asserted the following: "Hon. Wren's mines are also looking well and he is shipping a quantity of ore to the Richmond."[8] Wren was also legal counsel for the Richmond Company, plaintiff in a landmark dispute with Eureka

Consolidated over a valuable mining property. The suit began in 1877 and ended in 1881 with the Richmond's defeat.⁹ Wren was further described as "one of the foremost mining men of the state, had extensive business interests, was a jurist of unexcelled ability, especially as a mining attorney... and served as president for the Richmond Mining Company."[10]

Being prominently tied to the mining industry, Wren's personal loyalties rested naturally with the mine-owning class. The line between personal business affairs and professional ethics was blurred further by Wren's close association with Richard Rickard, superintendent of the Richmond, and with teamster George Lamoureux, as attested by the following news item: "A meeting of the stockholders of the Prospect Mountain Tunnel Company was held last Evening at the office of Hon. Thomas Wren. The following trustees were elected: R. Rickard, R.K. Morrison, George W. Lamoureaux [sic].... The stockholders are very much pleased with the prospects of the enterprise and its management."[11]

Although Wren's role as the top legal representative of the burners' adversaries is in itself irreproachable, his personal involvement with the local mining enterprise cast some doubts upon his professionalism. Having a personal stake in the speedy resolution of the trial as a result of his financial investments in the mining industry, Wren might have expediently assumed the dual role of prosecutor and plaintiff, pressing forward to see the burners' appeal to justice go unheeded. Because Wren's personal mining interests conflicted sharply with the burners' cause, the prosecutor might have approached the legal proceedings with a highly prejudicial mind-set, inclining him to tilt the scale of justice to secure a conviction. As a business associate of Lamoureux, another prominent plaintiff in the case against the charcoal burners, Wren could not have been reasonably expected to set aside partisanship in favor of the primacy of justice. Not only were Wren's business interests at odds with the coal burners' demands, but the prominent prosecutor also exhibited a racial intolerance toward the Chinese of Eureka.[12]

After being postponed as a result of the shooting at Fish Creek, the trial against nineteen charcoal burners charged with riot and conspiracy, presumably committed during the wagon disruptions, got under way on August 22 in the Eureka Justice Court. The summoned burners were confronted by Reinhold Sadler, the primary plaintiff, who charged the burners with "unlawfully conspir[ing], confederat[ing] and agree[ing] together unlawfully, forcibly to prevent R. Sadler and other citizens…from carrying on their business of hauling and sending charcoal thereby…committing acts that were and are injurious to both trade and commerce." The accused burners were G. B. Cordano, Severino Strozzi, G. Martinoli, Giuseppi Rossetti, Giovanni Cesoriolli, Angelo del Bondio, Garcia Defendetia, Antone Vebala, Luigi Pinola, G. Rodono, Georgeta Gentili, Parola Bianca, Dullenella Batistta, Consbandise Rosetti, Jacovio Sine, Bronda Antivill, Tom Pajorola, James Bassetti, and Joe Winkelreid.[13]

The trial was presided over by Judge Lawrence Washington Cromer, one of the best-known and most successful of the early businessmen of Eureka. A former military man whose career started in 1864, in Austin, Nevada, Cromer had been elected justice of the peace in 1876. Reportedly, "his judgments were so patently fair that only very few were ever reversed by higher courts." It was further stated that he was "conscientious and high-minded in official as well as in business relations."[14] The twenty arraigned burners appeared at the preliminary hearing, duly represented by Hillhouse & Cole and Beatty & Laspeyre. Conversely, the state was represented by Thomas Wren, W. W. Bishop, and G. W. Baker.[15] Although in theory the grievous occurrence at Fish Creek, with its troubling emotional effects still reverberating, was not to influence the trial, in practice it was virtually impossible to insulate the proceedings at hand from the charged emotions the shooting had generated only four days earlier.

Predictably, the plaintiffs' attorneys endeavored to cast the testimony of the teamsters, called as witnesses for the prosecution, in a favorable light, strongly sympathetic toward the posse's conduct at Fish Creek. The most damning testimony against the defendants was rendered by teamster E. N. Cornforth on August 25. Cornforth declared he had been prevented from loading coal various times by the "leading spirits" of the charcoal disturbance, namely, Giovanni Pedroni, Pompeo Pattini, and Giuseppe Martinoli. The teamster testified that he had heard the instigators make threats to kill Pete Strozzi, Bob Brown, Reinhold Sadler, Joseph Tognini, and Gabriel. (The identity of the last one of these men is unclear.) Cornforth added that the agitators also threatened to burn down the town unless they obtained thirty cents per bushel of charcoal.[16]

From the trial's onset, the counsel for the defendants assumed an unequivocally assertive stance. Hillhouse and his colleagues moved swiftly to have the charges filed against the defendants summarily dismissed, contending that the arrest warrants were inherently flawed and thus unenforceable. Indeed, the judicial writs bore fictitious names under which the burners' arrests were executed. Not only did the warrants fail to specify the names of the burners indicted, but they also omitted the defendants' specific occupations. Considerable counterargument ensued. In his rebuttal, Wren moved to deny the motion by appealing to the statutes of the state of Nevada, which presumably recognized the right of the justice of the peace to effect the arrest of any offender even when that person's name or occupation was unknown. The prosecution prevailed, and the true names of the defendants were inserted in the complaint.[17]

Other motions put forth by Hillhouse to clear the defendants were assiduously debated by the prosecution and overruled by Judge Cromer. One such motion requested that the complaining witness be made available to the defense attorneys for the purpose of cross-examination to ascertain his ability to identify the accused. This strategy was intended to place Sadler on record as the instigator of the arrests and to eventually hold him accountable for financial damages should the defendants be acquitted. The counsel for the state successfully opposed the motion.[18]

The first witness called at the burners' trial was Joseph Hausman, former secretary of the burners' association. Hausman asserted that no resolution had ever been adopted by the association inciting the membership to resort to force to implement the thirty-cent pledge. Hausman testified that the only resolution sanctioned by the association was the establishment of a rate of thirty cents per bushel, to which signatories pledged to adhere or incur a fifty-dollar fine per load for noncompliance. According to Hausman, the CBPA's roster listed between five and six hundred burners' names, not all of them full-fledged members of the association. Hausman added that a second resolution had also been adopted, authorizing the formation of four recruiting committees to be dispatched to the various coal camps to broaden the membership and rally support for the fledgling organization.[19]

The following day, as the events were reported in the *Leader* on August 23, 1879, several teamsters were called to testify. The first witness was W. M. Patterson, a resident of Pine Station in the employ of Hansen as a bookkeeper. Patterson testified about seeing Severino Strozzi at Pine Station on both August 10 and 11. Hansen's bookkeeper reported hearing Strozzi remark that no teams would be allowed to load unless two fundamental conditions were met. First, the charcoal was to be purchased by the teamsters at the newly established price of thirty cents a bushel. Second, the burners would be shown the charcoal receipts upon request. Patterson confirmed that all the incoming teams had already been stopped at Pine Station and at Alpha.

Patterson reported that Strozzi and a dozen cohorts were at Pine Station's saloon when their alleged threats were made. Presumably, the insurrectionists had been drinking, raising the suspicion that their grumblings were perhaps only the garbled effusions of inebriated tongues. One of them, a certain Andrew Delume, warned that "if [the burners] couldn't carry their point in any other way they would burn up the coal." Patterson testified further that all through the squabble, he witnessed no display of arms or violence by the burners except for some resistance shown by Strozzi toward the officer who arrested him at Pine Station.

The next witness was Fred White, another teamster who clashed with the burners. White readily confirmed the leading role exhibited by Severino Strozzi during the confrontation, in which sacks of coal that White was contracted to transport for Reinhold Sadler were dumped. The teamster stated that Strozzi openly admitted responsibility for ordering the dumping. White added that Strozzi warned defiantly that he would not be deterred by either officers or soldiers from stopping anybody from loading charcoal, pointing out the fact that he had already halted teams that belonged to Hansen, Burlingame, and McDonald.

Teamster Maximillian Siddle testified next that Strozzi and a band of about twenty burners targeted Tognini's ranch on August 10, causing the dumping of about 640 sacks of charcoal. Siddle divulged that Strozzi participated in the dumping raid by emptying some of the sacks himself. After identifying Strozzi among the prisoners in the courtroom, Siddle reported that the ringleader told him that the sacks were being dumped because the hardworking burners who filled them were working for nothing.

The next witness was an Italian burner named Natali Fobeli, seemingly an independent burner with no ties to the association. Fobeli testified to having contracted with Tognini to burn, sack, and load the charcoal on the wagons. Fobeli claimed he had about 850 sacks of charcoal on Tognini's ranch, ready for shipment, when Strozzi and his followers suddenly turned up and dumped nearly all of the contents. Following the dumping, Strozzi cautioned Fobeli to cease sacking charcoal under the threat of further consequences. For his part, Fobeli declared he was satisfied with the terms of his contract, adding that Tognini had never refused him access to the receipts. Following Fobeli's testimony, due to "a press of matter," newspaper coverage of the proceedings stopped.

However, when the trial resumed on Monday, August 25, the *Eureka Daily Leader* that day published an update of the testimonies that followed Fobeli's. Presumably, Antone Rapp had testified seeing Severino Strozzi with a band of about twenty-five Italians, seven or eight of whom were armed, emptying coal sacks at Tognini's ranch. Another witness, Louis Dequili, also placed Strozzi and his throng emptying coal sacks at Tognini's ranch on August 10. However, Dequili provided a higher count, putting the burners' number at thirty-five or forty. Dequili also revealed a new and troubling detail related to the burners' alleged threats. "Some of them," stated Dequili, "told me if I mentioned any names the penalty would be death from the Masonic fraternity."

E. N. Cornforth, a teamster of Antelope Valley, informed the court that he had been prevented from loading coal that belonged to his brother on several occasions. He then proceeded to identify some of the prisoners supposedly implicated in the coal stoppages. The teamster identified Giuseppe Martinoli, vice president of the association, whom he had met on July 15. At that time, Martinoli, accompanied by two or three burners, one of whom was Giovanni Pedroni, later killed at Fish Creek, told Cornforth that he and his cohorts were headed to Ackerman's Canyon to stop Pete Strozzi (relation to Severino undetermined) from loading charcoal.[20]

Cornforth was remarkably specific in his account of the number of armed burners engaged in the team stoppages. In fact, he asserted that out of a horde of forty-three burners, forty were armed with an assortment of weapons, including rifles, shotguns, pistols, knives, and pruning hooks. Presumably, Cornforth was afforded ample time to carry out such a minute inventory of the kind of weaponry brandished by the rioters. Cornforth testified that some burners warned the teamsters that before allowing the coal to be hauled to town for less than the pledged price, they would burn it, along with the wagons.

Cornforth identified Pompeo Pattini, another of the burners killed at Fish Creek, along with Joe Negrini and C. Rosetti. These men, Cornforth claimed, had talked of killing Pete Strozzi, Bob Brown, Tognini, and Gabriel, while they intended to hang Sadler. The witness also reported hearing Pedroni and Martinoli threatening to burn down the town unless the price of charcoal was raised to thirty cents a bushel. In the event the furnaces shut down their operations, Cornforth heard the burners threaten setting fire to the Richmond works, burning their own supply of charcoal stockpile, and then moving to California.

Cornforth said threats had been made against his person prior to the trial. Of the four men who cautioned him not to say much, Cornforth knew only one by name, a certain Jogette (Giorgetto?) Joseppi (Giuseppe), a friend and coworker of the witness. Presumably, the witness's brother was a member of the association and had agreed to hold his coal for thirty cents. However, Cornforth admitted in his testimony that he was unaware of his brother's involvement with the association. Finally, Cornforth attempted to dispel some insinuations of complicity with the burners, which arose during the trial. He denied telling Joseppi that the best thing the coal burners could do would be to kill Brown and hang Sadler and the rest of the contractors. At any rate, certain aspects of Cornforth's testimony seemed contrived and ambiguous.

As the examination of the charcoal burners drew to an end, grossly exaggerated reports of the number of belligerent burners engaged in the coal troubles lingered in some parts of the country. The *Leader* of August 25 reported on the numerical distortion: "A telegram to the *Chicago Times* in reference to our coal troubles states that the military force, under the command of General Sabin, were making a forced march to Fish river, where two thousand hostile Italians were encamped. Forced march is good." The telegram implied a stern condemnation of the burners' resistance, while flaunting support for the advancing military forces mobilized to quell the uprisings.

As of August 24, six days after the fight at Fish Creek, six of the coal burners engaged in the affray were still missing. One of them was known to have been shot in the shoulder, but since he was mounted, he managed to flee from the scene. After the shooting, friends of the missing vainly scoured the hills in search of them. Still hoping to find their comrades, a subscription was taken up in Eureka on August 23, and men were hired to continue the search.[21]

Meanwhile, on Saturday evening of August 23, while the trial of the charcoal burners was in recess, a formal complaint was filed in the Justice

Court by Michael Pattini, indicting all the members of the sheriff's posse for murder for the killing of his nephew Pompeo Pattini, presumably the leader of the strikers, at Fish Creek on August 18. The defendants cited in the murder allegation were Henry Storey, J. B. Simpson, Joseph Toomey, William Martin, Robert E. Brown, Marshall Rich, James Porter, G. H. Smith, and Thomas Arrivey. Arrest warrants were duly issued and handed to each individual officer for service.[22]

On Sunday, August 24, at five o'clock in the afternoon, all the posse members charged appeared in person before justice of the peace Judge Cromer, accompanied by their legal representatives, attorneys Bishop, General Sabin (who was also a lawyer), Wren, and Baker, while bail was determined at five thousand dollars each. Many influential citizens hastened to extricate the officers from their predicament. Without delay the bond was posted, and the lawmen were immediately released. The *Eureka Daily Leader* reported no dearth of prominent backers for the defendants: "Many of the substantial men of the county came forward without solicitation as bondsmen, and had it been necessary many thousands of dollars would have been easily given."[23]

Promptly, a notable list of the thirty-five bondsmen appeared in the press. While Sheriff Matthew Kyle was called to execute the official bond, the sureties for the defendants were published in the *Leader*. Whereas most bonds hovered around two thousand dollars, some were more than double that amount. Among the latter were listed some of the burners' staunchest adversaries, such as Joseph Tognini, John Torre, and George Lamoureux, each providing a five-thousand-dollar bond. The prominent Reinhold Sadler, another one of the burners' opponents, made available a ten-thousand-dollar surety. The *Leader* stated, "The bond is in excess of the amount required, and is about as solid a showing as could well be made." The promptness with which "many of the substantial men of the county" secured the release of the indicted lawmen lends further credibility to Prassel's assertion that western frontier lawmen frequently "functioned as the repressive arm of political institutions somewhat removed from public need."[24]

Anyone sympathetic to the cause of justice could readily detect the munificence bestowed by Eureka's magnates upon the defenders of the law in their hour of need. The readiness to post bail exhibited by Eureka's elite to secure the prompt release of the sheriff's posse contrasted sharply with the austere treatment of the destitute burners. Given the strong interdependence between the representatives of the law and the mercantile class on the western frontier, the eagerness of Eureka's bondsmen to rescue the troubled posse could be viewed as much as an expedient maneuver to reclaim control of a financial asset as a generous public gesture. In this regard, Prassel asserts that "for some prosperous concerns reliable support of county lawmen could be obtained more cheaply than hired guns." Prassel contends that "while such a situation did not occur with great frequency it could hardly be described as rare." Because only a thin line separated a posse from acting as vigilantes bent on apprehending presumed lawbreakers at will, some western jurisdictions endeavored to draw prospective members mainly from among upright citizens. Although by the turn of the century eligibility standards had been markedly raised, as in New Mexico, where "no person who may be under indictment or may be generally known as a notorious character, or as a disturber of the peace shall be eligible to serve as a deputy sheriff," in the 1870s it was not uncommon to hire known gunmen to enforce the law.[25]

The case of the sheriff's posse was scheduled to take place as soon as the hearing of the charcoal burners was completed. As reported by the *Leader*, the arrest of the posse revived the waning interest in the late tragedy, making the affair, once again, the foremost topic of conversation in town.[26] Remarkably, Simpson's arraignment was not the officer's first brush with the law. In fact, the *Eureka Grand Jury Minute Book* revealed that the posse leader had been indicted a few months earlier on a charge of assault with intent to kill. On February 5, Simpson was lounging at a dance hall, as was his custom, when he was suddenly drawn into a violent row sparked by two Italian patrons, Milito Batista and Billy Joseph, contenders for one of the dance girls. In the scuffle Simpson shot and fatally wounded Billy Joseph.[27]

The gravity of Simpson's previous arraignment cast some doubts upon the deputy's aptness at enforcing the law. Simpson's charge of assault with intent to kill reinforced the perception of a man prone to violence, rendering the burners' claim that the officers led by Simpson provoked the Fish Creek incident more probable.[28] On Monday, August 25, a week after the Fish Creek shooting, the hearing of the coal burners effected a digression to incorporate the testimonies of the sheriff's posse, defendants in the murder complaint filed by Michael Pattini three days earlier. Although the hearing was intended to deal primarily with the burners' conspiracy suit, the depositions made by those called to testify in the posse's murder suit were, as historian Phillip Earl has suggested, "obviously designed to influence public opinion in favor of the action taken by the lawmen."[29]

On August 26, 1879, the *Leader* published an account of the depositions. First to testify before Judge Cromer was Robert E. Brown, a teamster and coal burner. Brown alleged his teams were first stopped on July 20, while loading at Willow Station. Brown instructed his men to fill the coal sacks, but his order went unheeded by the intimidated workers, who feared for their lives. Shortly after, five horsemen and five footmen appeared on the scene. The intruders threatened to burn Brown's coal and wagons if the teamster insisted on loading. Yielding to the menacing rioters, Brown rode to Eureka, where he swore out a warrant for the arrest of five of the insurgents.

The following day Brown returned to his ranch with five additional men to load up the coal. This time, however, he was escorted by the sheriff and his posse. Predictably, sacking and loading proceeded smoothly until sometime that afternoon, when a party of about 150 burners descended on the ranch, ordering all operations to cease. The standoff was resolved later that evening when an order came from Maginni, commanding the strikers to leave Brown alone. Sacking and loading resumed, and Brown's charcoal activities proceeded unimpeded for a time. Brown went on to testify that his next quarrel with the rioters took place at Fish Creek a few days before the shooting, on either the thirteenth or the fourteenth of August.

On that occasion, the teamster rode up to Torre's ranch with fellow teamsters Gorman, Smith, Rich, and Arrivey to load and haul the charcoal sacks that lay in readiness at that location. Riding ahead of their respective freight wagons, the teamsters reached the loading station and found 9 burners sitting on the sacks, determined to prevent the loading. Brown knew all of the strikers and provided their names to the court. The teamsters asked the trespassers if they were there to fight. Hunching their shoulders, the marauders merely declared, "*No coal shall go.*" Then Brown spoke with Diola Bianca, who, according to the witness, pretended to be a friend and seemed disposed to help the teamsters. Bianca cautioned the haulers that they were going to have a hard fight because there lurked 150 burners in the nearby hills. Willing to help, Bianca asked the teamsters to provide him with a gun. Finally, the would-be friend urged the teamsters to refrain from loading the charcoal, for if they did not abandon their venture, they would surely all be killed.

Unmoved by Bianca's appeal, a boastful Brown retorted that he had no fear of the strikers. Positioning himself between the approaching teams to couple the wagons, Brown climbed aboard, eager to begin loading. Angered by Brown's temerity, the 9 strikers rushed forward to prevent any attempt at loading. A scuffle ensued. After repeated attempts by the insurgents to hold their ground, the teamsters, aided by their ranch hands, managed to disarm the strikers, and loading was completed. Brown testified that the strikers were armed with a rifle, a shotgun, two brush knives (similar to cleavers), and a dirk knife. The balance of the raiders wielded clubs. After disarming the assailants, Brown and Gorman placed them under arrest. Presumably, Brown had been deputized by the sheriff and carried a warrant for the burners' arrest, while Arrivey was a deputy constable.

Thomas Arrivey testified next. For the most part, his testimony corroborated that rendered by Cornforth and Brown. Arrivey recounted a solemn warning issued by one of the subdued strikers: "You may get this load, but the next time you come you bring half the men of Eureka, for there will be 200 armed men here, and will kill all of you." Arrivey identified the 9 defendants while also providing a detailed account of the fight to disarm them. After having been disarmed and placed under arrest, Arrivey continued, Gorman ordered the strikers to climb into his wagon to be taken to Eureka. However, the strikers, with unanimous defiance, declared they would not go to Eureka alive. Gorman retorted that he would force them to go. After talking among themselves, the strikers consented and climbed into the wagon for the trek to town.

Arrivey related an earlier occurrence when, prior to the escalation of the clash, he had warned the strikers that they would be arrested if they attempted to interfere with his loading. The strikers countered his warning by stating that they did not give a damn, that they had but one life to live and they would fight until they died before they would allow the coal to be hauled. Such ominous-sounding words were allegedly uttered by Diola Bianca himself, perhaps indicating the depth of his despair in regards to the struggle for a higher charcoal price.

Marshall Rich took the stand next. The teamster confirmed being in Fish Creek on both the thirteenth and the fourteenth of August, for the purpose of helping Fred Gorman with the loading of Brown's teams. Rich's overall deposition was congruent with the evidence already gathered. Rich elaborated upon his encounter with Bianca, with whom he was acquainted. Inquiring about the reason for his presence at the loading site, Bianca informed Rich that he was a member of the association and was there to prevent the loading of charcoal at less than thirty cents a bushel, as directed by the CBPA. Bianca told Rich that there were 100 men concealed in the rocks and warned the teamsters that they would get hurt if they attempted to load. Gorman then read out two warrants to the 9 rioters, after which, according to Rich, a scuffle broke out, resulting eventually in the disarmament and arrest of the strikers.

Plaintiff Reinhold Sadler, merchant and coal burner, testified on August 26. Sadler owned five teams engaged in hauling coal since 1876. Sadler testified that his teams had been interfered with and prevented from hauling coal during the current and previous months. Allegedly, the first stoppage took place at Cornforth's ranch, while the second one occurred in Newark Valley. The next interference with Sadler's loading operations happened at Fish Creek, and the last stoppage cropped up at Willow station. Sadler pointed out that the stoppages at these locations involved his own teams but that several other teams that hauled for him were also stopped at other sites.

During his testimony, Sadler related a conversation he had early on with members of the Charcoal Burners Protective Association, namely, Bassetti, the association's first president and subsequent secretary, and del Bondio and Cordano, both association members. Sadler was present at the union meeting when Bassetti was first elected and testified that the president told him that association members could no longer allow coal to be shipped at less than thirty cents a bushel and that all teams attempting to haul at below such a rate would be stopped. Sadler went on to relate a later conversation he had with del Bondio, on or about August 10. On that occasion, Sadler told del Bondio that the way the association members were going about getting their demands met was of no use and that it would be better to come to some understanding. Sadler also cautioned del Bondio not to interfere with his property, no matter at what price he chose to sell it.

At about the same time in August, Sadler had spoken with G. B. Cordano, another member of the association who expressed his willingness to accept a price compromise at twenty-eight cents. Sadler was favorably impressed by Cordano's sensible attitude: "He talked fair and tried to effect such a compromise with the other members, and after he had so tried he came to me and said that the price was not so much, but the coal burners wanted to see the receipts."

Sadler reassured Cordano that the coal burners could inspect his receipts to corroborate the quantity of coal transacted. Sadler identified Bassetti, del Bondio, G. B. Cordano, Louis Piccola, Giovanni Rodono, and Martinoli as among the indicted strikers who had been present at the coal burners' meeting of August 7. Sadler added that the association meeting culminated with the agreement to establish the price of charcoal at thirty cents while also stipulating a fifty-dollar fine to be paid by whoever shipped for less than the agreed rate. The witness also confirmed that the resolution was endorsed by an almost unanimous vote.

Shifting to the swearing of his complaint, Sadler declared that the warrant contained only fictitious names. Sadler went on to clarify that he meant to cite those individuals responsible for the interference with his business, whose names he did not know. The witness recalled about forty burners being listed on the complaint, all of whom had been arrested. Clearly, the underlying strategy was to isolate the more militant strikers from their less combative cohorts in the hope of containing the swelling crisis. Sadler's closing remarks approved of the manner in which the warrant had been executed and commended the sheriff for so doing.

A few more witnesses were slated to testify on August 27, the last day of the hearing, their testimony subsequently published in the *Leader* that day. The first witness to appear was J. C. Gardner, a teamster employed by Sadler. Gardner recounted that twelve or fourteen days earlier, sometime between August 15 and 17, he had been stopped by two dozen strikers on his first trip to Fish Creek. Gardner identified the perpetrators as outside parties determined to impose the association's terms despite the coal owners' willingness to load their product. The witness went on to recount that a fight was scarcely averted. Repelled by one of the insurgents armed with a Henry rifle, Gardner drove his team to Fenstermaker's ranch. From that location, he sent word to Sadler of the stoppage and awaited further instructions.

Gardner was unable to determine how many of the twenty-four-man party were armed but recalled seeing two rifles, three shotguns, and two pistols. Similarly, the witness failed to recognize any of the defendants present in the courtroom as members of the raiding party. Although Gardner claimed knowing three of the insurgents by sight in their customary appearance, namely, covered with black coal dust, the witness could not swear whether he could recognize the same individuals once they appeared washed and wearing clean clothes.

Eventually, after a two-and-a-half-day layover at Fenstermaker's ranch, Gardner returned to the coal pits, escorted by a force of six men. Confronted by the armed party, the lone insurgent left to guard the coal pit relented, allowing the loading to proceed unimpeded. Nonetheless, the striker cautioned the loading party that the coal they had just loaded would be their last shipment. The lone sentry declared that on that day he was not prepared to fight, but that he intended to go to Eureka to obtain both men and arms to prevent all teamsters from loading any more coal at that location. As he concluded his testimony, Gardner declared that the lone burner was not among the defendants.

The next witness to be sworn in was David Keen, a coal rancher and a teamster. Keen testified that two weeks earlier, around the thirteenth of August, about fifteen or twenty burners had ridden to his ranch to tell him not to load any more charcoal. Keen identified the intruders as either Swiss or Italians. As the legitimate owner of the coal, Keen asked the strikers why they were stopping his activity. The insurgents replied that they were stopping everybody's teams. Sometime later, on the following Friday night, Keen received a visit from Alex McKay and George Smith, who informed the teamster that they had a warrant for the arrest of the Italian leader named Ferretti. The following day Keen drove his team to the pit with the intention of loading coal. Upon reaching the site, Keen noticed the presence of several armed strikers, led by George Ferretti, who did the talking. Keen ended his testimony by disclaiming any personal membership with the Charcoal Burners Protective Association, while also identifying himself as a native of the United States.

Subsequently, Sheriff Matthew Kyle took the witness stand, confirming the arrest of four charcoal burners on the evening of August 13, on the other side of Pinto Summit, between Eureka and Fish Creek. The reason given by Sheriff Kyle for their arrest was suspicion of being parties guilty of stopping teams from loading coal. Assisted in the arrest by Special Deputies

H. J. McKee (a teamster who, like other teamsters, had his teams prevented from loading charcoal at Fish Creek on August 10) and Hank Storey, the lawman confiscated six six-shooters, a shotgun, and a bowie knife from the four suspects. Last, Sheriff Kyle identified the four defendants. One of the arrested rioters was a suspect for whom a warrant for stabbing someone in a Eureka hurdy house had been issued a year earlier.[30]

The next witness was James H. Mannion, a hostler who resided at Fitzpatrick's Station. Mannion testified about seeing the sheriff and his posse escorting four men through that location on August 11 or 12. Presumably, the men in custody were the same men Mannion had seen passing through earlier and heading south. The witness explained that, upon noticing a load of coal in transit at that location, the four rovers stopped to inquire. Mannion heard one of the men asking where that load of coal had come from, to which the teamster in charge indicated an unnamed place "down...aways." One of the burners then warned that it would be the last load to leave the ranch. Because the four suspects had stopped only fleetingly, Mannion was unable to recognize the men among the defendants. The hearing continued with the brief testimony of W. H. Thompson, a swamper (handyman) for Billy Powell's team, and Robert Abrams, Powell's teamster. Their testimonies did not reveal anything salient.

The examination of the twenty Italian charcoal burners charged with riot and conspiracy was concluded on the afternoon of August 27. The decision by the court was to hold all twenty Italians to answer before the grand jury. Of the twenty defendants, sixteen were released on their own recognizance. Giuseppe Martinoli, Guido Bassetti, Severino Strozzi, and John Radoni were held on a bond of five hundred dollars each. While the first three were all officers of the Charcoal Burners Protective Association, perhaps warranting the posting of greater securities to obtain their release, Radoni was not an officeholder. Nonetheless, bail for all four was expected to be posted later that evening. On August 28, Antonio Invernozzi and Gregorio Marconi, the last two of the charcoal burners arrested at the Fish Creek fight and subsequently jailed on a charge of rioting, were also released on a bond of five hundred dollars.

The attorneys for the burners implicated in the alleged wagon stoppages were Hillhouse, Cole, and Laspreyre.[31] The lawyers called to represent the

State of Nevada as plaintiff in the wagon-stoppages suit, namely, G. W. Merrill, W. W. Bishop, Thomas Wren, and G. W. Baker, were also engaged in the defense of the sheriff's posse charged with the Fish Creek burners' slaying.[32]

Given the complexity and the overlapping nature of the case, Eureka's legal establishment combined the two pending suits, the posse's murder suit and the burners' conspiracy suit, into a single grand-jury inquest. Because of the burners' inability to effectively participate in the legal proceedings in English, interpreters were assigned by the court to represent the respective parties. Louis Monaco, a declared advocate of the strikers' cause, served the charcoal burners. Conversely, Joseph Tognini, an influential Italian merchant, was selected as Monaco's counterpart.[33]

The preliminary list of prospective grand jurors initially considered for the review of the thorny case against the officers charged with murder raised doubts about the fairness of the impending proceedings. Among the citizens summoned as potential grand jurors were some of the same influential bondsmen who had aided the arrested posse. They (and the bonds they furnished) included J. L. Hinckley (three thousand dollars), John Torre (five thousand dollars), H. Donnelly (five thousand dollars), C. C. Carpenter (two thousand dollars), F. Doutrick (twenty-five hundred dollars), George W. Lamoureux (five thousand dollars), Joseph Mendes (five thousand dollars), and C. L. Broy (two thousand dollars).[34]

Deeming them equally suited to serve with fairness in the imminent proceedings, the *Eureka Daily Leader* stated that "these men are representative citizens, and will deal justly with the important matters that they will be called upon to consider."[35] Though qualified to serve in any other trial, some of the prospective jurors would have a conflict of interest by today's standards in the legal action against the officers.

Although not directly embroiled in the charcoal crisis, J. L. Hinckley and Frank Doutrick were also among the prospective grand jurors who had posted bail for the arrested posse. Donnelly, Torre, Lamoureux, Hinckley, and Doutrick were ultimately excused from serving as grand jurors together with seemingly neutral candidates such as R. L. Chase and M. Smith. Predictably, Louis Monaco, tireless defender of the charcoal burners, was also excused from serving on the grand jury.[36]

Ultimately, only C. C. Carpenter, John Torre, and W. H. Remington were chosen to be grand jurors. Oddly, the latter had been drawn not by venire but by some other undisclosed process. Remington also figured among the substantial bondsmen who aided the sheriff's posse with a surety of twenty-five hundred dollars. Of the three so-called representative citizens impaneled, John Torre, teamster and charcoal rancher directly implicated in the charcoal dispute, had a personal stake in the outcome of the grand-jury inquest. The final seventeen-man grand jury was thus composed: John E. Plater (foreman), Max Oberfelder (secretary), H. R. Kemp, J. A. Porter, A. D. Rock, H. Johnson, James P. Moore, W. O. Mills, J. C. Powell, A. Skillman, C. C. Carpenter, W. H. Remington, John Torre, C. L. Broy, R. K. Morrison, Joseph Mendes, and D. A. Haskell.[37]

A cursory glance of the foregoing list will also reveal that the judiciary body included only a single Italian, John Torre, whose interests were diametrically opposed to those of the burners on trial. In fact, Torre's ranch was the site of the last charcoal stoppage carried out by the strikers before violence at Fish Creek erupted. With a personal ax to grind, Torre was not a disinterested candidate for the grand jury, for his business aims naturally conflicted with the inquest. The exclusion of common Italians from the grand jury might have been prompted by their limited fluency in English and by the fact that most were not citizens. The members of the grand jury thus assembled were likely to hold views of the events unsympathetic to those of the charcoal burners.

Not only was the composition of the grand jury ethnically imbalanced, but it was also significantly skewed in terms of the jurors' socioeconomic backgrounds, prejudicing further the evaluation of the evidence presented during the inquest. Far from being a representative sample of the Eureka population, a significant number of influential Eureka citizens, naturally inclined to side with the status quo, made up the grand jury. Out of the seventeen-man jury, six members—Plater, Oberfelder, Johnson, Moore, Remington, and Torre—belonged to Eureka's elite, thus making up an influential 35 percent of the entire judicial body.[38]

That the selection of a balanced jury was no trivial matter had been soundly expressed by Edward Probert, manager of the Richmond mining company in 1873, when his company was sued by Eureka Consolidated over title to the Look Out lode, bordering the two. Dismayed by the individuals summoned to impanel the jury, Probert objected: "A jury picked up in the streets—holding out their hands to both sides.... Our counsel might as well have spoken to the winds as to that jury." Feeling hopeless about the verdict that could be rendered by such a flawed jury, Probert decided to settle the dispute out of court.[39]

In 1877 the Richmond was sued once more by Eureka Consolidated for claim jumping in what became one of the most prominent cases in the history of mining law.[40] Anticipating yet another unfavorable court decision, the *Mining Journal* lamented, "The paramount design of the American judges seems to be to favour their own countrymen, and to refuse justice to all aliens."[41] Given Probert's misgivings about the jury and the *Mining Journal's* criticism of "American judges," legitimate doubts arise regarding the legal treatment of the Italian strikers. If a balanced jury and fair-minded judges were difficult to obtain for a colossal smelting company like the Richmond, how much more arduous of a task would it have been for a throng of destitute, non-English-speaking foreigners to receive just treatment?

Notwithstanding such obvious limitations in the makeup of the grand jury, the official investigation in a highly complex and emotionally charged legal case got under way on September 2. However, before embarking upon a detailed analysis of the inquest, a temporary digression to acknowledge the involvement of the Italian consul in the intricate affair is in order.

Notes

1. *Leader*, August 21, 1879.
2. Ibid.
3. *Sentinel*, January 5, 1879.
4. *Leader*, August 11, 1879.
5. *Sentinel*, September 2, 1879.
6. Reichman, "Early History of Eureka County," appx. C, 131.
7. Robert Sobel and John Raimo, eds., *Biographical Directory of the Governors of the United States, 1789–1978*, vol. 3.
8. *Leader*, August 15, 1879; *Sentinel*, August 26, 1879.
9. Richmond Consolidated Mining Co., *Annual Report*, year ending February 28, 1882, cited in Clark C. Spence, *British Investments and the American Mining Frontier, 1860–1901*, 127.
10. Thomas Wren, *A History of the State of Nevada: Its Resources and People*, 758–59.
11. *Sentinel*, August 29, 1879.
12. Wren's opposition to Chinese immigration to the United States was implied in a press announcement released a month before the shooting at Fish Creek: "Anti-Chinese Meeting: A meeting of the Anti-Chinese Association will be held some

evening during the present Week, and it will be addressed by Hon. Thomas Wren upon the probable future action of Congress upon this important question." Predictably, Wren's participation in a trial involving several members of a despised ethnic minority, such as the poorer Italians of Eureka, would likely cast a shadow, once again, over the prosecutor's personal motives. *Leader*, August 15, 1879.

13. Justice Docket, *Criminal Docket and Marriages*, in Justice Court, Eureka Township, Eureka County, NV, L. W. Cromer, JP, no. 202, quoted in Grazeola, "Charcoal Burners War of 1879," 103–4.
14. Wren, *History of the State of Nevada*, 641–42.
15. *Leader*, August 22, 1879.
16. Ibid.
17. Ibid.
18. *Sentinel*, August 22, 1879.
19. *Leader*, August 22, 1879.
20. *Leader*, August 25, 1879; *Sentinel*, August 26, 1879.
21. *Sentinel*, August 24, 1879.
22. *Leader*, August 25, 1879.
23. *Leader*, August 25, 1879; *Sentinel*, August 26, 1879.
24. *Leader*, September 2, 1879; Prassel, *Western Peace Officer*, 93.
25. Prassel, *Western Peace Officer*, 112; *New Mexico Statutes* (1905), 15-40-10, quoted in ibid., 98.
26. *Leader*, August 25, 1879; *Sentinel*, August 26, 1879.
27. *Sentinel*, February 6, 1879.
28. *Grand Jury Minute Book*, 76.
29. Earl, "Nevada's Italian War," 77.
30. *Sentinel*, August 14, 1879.
31. *Leader*, August 22, 1879.
32. *Leader*, August 25, 1879.
33. Grazeola, "Charcoal Burners War of 1879," 104.
34. *Leader*, September 2, 1879.
35. *Leader*, September 19, 1879.
36. *Leader*, September 20, 1879.
37. Justice Docket, *Criminal Docket and Marriages*, in Justice Court, Eureka Township, Eureka County, NV, L. W. Cromer, JP, no. 202, referenced in Grazeola, "Charcoal Burners War of 1879," 104.
38. Grazeola, "Charcoal Burners War of 1879," 104.
39. Report of meeting of the Richmond Consolidated Mining Co. (December 3, 1872), *Mining World* (December 7, 1872), cited in Spence, *British Investments*, 126.
40. Spence, *British Investments*, 126.
41. *Mining Journal* (September 1, 1877), 964, cited in ibid., 127.

XII

Italian Diplomacy

Suspicious of the claims made by the sheriff's posse in justification of the Fish Creek Massacre and skeptical of the judicial system that seemingly condoned the carnage, Eureka's Italians sought redress from the Italian authorities in San Francisco. Boasting the largest Italian immigrant population in the West, San Francisco was a bastion of ethnic solidarity for the Italians scattered across the western frontier. Most Italian immigrants who sailed to California disembarked in the "City by the Bay" before reaching the more remote destinations of the interior. Many chose forthrightly the city that bore the name of one of their most venerated of Italian saints as their permanent home. Consequently, most itinerant Italians who crisscrossed the western mining frontier in search of opportunity counted some relatives, friends, and acquaintances among San Francisco's ethnics. Despite the laudable endeavors put forth by the Italian envoy, Consul Diego de Barrilis, in seeking redress for the beleaguered burners of Eureka, his intercession produced only palliative effects. Notwithstanding his personal desire to tip the scale of justice in favor of his impoverished conationals, the Italian emissary yielded to the precepts of diplomacy.

Even though San Francisco, according to the 1880 US Census, was home to the largest Italian community in the American West when the Fish Creek incident occurred (numbering close to twenty-five hundred Italians), the Bay press had not covered any of the troubling events that preceded the fatal shooting at Fish Creek. In fact, it was not until August 20, two days after the shooting, that the *San Francisco Chronicle* and the *Daily Alta Californian* reported the dreadful incident. Reliant on a special dispatch received from Eureka, the *Chronicle* merely echoed those accounts already widely circulated in the general press, propagating further the biased perception that the burners had provoked the shooting at Fish Creek. By contrast, the *Californian* went beyond reiterations and provided a resolute editorial column of its own, titled "The Slaughter at Fish Creek." The commentary stated: "None of the Sheriff's posse received a scratch in the fight. This causes many people to believe that the coal-burners were not armed. As yet, no sufficient reason, no excuse is given for the taking of human life by the wholesale, as reported to have been at Fish Creek, Nevada."[1]

Learning suddenly of their ill-fated countrymen in the remote mountains of Nevada, the Italians of San Francisco reacted with strong emotions. Unaware of what had fueled the violent culmination at Fish Creek, San Francisco's Italians attempted to deal with the devastating news prudently. Sensing that their compatriots had likely been victims of foul play perpetrated by unsympathetic interests, San Francisco Italians vented their anger publicly while calling for a swift investigation of the affair.

In response to the alarming reports hailing from Eureka, San Francisco Italians staged a massive solidarity gathering in the Fifteenth District courtroom on Saturday, August 23. The assembly was rife with enmity for the fate suffered by their compatriots in Eureka. On August 25, attuned to the emotional fervor and the sense of urgency that stirred San Francisco's Italian community, the city press reported on the momentous event organized by the civic-minded Italians. The spirited meeting was characterized as an "indignation meeting" at which the consensus was that "the Eureka Italians have been unfairly dealt with by the authorities. A Committee of five was appointed…which was given full powers to use every means to have the affair thoroughly investigated, with or without the aid of the Italian Consul in the city. The Committee was empowered to employ counsel and a subscription was opened to defray all necessary expenses."[2]

The *Californian* also reported on the formation of the Indignation Committee, adding that a subcommittee would be dispatched to Eureka. "If there has been any abuse of power or criminality in the proceeding, the Italians here are resolved to protect their countrymen in Eureka, and bring the criminals to justice."[3] The newly formed solidarity committee was intended to operate in complete autonomy from the Italian consul general.[4]

As might be expected, San Francisco Italians' resolution was not viewed benignly by some of Eureka's citizens. Indeed, the very creation of an investigating committee in a distant city insinuated that the Eureka inquest was flawed. The *Eureka Daily Sentinel* issued a caustic response, characterizing the San Francisco Italian gathering as a "ridiculous effusion of bombast and bravado." It further indicated that in Nevada, the rule of law prevailed and that the rights of individuals or citizens, whether native or foreign born, were equally defended. Eager to dispel all doubts about the reliability of Eureka's judicial system, the *Sentinel* declared its unconditional faith in the integrity and efficiency of the local authorities, who could be trusted completely to ensure that "justice will be done." Then, as if to put the forthcoming committee on notice, the *Sentinel* released a veiled warning that "justice...will not be influenced by any threats, open or implied, that may come from San Francisco or any other quarter."[5] For unknown reasons, the San Francisco–based Italian solidarity committee never fulfilled its mission, and its promise to investigate fully the legal case of the slain Eureka charcoal burners never materialized.

On August 31 the *Californian* published an extensive account of the shooting at Fish Creek. The article had been provided first to the editor of *La Voce del Popolo*, the largest Italian newspaper on the West Coast, and was authored by Veritas, a.k.a. Louis Monaco, Eureka photographer and supporter of the burners' cause. The highly detailed commentary represented most closely the charcoal burners' view of the bloody incident. The author pointed the accusatory finger unequivocally at the lawmen for the bloodshed: "The Deputy Sheriff looked around, and, stepping aside, cried, 'Fire!' and he and the posse fired upon the unsuspecting coal-burners, killing five outright.... [T]he muzzle of the guns must have been within a few feet when fired, as still powder marks were visible on their chests."

The article also emphasized the arrested burners' unflinching determination to demonstrate their innocence: "The parties that are now under arrest for conspiracy, etc. were ordered to allow the matter to drop, but this they peacefully declined. If wrong, they will accept punishment and if right, want redress." In closing, Veritas appealed to the impartiality of justice for the truth to triumph: "Now, Mr. Editor, what we most need is some one who will faithfully plead our cause before the Judicial Tribunal. The Press and police are against us, but public feeling and truth are with us."

Meanwhile, a group of Eureka Italians wired the Swiss and Italian consuls in San Francisco, pressing them to travel to Eureka to help defuse the mounting crisis. The urgent diplomatic intervention requested was met with the approval of the *Eureka Daily Leader*'s editors, who hoped representatives of the two consulates could steer the affair toward an amicable resolution.

The consular response came in the form of a telegram the Italian diplomats sent to Lambert Molinelli, apparently cast in the role of conciliator. It is unknown whether the telegram was prompted by the Eureka Italians' request or by the reports of the Fish Creek shootings published in San Francisco's newspapers on August 20. In his missive Consul de Barrilis expressed his deepest regret over the whole incident, while urging Eureka businessman and former CBPA vice president Molinelli to appeal to Eureka Italians' sense of moderation and trust in the law. The dispatch entrusted Molinelli with the arduous task of dissuading his fellow countrymen from seeking retaliation, as presumably advocated by reckless instigators. Although forwarded to Molinelli, the Italian consul's telegram was translated into English by Louis Monaco and subsequently printed in circular form to be distributed to all the coal camps in the county.[6] Essentially, the document issued by Consul de Barrilis exhorted Eureka Italians to remain law-abiding citizens: "The Italians here are profoundly affected over these deplorable events. I am looking to [Molinelli] to counsel and advise calmness and moderation. The inquest will demonstrate who is in the right. Meanwhile desist from any opposition. Don't trust to the advice of those interested or excited, but trust in the justice of the law and the support of its authorities."[7]

Whether the charcoal burners heeded the paternalistic plea issued by the Italian consul is unknown. The telegram did convey the Italian authorities' grave apprehension about the "deplorable events," reflected in their appeal to avert further trouble and even bloodshed. The consul's consternation seemed evidenced in the telegram by the use of capital letters in the key words CALMA (calmness) and MODERAZIONE (moderation). The English translation did not reflect such an emphasis. Though openly addressed to the Italian collectivity of Eureka, the telegram entrusted Molinelli to mitigate the tensions. Such a reliance by the Italian diplomats upon Molinelli, whose public credibility had been greatly weakened in the eyes of many embittered burners, seemed to obfuscate the Italian envoys' aims. Although Molinelli ranked among the most qualified diplomatic proxies in Eureka, the Italian consul either did not know or overlooked the fact that Molinelli was a significantly compromised figure, one whose ethnic solidarity had proved fragile.

Having resigned early on as vice president of the CBPA, in protest against the wagon stoppages carried out by the strikers, Molinelli was viewed by many as a driven and ambitious man, in constant pursuit of self-aggrandizement, and consistently involved in various business sidelines.[8] Perhaps the greatest damage to Molinelli's credibility stemmed from the fact that all through the charcoal dispute, he maintained close ties with the furnace superintendents, thus casting strong suspicions upon his true allegiance.[9]

After his disassociation from the CBPA at the end of July, Molinelli resumed his entrepreneurial activities, among which the publication of his *History of Eureka* figured prominently. Presumably, as the charcoal crisis was spiraling fiercely out of control, Molinelli was in San Francisco, finalizing the publication of his book. During his stay Molinelli visited the Italian consulate, perhaps to elicit support for his publishing endeavor.[10] Undoubtedly, Molinelli's meeting with the Italian consul in San Francisco, as fortuitous as it might have been, would have provided the consular authorities with a firsthand account of Eureka's intricate charcoal crisis.

Although Consul de Barrilis's telegram conveyed a strong conciliatory message, certainly the best advice under the volatile circumstances, its rhetorical tone must have rung hollow to the ears of those distraught burners thirsting for justice. After all, Eureka's marginalized Italians were being exhorted by their own compatriots to place their trust "in the justice of the law," the very law that in their minds had sanctioned the injustice perpetrated against their slain countrymen—the same law wielded by the burners' oppressors to ensure their perpetual servitude. Paradoxically, precisely because they mistrusted the local authorities, Eureka Italians had turned to their government representatives in San Francisco to seek redress.

For his part, wishing to avert a deeper diplomatic crisis, the Italian consul acknowledged categorically the supremacy of the law of the land, to which Eureka Italians were urged to adhere. As if assuming the role of a benevolent father rescuing children in peril, embedded in the consul's appeal lurked a stern paternalistic warning: "Don't trust to the advice of those interested or excited." Although seemingly a vague allusion, quite likely the consul, in an attempt to bring the riotous burners within the fold of the law, was making deliberate reference to the so-called instigators of the crisis. Indeed, "those interested or excited" could only belong to the ranks of the discontented burners who had grown disillusioned with the ineffectual leadership of the association.

Similarly, the Italian consul might have perceived the San Francisco "solidarity committee," formed immediately following the violent outbreak at Fish Creek by San Francisco's angered Italians, as "interested or excited," and thus ill-disposed and nonaligned with the diplomatic strategy dictated by consular protocol. The Italian consul might have felt its authority threatened from within its own constituency by factions perhaps deemed too "excited" to be allowed to influence the mediation of the delicate affair. Accordingly, the Italian consulate might have sought to put its own house in order before dealing with its external adversaries. Perhaps in an effort to dispel any intimation of internal dissent regarding the Fish Creek incident, the Italian envoys strove to create the perception of a unified front, represented solely by the Italian diplomatic establishment. Somehow, San Francisco's "solidarity committee" and the "excited" elements in Eureka were effectively silenced. The Italian consul's malleable posture toward the resolution of the crisis, as expressed through the telegram, was readily praised by Eureka authorities, as suggested by the headline "Good Advice from the Italian Consul at San Francisco."[11]

The Italian government representatives were originally expected to arrive in Eureka on Wednesday, August 28. Anxiously awaiting the diplomats' arrival, a large crowd of Italians gathered at the train depot that evening to greet them. To the great disappointment of the fervent throng, the Italian emissaries did not arrive as scheduled. Dismayed at waiting in vain, "they vented their curses loud and deep."[12] The diplomatic delegation arrived a day later, on Thursday evening. The cause of their delay was never disclosed. Given the high tensions that pervaded Eureka, the consuls' arrival had been eagerly expected. Whatever the reason, the missed encounter proved anticlimactic for Eureka's Italians especially.

The consuls' delayed arrival was not the only deviation from the envoys' originally scheduled plan. Although reservations had initially been made for the consular delegates to stay at the Jackson House, conveniently located right across from the imposing courthouse, the diplomats ended up staying at the Turner House.¹³ Located on the same side of Main Street as the courthouse, a short distance south of the stately edifice, the Turner House was a less conspicuous site.

The consular representation delegation was constituted by Consul Diego de Barrilis and Vice Consul Ferrario Sacco (reported as "Zocchi Fiareryo" by the *Sentinel*).¹⁴ Although the Italian diplomats received a cordial reception upon arrival, their presence seemed fretfully tolerated by the community at large. As if catering to the anxiety of those who viewed the diplomats as unwelcome intruders, the *Sentinel* pointed out the futility of the Italian officials' mission: "They come for the purpose of investigating the Fish Creek affair.... What good can they accomplish is not apparent, as all the facts in the case will be brought before the Grand Jury."¹⁵

The delegation's first day in Eureka was spent, for the most part, meeting with a large number of leading Italian citizens. Invitations were extended to the Italian envoys by Richmond superintendent Richard Rickard to visit the company's mine and furnaces and accepted by the guests. In the evening, the Italian consul dined at Nick Millich's saloon in the company of Donnelly and Rickard, of the Eureka and Richmond mines, respectively, with whom the various aspects of the charcoal dispute were discussed.¹⁶

In a subsequent reassessment of the Italian consul's mission, the *Sentinel* tempered its earlier pessimism: "There is but little doubt but that an amicable settlement of the whole affair will be reached." As the Italian consul's "endeavors to get at the bottom of the Fish Creek affair" steadily proceeded, the *Sentinel* praised the zeal with which the diplomat carried out his assignment. Recognizing the diplomat's perspicacity and his determination to hear all voices, the newspaper conceded that the outcome of the investigation still hung in the balance. "The Italians have no better idea as regards [the consul's] opinions [of the Fish Creek affair] than have the Sheriff's posse." The paper added mordantly: "The Consul is evidently possessed of a judicial mind and proposes to judge the case purely upon its merits." To the consul's presumed intent, the *Sentinel* pledged its "hearty cooperation."¹⁷

On the evening of August 30, Consul de Barrilis and Vice Consul Sacco met with Sheriff Kyle in Lambert Molinelli's office, during which "the whole affair was freely discussed."¹⁸ During the friendly exchange, the respective positions were made transparently clear. The Italian consul dispassionately declared that he was merely fulfilling a mandate issued by the Italian minister in Washington. De Barrilis's admission of his subordinate rank within the diplomatic hierarchy, while an outwardly self-effacing remark, was probably intended to put the sheriff on notice. Somewhat disadvantaged by the remoteness and unfamiliarity of the setting, de Barrilis probably tried to equalize the contest by summoning the power of his government, reminding the lawman that he was not dealing with just a lone Italian diplomat, way out there on the desolate western frontier, but, rather, the representative of a modern and mighty nation.

On a more pragmatic note, de Barrilis admitted being "desirous of getting the whole truth." Undaunted by the Italian consul's assertion of diplomatic strength, Sheriff Kyle countered "plainly and forcibly." While Kyle expressed regret for the unfortunate incident, he was quick to point out that under the precarious circumstances, his officers did not have any other alternative but to resort to force. Summing up the gist of the exchange between de Barrilis and Kyle, the *Sentinel* reported: "The interview was a pleasant and social one throughout, and served to bring about a better feeling as regards the unfortunate occurrence." It was only on August 31, one day before his departure, that Consul de Barrilis finally met with representatives of the CBPA. Perhaps overly eager to see the deplorable affair swiftly discarded, the *Sentinel* all too hastily declared the dispute resolved based solely on the consul's promise that he would advise the officers of the CBPA to "desist from further acts of violence and to abide by the decision of the recognized officers of the law."[19]

No one knows how the consul's busy schedule was developed. Presumably, it was carefully crafted in advance, and as such meeting with the charcoal burners last might have been indicative of their low-priority status. Notwithstanding the short time allotted to the consul to investigate the convoluted incident, with the scent of blood still in the air, it would have seemed imperative that the Italian representatives paid their first respects to the injured constituency, regardless of who was to blame for the slaying. After all, the Italian diplomats were called to Eureka to investigate a massacre.

Moreover, by the time the Italian consul met with the CBPA representatives, it is uncertain to what degree the association was still reflecting the burners' interests or their will. It is also unknown whether de Barrilis actually met with any union members besides the association's leaders. However, sixteen depositions, unanimous in their claim that the sheriff's posse had been the instigator of the fight by firing the first shot, were sworn by burners who had participated in the conflict at Fish Creek. How Consul de Barrilis obtained these affidavits, whether directly from the burners or circuitously at some time during his stay, is not stated in the historical records.

On September 1 the two Italian diplomats departed from Eureka, bound for San Francisco. Although the *Sentinel* commended the Italian officials for having defused antagonistic tensions through their judicious mediation of the conflict, emotions still ran high over the enduring affair. Attesting to the resilient passions still stirring within the weary community, the *Sentinel* reported, "There was a lively scrimmage on Main Street last evening, growing out of the coal troubles."[20] The paper did not specify whether the brawl was interethnic or involved only members of the Italian enclave. Nonetheless, the outbreak evidenced a conflict still smoldering.

In his early communication with Italian ambassador Albert Blanc in Washington, on August 20, 1879, Consul de Barrilis had characterized the sequence of events leading to the incident in purely tentative terms. De Barrilis stated, "At this moment we do not have precise details and it remains unknown whom of the two parties, the public authority and the strikers, first opened fire."[21]

Nonetheless, even before his trip to Eureka, Consul de Barrilis had formulated a confident hypothesis that placed the blame for the shooting at Fish Creek squarely on the sheriff's posse. Hence he asserted, "However, the fact that among 15 or 16 Italians taken prisoners only three were found in possession of firearms, would seem to suggest they had no intention of carrying out their earlier threats, and that therefore Eureka's authorities acted with a swiftness totally unjustified."[22] Perhaps sensing an inauspicious legal outcome from the local authorities' investigation into the death of the slain burners, Consul de Barrilis advised Ambassador Blanc to consider whether "the *Regia Legazione* (Royal Government) should intervene in the proceedings in support of the victims of the deplorable incident."[23]

Notwithstanding Consul de Barrilis's genuine desire to shield the Italian charcoal laborers of Eureka from public condemnation, the diplomat betrayed a rather paternalistic and disapproving attitude toward the extreme militancy exhibited by the radicalized faction of the unionized burners. In a perhaps well-meaning attempt at exonerating the majority of the burners from culpability, the consul seemed to attribute responsibility for the tragic occurrence to a handful of ill-disposed and hot-tempered ringleaders. In describing the burners' initial organizing efforts, de Barrilis wrote, "Up to this point the charcoal burners stood perfectly within the law, but subsequently they initiated their illegal acts.... [I]ll advised by some ringleaders and instigators, whose kind are never absent in circumstances such as these, they began to organize themselves in armed bands, patrolling the mountains for the purpose of preventing by force the hauling of the coal to the city."[24]

While acknowledging that the burners' attempts to rectify their circumstance through violence was misguided, de Barrilis remained doubtful about the lawmen's conduct prior to the shooting. Indeed, the accounts provided by the charcoal burners regarding the antecedents of the shooting at Fish Creek revealed a consistency, clearly evidenced in the sixteen sworn depositions collected by de Barrilis at Eureka. Subsequently, he wrote, "If it is true that the Italians carried out deeds of violence and hurled threats, as it has been claimed, it is equally certain that the law officers acted all too precipitously, opening fire on the Italians without first issuing a warning, while the latter never discharged their weapons, neither before the shooting nor after."[25]

Foreseeing a ruling unfavorable to the slain burners and resulting in the absolution of the officers, Consul de Barrilis favored a financial reparation to be accorded to the victims' families. "It seems to me that should the murderers be found guiltless for their criminal actions, they should at least be held responsible for the damages and be required to pay a fair indemnity to the families of the victims."[26]

In his thorough report to the Italian ambassador in Washington, de Barrilis also acknowledged a crucial detail that, if admitted as evidence in the inquest, could have substantially strengthened the burners' case against the law officers. The Italian consul made specific reference to the testimony provided by an Italian witness, which, lamentably, was fated to remain outside the scope of the official proceedings. De Barrilis stated that such "a testimony would greatly undermine the position of the public authority.... [O]ne of the men who escorted the Sheriff...told [the consul] that he was armed to go and kill Modoks," a name of an American Indian tribe in California, applied disparagingly to Italians by many Anglo-Americans of Nevada.[27]

Keenly attuned to the general mood that pervaded Eureka County in regards to the Fish Creek incident, the perceptive diplomat discerned unpromising signs for the fulfillment of justice, as gleaned from his report: "The general opinion in Eureka, I gather, is that the District Attorney will announce the cessation of all legal proceedings; generally the reason given is that, should the law officers be found guilty, such an outcome would cause the County a severe hardship, requiring it to pay for both the legal proceedings as well as the victims' indemnity."[28]

Notwithstanding the fact that the indicted Italians received legal representation for the duration of the trial through the Eureka County District Attorney Office, de Barrilis bemoaned the fact that an independent counsel was unavailable to the Italians on trial: "Furthermore, the Italians are without a lawyer due to their lack of financial means to pay the required legal fees, that in this country are exorbitant," echoing Monaco's previous lament that the burners "cannot afford to hire lawyers...to keep up a war of pen and ink" (see chapter 5).[29]

Quite likely, the intercession of the Italian diplomatic delegation on behalf of the Italians of Eureka in the wake of the Fish Creek Massacre shielded the disenfranchised burners from further brutality. Once news of the gruesome incident at Fish Creek reached the world beyond Eureka, the burners' appeal for justice, or at least for the cessation of violence at the hand of the local authorities, could not be disregarded. The mere presence of official representatives of the Kingdom of Italy in Eureka, hard on the heels of those presumed responsible for the killings of the Italian burners, certainly deterred further aggression toward the surviving burners by vigilante-style lawmen. Although it cannot be asserted that the intervention of the Italian consuls rescued the oppressed burners of Eureka from the throes of exploitation, the arrival of the Italian diplomats upon the scene of the Fish Creek tragedy defused, if only temporarily, a dangerous impasse between an alienated foreign minority and an apprehensive mining community.

However, the salutary influence exerted by Italian diplomacy upon Eureka's political crisis was limited in scope. Among the most adamant insurgents, those individuals Consul de Barrilis labeled "interested or excited," skepticism regarding the role Italian diplomacy would play in the amelioration of the burners' plight prevailed. Prone to doubt the motives of a fledgling Italian government whose disastrous policies had forced multitudes of new Italian citizens to abandon their native land in search of a dignified life in America, these reproachful burners were unlikely to trust that same government's emissaries now on foreign soil or the rhetoric of their diplomacy.

Notes

1. US Department of the Interior, Census Office, "Compendium of the Tenth Census" (June 1, 1880), pt. 1, table XVI, pp. 540–51; *San Francisco Chronicle*, August 20, 1879 (hereafter cited as *Chronicle*); *Californian*, August 20, 1879.
2. *Chronicle*, August 25, 1879.
3. *Californian*, August 25, 1879.
4. *Sentinel*, August 26, 1879; *Chronicle*, August 20, 1879.
5. *Sentinel*, August 26, 1879.
6. *Leader*, August 20, 21, 1879.
7. *Leader*, August 20, 1879.
8. *Sentinel*, September 2, 1879.
9. *Leader*, September 2, 1879.
10. *Leader*, August 25, 1879.
11. *Sentinel*, August 21, 1879.
12. *Sentinel*, August 29, 1879.
13. Ibid.
14. Ibid.
15. *Sentinel*, August 29, 1879.
16. *Sentinel*, August 30, 1879.
17. *Sentinel*, August 31, 1879.
18. Ibid.
19. Ibid.
20. *Sentinel*, September 2, 1879.
21. ASDMAE, Rappresentanza Diplomatica Italiana a Washington (1861–1901), b. 35, f. 60, Piazzale della Farnesina I 1-00194 (dispatched by the Italian consul in San Francisco to the Italian Embassy in Washington, DC, August 20, 1879), cited in Salvetti, *Corda e sapone*, 4.
22. Ibid.
23. Ibid.
24. Ibid., 5.
25. Ibid.
26. Ibid.
27. Ibid., 6.
28. Ibid.
29. Ibid.

XIII

Grand Jury Decision

Their consular assignment completed, the Italian diplomats departed for San Francisco on September 1 but not before exhorting their embattled constituency to renounce violent means and yield to the law. Approving of the sensible manner in which Consul de Barrilis and Vice Consul Sacco investigated the Fish Creek incident, the editors of the *Eureka Daily Sentinel* lauded the diplomats' endeavors to lessen tensions.[1] However, despite the mediators' best intentions, discord among the dejected burners persisted. The widespread publicity elicited by the Fish Creek shooting bred strong opinions about the cause of the tragedy and those presumed responsible for it. By the time the trial of the sheriff's posse rolled around, hardly any resident in Eureka County had not formulated an idea about the affair. Fanning the winds of controversy, the press added fuel to an already heated debate. Decidedly supportive of the sheriff's posse, the *Tuscarora Times-Review* of Elko County, Nevada, wrote:

> According to the local papers the action of the Sheriff's posse in the Fish Creek affair is quite severely censured by some of the people of Eureka. This was to be expected. There is a class of persons in every community who are always ready to heap abuse upon the officers of the law upon general principles, and it is this class, we are confident, who are adversely criticizing the acts of Officer Simpson and his companions. If the latter had done less than they did they would have been derided by the cavilers as dastardly cowards. The only way that they could have escaped the censure of these critics was to have stood and [done nothing].[2]

Indeed, the notoriety attained by the case would have made the selection of a fair and impartial jury arduous at best. A sarcastic allusion to the larger bonds imposed on the lawmen implicated in the Fish Creek fight appeared in the *Ruby Hill Reporter*, published in the township adjoining Eureka: "This is a glorious country. They put men under $5,000 bonds for obeying and enforcing the laws."[3] Though the town of Eureka could have hardly been considered a neutral venue for what was to become one of the most prominent legal cases in the history of the county, on September 1, 1879, the preliminary hearing for the officers charged with the murder of the five charcoal burners got under way.

On September 2, a new bond was filed by Sheriff Matthew Kyle on behalf of the officers. The *Eureka Daily Leader* provided an exhaustive list of the bondsmen, and their respective sureties, who came forward to aid in the release of the sheriff's posse. Among the prominent citizens who posted the bonds, there were two Italians, Joseph Tognini and John Torre, both charcoal contractors, who provided five thousand dollars each. Reportedly, the bond was in excess of the amount required, signifying a solid showing of support for the officers.[4]

On that same day, the painstaking process of hearing the burners' testimonies on the examination of the officers of the posse began in earnest before the grand jury. The proceedings were expected to establish the truth of the facts culminating with the Fish Creek massacre. The first witness to appear was Joseph Lucca, an Italian speaker who did not understand English and thus required the services of an interpreter. The court assigned the task of translating to Angelo Noce. Lucca stated plainly that Rich had sparked the violent outburst when he fired the first shot. Lucca also declared that no shot was fired by the Italian burners.[5]

As if to denigrate the witness's character, the *Eureka Daily Sentinel* published a sardonic account of Lucca's testimony: "The whole afternoon was consumed in the examination of a single witness, an Italian who did not understand English...[and] also made the astounding statement that the posse kept up a continuous fusillade for three-quarters of an hour. If the witness is as deficient in all things as he is in regard to his estimate of time, the prosecution will make but little headway through any evidence he may give."[6]

The second witness, Domenico Quadro, testified that he was a member of the Italian throng present during the fight. Quadro estimated there were between eighty and ninety burners gathered at Fish Creek at the time the fight erupted. According to the witness, the band of burners had been roaming through the locality, aiming at intercepting coal teams and preventing them from loading. Quadro corroborated Lucca's earlier testimony, reiterating that it was the officers who opened fire first. Quadro asserted that he had spurred his horse onward, away from the scene, as soon as the shooting commenced, thus absolving himself of any involvement in the fight. However, after he signed his testimony, Quadro was promptly arrested by Officer Fred Gorman and charged with the attempted murders of Joe Toomey and William Martin.[7]

In summing up the evidence heard during the first day of the proceedings, the *Sentinel* aired much skepticism regarding some of the claims made by the Italian witnesses. The newspaper took issue with the length of time the witnesses alleged the officers fired their weapons at the burners. Certainly, the disparaging editorial seemed to challenge the witnesses' credibility.

> Analyzed, the testimony given was as weak as that given by the first witness on two points the witnesses agree, namely, no shots were fired by the strikers, and the officers continued firing from one-half to three-quarters of an hour. Does any sane man believe that a body of men would stand that length of time and allow themselves to be made targets of by such dead shots as composed the posse, and if they did would not the officers have succeeded in killing more than five; or in case they fled at the first fire, is it reasonable to suppose the officers would have remained on the ground for the length of time mentioned, and amused themselves by firing into vacancy? A child of half a dozen summers could make a distinction between three minutes and three-quarters of an hour, and if the witnesses are so utterly unreliable in one thing, all their evidence will be taken with many grains of allowance.[8]

Although the witness estimated wrongly the extent of the firing, the article abounds with slights that dispute the witnesses' sanity, intelligence, and reliability altogether. In a perplexing change of attitude, the *Sentinel*, previously extolled by Louis Monaco as having "always been the champion of the rights of the people," appeared to withdraw its earlier support for the burners' cause.[9] Perhaps fearful of jeopardizing the approval of the burners' powerful antagonists, wealthy merchants, and influential leaders, some of whom were probably financial contributors to the paper, the *Sentinel* sided with the status quo. Indeed, the *Sentinel*'s analysis exhibited the trappings of hyperbolic journalism, bolstering significantly the legal arguments presented by the defense counsel for the officers.

The next witness to appear was Giuseppe Negrini; his testimony, also mediated through the interpreter, lasted through one o'clock of the next day. Negrini declared that he lived in Antelope Valley and had joined other members of the CBPA on their way to Fish Creek to prevent the loading of coal on the day of the fight. Thus present when the violence erupted, Negrini testified that he saw Bob Brown shoot Pompeo Pattini. However, Negrini added that the firing started before Brown fired his weapon, admitting he did not know who fired the first shot. Negrini also shed some light on the burners' preemptive strategy.

Negrini stated that before the shooting began, he was mounted on a red horse just to the left of Pattini. While displaying a rifle, Pattini had reassured Negrini that it was merely a front: "Don't get scared, it's only powder." An instant after uttering those words, Pattini's life was taken. Right before Pattini was shot, Negrini heard Bob Brown curse, "God damn son of a bitch." As soon as the shots rang out, Negrini turned and ran but did not see or hear any Italian shoot. Negrini went on to state, "There were no captains or leaders of the Italians, all were alike."[10]

Negrini's lengthy testimony was followed by Giacomo Ceressi's brief account. Being present at the Fish Creek fight, Ceressi asserted seeing Martin, Smith, and Rich shoot; allegedly, they fired at him. Although Ceressi was carrying a shotgun, he fled the scene immediately after the firing began. Though he did not know who fired the first shot, Ceressi claimed that the shooting lasted about fifteen minutes.[11]

Lamenting the sluggish pace at which the examination of the officers was progressing as a result of the bilingual proceedings, the *Leader*, almost begrudgingly, reported daily on the progress of the hearings. Exhibiting a dismissive tone, the newspaper characterized the testimonies as "tedious details that have been published several times over and over, and are of no interest to the public."[12]

The examination of Italian witnesses continued with the testimony of Gregorio Marconi, the burner who had allegedly drawn a pistol on Rich during the wagon stoppage the morning before the fight. Consistent with the previous witnesses, Marconi testified that the officers were the sole perpetrators of the shooting rampage, which he claimed lasted for thirty or thirty-five minutes. Supposedly, Marconi, like the rest of his countrymen, dispersed as soon as the shooting began. He testified that when the gunfire ended, Rich advanced toward the buggy where Marconi had absconded during the shooting.[13]

Marconi was on his knees when Rich leveled his cocked shotgun at him. The burner stated that his life was spared on account of Deputy Simpson's magnanimous intervention. Had Rich carried out his vile deed by killing Marconi in cold blood, the culpability of the posse would have seemed flagrant. The burner also swore he did not draw his pistol on Rich. Marconi was arrested immediately after stepping down from the witness stand on a perjury charge leveled against him by Marshall Rich, who alleged that the witness did threaten him at gunpoint. Unable to post the one-thousand-dollar bail, Marconi was promptly jailed.[14]

Persisting in its shoddy approach, the *Leader* of September 4 stated categorically that general interest in the Justice Court proceedings was rapidly dying out on account of the wearisome nature of the testimonies being rendered. The less-than-balanced style exhibited by the Eureka press in its coverage of the legal proceedings pertaining to the Fish Creek shooting did not go unnoticed, as evidenced by a letter sent to the *Sentinel* condemning the apparent bias. Though the target of the criticism, the *Sentinel* exhibited journalistic fortitude by publishing the acerbic anonymous epistle:

> While the hearing of the twenty Italian prisoners...was going on, all, or nearly all, the depositions of one side were given in full in the columns of said paper.... On one occasion...(Mr. Sadler's examination) everything was related, but the cross-examination...was by the same paper very judiciously omitted, although the direct examination was inserted. Again, on the occasion of the Coroner's Jury trial of the Sheriff's posse, every word of their deposition was carefully related...while in the case of the present testimony in yesterday's and tonight's issue of that paper, everything is hushed up.... There have been three or four witnesses put on the stand these last two days, and very plainly and fairly examined and cross-examined,

but nothing of the kind can be learned from that paper but a sarcastic hint or two where...the witness might have got off a trifle on matters of no bearing to the case. *"Tell it all, sir, or none."* Exhibition of one side and silence on the other smells strongly of trying to raise prejudice.

— *Watchfulness.*[15]

Admittedly, the incisive style in which the missive was written was strongly reminiscent of the piercing prose previously encountered in Veritas's press commentaries. Balanced and lucid in the meticulous exposition of the arguments, "Watchfulness" demanded the absolute disclosure of the truth, with all its inherent subtleties, no matter the effort expended in the process.

The examination of Marconi was followed by those of Giuseppe Gaspari and Eunice Pedroni. The latter, besides being the brother of Giovanni Pedroni, one of the five slain burners, was also the first witness to be examined on behalf of the prosecution who understood English sufficiently not to warrant the services of an interpreter. Both witnesses pointed out Rich as the provoker of the fight, the one who fired the first shot that killed Pattini, while identifying Brown as the man who killed Giovanni Pedroni.[16]

About four more witnesses remained to be examined by the prosecution. However, as the *Sentinel* stated, should the defense forgo additional testimony, thus allowing the matter to go before a higher tribunal, as the circumstances seemed to suggest, the trial then would be concluded within the week.[17] As predicted, the *Leader's* evening edition of September 5 announced that the evidence in the examination of the sheriff's posse had been concluded that afternoon in the Justice Court. Further, a postponement of additional proceedings had been decided until October 1, leaving open the possibility for a settlement by the grand jury during the interim. Nonetheless, the officers would remain out on bail, pending the resolution of the case. Incidentally, on the following day, as reported in the "Local Lines" of the *Leader*, the Italians who had been previously jailed on charges of assault with intent to kill and perjury were also released on bail.

The testimonies rendered by the witnesses were consistent regarding the shooting at Fish Creek and who commenced it. Arguably, given the considerable amount of time that had elapsed between the day of the fight and the time in which the testimonies were heard, the burners could have had ample time to conspire and reiterate in unison the same exculpatory account. However, the existence of an earlier report corroborated the witnesses' claims. In fact, less than forty-eight hours after the Fish Creek shooting occurred, on August 21, the *Sentinel* had published a succinct yet insightful account reported by an Italian witness who wished to remain unnamed. This early Italian version (see chapter 9) proved thoroughly consistent with the testimonies just heard by the grand jury.

Remarkably, despite its substantial claims, the earlier anonymous account failed to exert any significant influence upon public opinion or the grand jurors evaluating the case. Conceivably, the critical report might have been summarily dismissed because of its unidentified source, thus fostering the perception of a contrivance. Conversely, the report could have been deliberately ignored in order to defuse its potentially damaging impact upon the inquest.

Three weeks after the adjournment of the investigation, on September 25, the grand jury's official, and much-anticipated, report was made public, thus marking the end of the inquiry into the Fish Creek tragedy. Reading the entries listed at the top of the column of the grand jury's decision spawned the misleading impression that the judicial body had reached a decision favorable to the charcoal burners. In fact, the various indictments previously lodged against the striking burners, namely, Marconi's perjury charge, Quadro's charge of assault with intent to kill, as well as the collective-conspiracy charge involving the other twenty burners, had all been dropped.[18]

However, in the same breath, the grand-jury report unequivocally stated that the murder charges filed against the sheriff's posse had also been dropped. At least on the surface, it appeared as if both contending sides had achieved a victory, what in legal parlance amounted to a quid pro quo. Yet in no significant way did the grand-jury ruling exact a penalty for the five burners slain by the sheriff's posse at Fish Creek. Indeed, the unalterable verdict bequeathed no real solace to the multitudes left to grieve the violent and senseless death of their countrymen.[19]

Not only did the grand-jury decision fail to do justice to the slain burners, but it also sanctioned the branding of the strikers on trial with the degrading stigma of conspirators. Although the grand jury did spare both the burners and the sheriff's posse from further retribution, the former remained weighed down unfairly by the blemish permanently affixed to their character, as alluded to by the closing remarks of the report:

> In view of the occurrences connected with an incident upon what is commonly known as the Italian War, the Grand Jury regards this as a proper occasion for expressing their entire approval of the action of the Sheriff's posse in their determination to enforce the law at all hazards, and while the unfortunate result of this determination on the part of the said officers must be regretted by every good citizen; yet, if such results are the consequence of demonstrating the power of the people, represented by their legal officers, to protect themselves in the free enjoyment and disposal of their property as to each seems best, then all acts on the part of the individuals, or organized bodies of men, which in any way contravene or interfere with the rights guaranteed by the law to each citizen, must be considered and regarded as acts to be resisted, even if death is the inevitable result.[20]

The undemonstrative tone of the report exuded a cruel indifference toward the brutal killings perpetrated by the sheriff's posse. Despite the glaring contradictions that marred the officers' testimonies throughout the inquest, only a slight trace of doubt seemed to permeate the austere opinion articulated by the grand jury. Denoted merely by a faint *if*, as in "yet, *if* [author's emphasis] such results," the grand jurors seemed to concede, if only tenuously, the sincerity of the victims' unshakable assertions. Further, the report extolled the inalienable rights of people to "the free enjoyment and disposal of their property," rights the oppressed burners, though misguidedly, also avowed, ultimately paying with their lives.

The report, though implicitly, exalted the inviolability and primacy of private property above all other human entitlements, in sharp contrast to the ranking posited in the Declaration of Independence. While declaring that "all men are created equal," the framers of the American Republic, inspired by John Locke, further affirmed that "they are endowed by their Creator with certain unalienable Rights, that among these are *Life, Liberty and the pursuit of Happiness,*" the last one formerly "Property," as formulated by Locke, later modified by Thomas Jefferson. Revered as the most quintessential of American principles, the order in which such rights were listed implied that the right to life trumped all others, for the right to life is ultimately the source of all rights. Unable to control the price of their product, from which their livelihood was sustained and with their very survival threatened by starvation, the burners, impelled by the instinct of self-preservation, considered the first law of nature, asserting their right to life, though unlawfully, over the "free enjoyment" of other people's property.

The preeminence of private property was indeed a fundamental tenet of the materialistic ideology pervading nineteenth-century industrial America. The extremes to which the defenders of property were willing to go was clearly evinced by the 1873 legal dispute between the Richmond and Eureka Consolidated. After being sued by Eureka Consolidated for trespassing, "Immediately the sheriff seized the mines of the Richmond...compell[ing] [the company] to post a 20,000 pounds bond." While the case was being aired in court, the Richmond positioned "ten men 'armed to the teeth' to hold the mine behind barricades."[21] If the two Eureka smelting giants, prestigious and legally constituted entities with abundant legal means at their disposal to assert their claims, were ultimately willing to resort to armed confrontation to resolve their dispute and protect their alleged property, it can be easily imagined how much more volatile were the circumstances that pitted the striking burners against Eureka's authorities.

Reminiscent of the incompleteness with which the coroner's inquest was brought to a sudden end on the basis that it was "taking too wide a range," one wonders if the grand-jury proceedings were also halted prematurely as if to thwart the surfacing of inconvenient truths.[22] Though the interruption of the grand-jury proceedings smacked of expediency, it could have been anticipated. After all, even Consul de Barrilis, during his brief stay in Eureka, sensed the imminent demise of the inquest. Fearing that the investigation would have ultimately demonstrated the lawmen's guilt, de Barrilis predicted that the district attorney, compelled to spare the county the severe financial burden of covering all legal expenses and the resultant indemnities owed to the victims' families, would bring the proceedings to an end.[23]

Thus swayed by strong pecuniary pressures to absolve the sheriff's posse, the proceedings ground to a halt. While Eureka taxpayers were thus shielded from a costly public expense, profound and troubling truths had been glossed over, spawning the corrosive feeling that a grievous miscarriage of justice had irreparably occurred. While the infamous case of the Fish Creek Massacre was thus brought to an end, legitimate misgivings lingered.

Notwithstanding "the unfortunate result" lamented by the grand-jury report, the burners' previous offenses remained outstanding and indefensible, begging the question of why the judicial body dropped the charges against the lawbreakers altogether. Indeed, the inquest outcome contradicted the investigation findings. After all, the burners had clearly violated the law and were relentlessly pursued by the officers throughout the crisis. Thus, as Grazeola keenly observed, "One might reasonably expect the burners to suffer penalties that were commensurate with the seriousness of the charges against them," rather than being granted a wholesale pardon.[24] Had the grand jury been truly impelled by a genuine pursuit of justice, its decision would have been consistent with the guilt demonstrated by the facts.

Evidently, the quid pro quo deal represented the most auspicious bargain for the county. Surely, a punitive verdict would have incited the collective wrath of the hundreds of burners, who had manifested, mightily and unmistakably, their vehement condemnation of the authorities' brutal killings in an epic display of ethnic and human solidarity at the victims' funeral. The hostility that a punitive sentence could have engendered among the embittered charcoal burners could have led to a permanent stoppage of their unrewarding occupation. In turn, disruption of the charcoal production would have spawned precisely the kind of commodity shortage that the mining industry had sought to vigorously avert prior to the blood drawn at Fish Creek.

Clearly, some substantial concession was long overdue to the trampled burners, and now it could assume the more legitimate form of a blood debt. Hence, the pardon, which, unintended as an admission of guilt on the part of the authorities, could represent a perfunctory act of reconciliation with an alienated labor force whose commodity was vital to the county's prosperity.

If the mining interests were eager to mend their ailing relationship with the slighted burners, the enforcers of the law were even more impatient to see the whole affair permanently thrust aside. The officers' anxiety probably stemmed from their awareness of the flagrant inconsistencies that plagued their flimsy testimony, flaws that certainly would have become exposed in a new trial, had the burners been adversely sentenced by the grand jury. Had further investigative proceedings been warranted by a guilty verdict against the burners, all of the evidence previously examined would have been resubmitted for an even more scrupulous scrutiny than the first probe entailed.

Undoubtedly, a second investigation into the tangled affair could have produced not only damaging consequences for the dubious officers of the law, but, perhaps, even more detrimental effects upon those influential Eurekans who had vouched unconditionally for the officers' ethical conduct. Ultimately, reopening the inquest would have undermined the presumed validity of the preceding investigation. The ominous implication of the reexamination of the case would have certainly exacerbated the tensions that had recently gripped the beleaguered community, perhaps running the risk of shattering Eureka's reputation as a community where the rule of law prevailed and justice reigned.

In light of all the troubled county stood to lose, a sentence of clemency for the burners must have seemed an uncomplicated and exceedingly palatable bargain to those anxious to relegate the harrowing incident to the dusty annals of history. Indeed, that an early settlement of the case was likely had been hinted at by the *Leader* early on. The next day, September 6, the Italians who had been jailed on charges of assault with intent to kill and perjury were released on bail.[25]

The grand jury's ruling marked the irrevocable end of the Fish Creek affair, and it seemed that Eureka returned to a semblance of normalcy, approximating life before what might have been the first Italian massacre in the American West. Paradoxically, it took the blood of five presumed innocent burners to extinguish the charcoal dispute, but at last a fragile harmony had been awkwardly restored. In fact, all contending factions implicated in the conflict attained something, but some more than others. The burners indicted on conspiracy charges, though unrewarded, were free to return to their deunionized occupation, having relinquished the cherished rights they had so desperately fought for, namely, an increase in the charcoal price and access to the shipping receipts. Cruelly, the burners' losses translated into further gains for their antagonists, the smelter operators, the teamsters, and the merchants. Ultimately, after a short-lived challenge to its rule, the Darwinian law of survival of the fittest had reasserted its hegemony within Eureka's marketplace. In what could perhaps be viewed as an ironic twist of fate, on August 16, 1880, two days shy of the first anniversary of the Fish Creek Massacre, the town of Eureka was devastated by yet another dreadful fire. The financial loss was estimated at one million dollars.[26]

Given the virtual dearth of information exhibited in the local press after the grand jury's verdict, the subsequent conditions of the charcoal burners remained unknown. Historian Hubert Howe Bancroft claimed that "the price of charcoal was subsequently reduced to 22 cents." Bancroft further asserted that "in 1884, 165,000 bushels were burned" in Eureka. Compared to Eureka's heyday of mineral production, the late 1870s, when Eureka's furnaces consumed more than sixteen thousand bushels of charcoal per day, the scanty 1884 figure cited by Bancroft is indicative of the vast decline in Eureka's mineral output in the years following the ill-famed Fish Creek incident.[27] Indeed, the 1880s marked the end of an unprecedented era of mineral productivity in Eureka, as well as in many other mining districts of Nevada, and the beginning of an inexorable period of industrial stagnation.

Eureka's once prosperous mines eventually shut down, impelling multitudes of miners and charcoal burners to seek opportunity elsewhere. Once rated the second most populous mining center in Nevada, the "Pittsburgh of the West" went from a community of nine thousand residents in 1878 to a sparsely inhabited modern town at the dawn of the new millennium, though still clinging proudly to its notable past.[28]

However, the ubiquitous footprints left by scores of Italian charcoal burners across Eureka's landscape have not been totally erased by the winds of time. In fact, several descendants of the early charcoal burners have laid deep roots in the soil trodden by their hardy ancestors, bestowing upon Eureka the gifts of their rich Italian heritage. Whether browsing through Eureka's telephone directory or glancing at a topographic map of Eureka County, the mindful traveler will readily notice tangible proof of the indelible legacy the Italian charcoal burners left upon the "Pittsburgh of the West."

Notes

1. *Sentinel*, September 2, 1879.
2. Quoted in *Sentinel*, August 29, 1879.
3. Ibid.
4. *Leader*, September 2, 1879.
5. *Sentinel*, September 2, 1879.
6. *Sentinel*, September 3, 1879.
7. *Leader*, September 3, 1879.
8. *Sentinel*, September 3, 1879.

9. *Sentinel*, August 15, 1879.
10. *Leader*, September 3, 1879.
11. Ibid.
12. Ibid.
13. *Leader*, September 4, 1879.
14. Ibid.
15. *Sentinel*, September 4, 1879.
16. *Sentinel*, September 5, 1879.
17. Ibid.
18. *Leader*, September 25, 1879.
19. Ibid.
20. Ibid.
21. Report of meeting of the Richmond Consolidated Mining Co. (December 3, 1872), *Mining World* (December 7, 1872), cited in Spence, *British Investments*, 125–26.
22. *Leader*, August 21, 1879.
23. ASDMAE, Rappresentanza Diplomatica Italiana a Washington (1861–1901), b. 35, f. 60, Piazzale della Farnesina 1 1-00194 (dispatched by the Italian consul in San Francisco to the Italian Embassy in Washington, DC, August 20, 1879), cited in Salvetti, *Corda e Sapone*, 6.
24. Grazeola, "Charcoal Burners War of 1879," 110.
25. *Leader*, September 5, 6, 1879.
26. *San Francisco Evening Bulletin*, August 19, 1880.
27. Bancroft, *History of Nevada, California, and Wyoming*, 285; Molinelli, *Eureka and Its Resources*, 103.
28. Paher, *Nevada Ghost Towns and Mining Camps*, 181–88.

Conclusion

What did really happen at Fish Creek on the evening of August 18, 1879? Although my search for the elusive answer has led me on an arduous journey of historical exploration, I feel I reached the poignant site of the massacre too late in the day. Indeed, by the time I arrived at the canyon on the western slope of Dave Keane Mountain, at the southern end of the Fish Creek Range, where the slain charcoal burners breathed their last, darkness had already drawn its unretractable curtain. With the few fragments of truth still remaining on the charcoal-covered ground and with a burning desire to understand the tragic incident, I endeavored to piece together a diligent account.

In the bitter struggle to improve their bleak lives, the Italian charcoal burners of Eureka determined to defy the status quo. Their defiance was aimed at exposing what, in their eyes, was fraudulent commerce and the unsympathetic economic law of supply and demand that legitimized their oppression while it protected their callous antagonists. In an unforeseen turn of events, the charcoal burners, victims of a subtle system of graft devised by the powerful Eureka teamsters to further their profits, became the villains in a tragic drama. The burners' daring violation of Nevada law that regulated state commerce cast them in the unwitting role of outlaws. Their audacious interference with local industry, manifested as coal stoppages, threatened Eureka's economy.

In response to such a threat, Eureka's business class exerted pressure upon local and state authorities for a prompt resolution of the charcoal crisis and a normalization of commercial activities throughout the beleaguered county. Although no overt appeal to violence to restore order was ever advocated by Eureka's commercial interests, their request that the state militia intervene to quell the uprisings was intended to intimidate the burners.

Denied an opportunity of escape from an undignified and cruel existence, the burners, perhaps inspired by the old Italian adage "Non tutto il male viene per nuocere" (Not all evil engenders evil results), resorted to illegal means with the hope of achieving just ends. Having mustered their collective strength, the desperate burners launched a concerted attack against those who thwarted their economic progress. In their adamant struggle for economic justice, the burners placed themselves outside the law. Whether they had anticipated the bloody outcome that stole the lives of five of their comrades will never be known. However, the deliberation with which the sheriff's posse faced the striking burners at Fish Creek leaves little doubt about its aggressive intentions.

The appalling misdeed could not have been carried out without the posse's unrivaled weaponry. As learned from Deputy Sheriff J.B. Simpson's testimony, the nine men of the posse had five Henry rifles, five Navy revolvers, three additional revolvers, and three double-barreled shotguns.[1]

Undoubtedly, the posse members wielded superb weapons, capable of great accuracy, sure to engender deadly consequences when placed in the skilled hands of adept shooters. What remains to be ascertained is whether the officers who brandished the ominous weapons had sufficient time to aim intentionally at their human targets, thus explaining the deadly precision with which the wounds were inflicted. The preponderance of the testimony rendered by the law enforcers clearly suggests an affirmative answer. Deputy Sheriff Simpson readily testified that the posse he led to Fish Creek ranged itself in a straight firing line about thirty feet long, facing squarely the assembled burners.[2]

Similarly, Marshall Rich admitted having his "shotgun cocked," a fact perfectly consistent with Rich's subsequent statement that "everybody was prepared, and had their guns all ready."[3] Then, immediately after the shooting commenced, Rich testified that Simpson incited the posse by uttering words to the effect of "Give it to 'em, boys!" It can thus be inferred from such detailed testimony that most of the law officers were indeed cognizant members of a "fighting posse," as many perceptive Eurekans had previously suspected, impelled by premeditated aggression thinly disguised as peaceable mediation. Thus, the posse was clearly predisposed to resort to violence before the unsuspecting burners could read the lawmen's true intentions.

Naturally, the eagerness to employ violence gave the posse the crucial advantage of mounting a surprise attack on the unwary strikers, ultimately accounting for the accuracy of the physical wounds suffered by the slain burners. Further, the implication of premeditation embedded in the officers' testimony substantially validates the claim advanced by the anonymous burner, who stated that one of the officers handed a paper to an Italian, after which the posse ranged themselves and—following the order "Fire!"—began shooting.[4] The informer, a direct witness to the shooting, claimed that "his countrymen were murdered, and that the shooting was malicious."[5]

The convergence of testimonies stemming from disparate sources renders the evidence thus obtained more unmistakable, dispelling Thomas Arrivey's contention that the posse "immediately separated and opened fire" only after an unidentified shot hailed from behind a clump of cedars some distance away.[6] The systematic pattern exhibited by the fatal wounds undermines the theory of a randomly arranged posse startled into action by an unexpected shot.

That the intentions of the distraught burners were other than bellicose is ultimately supported by the types and conditions of the weapons found in their possession following the shooting. Indeed, the assortment of arms that Simpson seized from the surrendered strikers clearly indicates that the burners' true force rested with their numbers rather than with their weapons. The impounded hardware included seven six-shooters and three shotguns. Not surprisingly, the shotguns were found all empty. Of the remaining six-shooters, one was found totally vacant, four had some shots in their chambers, while only two were completely loaded.[7] Yet as harmless as the burners' intentions might have been, the outnumbered posse could not have known their true purpose.

A truly pugnacious horde bent on waging war on a formidable opponent armed to its teeth, as the law officers were, would surely not rely on such a meager arsenal. The brandishing of the innocuous weaponry by the burners was more a tactic of psychological warfare than an authentic display of hostility, deemed sufficiently menacing to disrupt the teamsters from carrying on their usual charcoal loading activities. That such a bluffing strategy was an integral component of the strikers' harassment campaign was clearly substantiated by Negrini's testimony, as it related to Pattini's "rifle" (in reality a shotgun). Recounting his companion's reassuring final words—"Don't get scared, it's only powder"—Negrini confirmed the supposition that the burners' intent was merely to create the appearance of might.[8] Dreadfully, artifice became reality.

Trusting wholly the menacing effect of their audacious display of inferior arms, the strikers gravely miscalculated the risk of their gamble. Admittedly, no dispassionate observer outside the burners' inner circles could have possibly inferred, given the hostility exhibited by the burners' demeanor, that their weapons were essentially hollow decoys. Tragically, the burners' boldness provided the spark that, fanned by the highly combustible tempers of "such men as Simpson, Martin, and Toomey… quick to resent an insult which more moderate men would overlook in order to avoid trouble," erupted into a dreadful carnage.[9] The burners had disastrously underestimated the inflaming power of their passion play, unaware throughout their struggle that their cause would eventually stir up a terribly destructive force.

Ultimately, it is quite unlikely that the anguished burners had even the slightest intimation of the thunderstorm that was swiftly gathering around them on that evening of August 18, 1879. Although ominous clouds hung gravely over Eureka's sky, the Italian strikers stood their ground, utterly oblivious of the blood about to be spilled. By contrast, the law officers, as denoted by their overpowering weaponry and the lethal injuries they sowed, traveled to Fish Creek expecting to mete out a sanguinary brand of justice in fulfillment of the "at all hazards" resolve declared by Sheriff Matthew Kyle.

For certain, Sheriff Kyle did keep the promise made to his constituency to resolve the charcoal crisis expeditiously and inexpensively.[10] When the Board of County Commissioners met on September 2, 1879, among the bills allowed were "T. S. Douglas, rent of room for jail [arrested coal burners] $47… C. W. Schwamb, burial of five men [burners killed by sheriff's posse at Fish Creek] $234.25."[11] Indeed, in the space of a week, from Monday evening, August 11, when Kyle's "at all hazards" declaration was first uttered, to Monday evening, August 18, when the Italian burners were killed, the coal crisis had been, in point of fact, resolved for a total expense to Eureka's taxpayers of $281.25.

The annals of history abound with instances of interethnic conflict involving people of distinct cultures and nationalities clashing in their struggle for economic hegemony. Being recent arrivals and making up one of the largest ethnic groups in Eureka County, the Italian charcoal burners were, predictably, relegated to the lowest rungs of Eureka's occupational ladder. Although cultural differences of custom and language might have caused apprehension within the host community, the oppressive treatment endured by the Italian charcoal burners of Eureka perhaps can best be understood in terms of class conflict rather than ethnic discord.

While social class and ethnicity are closely intertwined, the role of class seems predominant in the clash between the Italian charcoal burners and Eureka's establishment. Emphasizing the role of class over ethnicity in explaining social conflict, Ralf Dahrendorf posits that the greater the deprivation in economic resources, social status, and social power suffered by the members of a social class, the greater the likelihood that such members will resort to violent means to improve their status. That ethnicity played a lesser role in the unfolding of the coal crisis is supported by the presence of numerous Italians within the upper stratum of Eureka's society. According to Frehner, "The sixty-two Italians listed in the 1875 tax rolls owned under 1.75% of all taxable property in Eureka even though Italians made up 7.5% of the entire population. By 1880 Italians owned 7.5% of all taxable property and represented 15.1% of the population."[12] Seemingly, Eureka was flexible and progressive enough to allow Italian immigrants the opportunity to actively participate in the growth of the host society based on their personal attributes rather than upon their ethnic background.

Just as ethnicity did not appear to hamper markedly Italian entrepreneurship and economic success in Eureka, a shared cultural heritage did not seem to significantly enhance cohesiveness among Eureka's Italians, either. Though Eureka's dominant class counted several successful Italians within its ranks, including some of the merchants and teamsters embroiled in the coal controversy, the wealthier Italians manifested few bonds of ethnic solidarity toward the impoverished burners. Quite the contrary—the Italian *prominenti* were among the major instigators of the reprisals unleashed against the burners by the local authority. Among them, Joseph Vanina and Joseph Tognini were powerful forces in the vehement crusade to keep the price of charcoal down.

Not only were the two affluent businessmen among the leading petitioners of the fervent appeal to Governor John H. Kinkead for military intervention to quell the charcoal troubles,[13] but Vanina and Tognini also revealed themselves adamant defenders of the unbridled capitalism that pervaded the United States in the last quarter of the nineteenth century. Espousing the mercantile rhetoric of the period, Vanina and Tognini appointed themselves spokesmen of Eureka's Swiss Italian business class as they repudiated Veritas's condemnation of their presumed intraethnic bigotry in the local press. In Frehner's view, the glaring conflict of interest between the Italian laborers and their entrepreneur counterparts was further exacerbated by the geographical distance entailed in their contrasting occupational activities, which precluded the two groups from developing an "ethnically cohesive community."[14]

The economic chasm that divided an otherwise homogenous ethnic community on the remote mining frontier of the American West in the late nineteenth century demonstrates that, given particular conditions, allegiance to class supersedes ethnic loyalties. Indeed, the coalescing power of class interests, be it labor unions or business alliances, seems to transcend ethnicity. Regrettably, the bonds of ethnic solidarity among Eureka's Italians were too fragile to deter the slaying of the five striking burners at Fish Creek. Sadly, the intraethnic dimension of the protracted coal crisis and its culmination with the Fish Creek Massacre represent one of the most perplexing and disheartening aspects of the incident.

Understandably, cynics will contend that the burners were the transgressors who reaped the bitter fruit of the seed they themselves sowed. In their desperate search for a solution to their grievances, the burners underestimated the dangers of their aggressive protest and thus persisted in courting disaster with the unshakable conviction that theirs was a just cause. That theirs was a flawed strategy cannot be denied. Nevertheless, despite their lawless acts, the punishment hardly fitted the crime.

While poised fingers pulled the deadly trigger, time and place conspired to seal the burners' fate. The slain Italian strikers suffered the aggravated misfortune of living at a violent time in US history in the remote American Far West, where frontier lawmen enjoyed an unprecedented degree of discretionary enforcement. As asserted by historian Robert M. Utley, "The man behind the badge practiced a highly personal, capricious brand of enforcement." Although most western peace officers were diligent and honorable men, a few rogues plied the trade as well. Partly due to a dearth of qualified candidates in some parts of the frontier, officers of the law frequently "came from the ranks of local toughs, on the theory that such persons would most easily gain the fearful respect of the region's criminal element."[15]

That individuals with latent criminal tendencies were, though sporadically, entrusted with the power of the badge is confirmed by an early account reported in the *Esmeralda Star*, of Aurora, Nevada: "No sooner had the Marshal been sworn in than the worst villains that ever infested a civilized community were appointed policemen, and with but few exceptions they were composed of as hard a set of criminals as ever went unhung." Among the indictments for improper conduct leveled against western lawmen of the nineteenth century, the "indiscriminate use of firearms resulting in culpable homicide" was a frequently cited accusation.[16] While in most instances western lawmen saved lives, in some regrettable cases they killed more innocent people than did the outlaws.[17] "Because hung to every man's belt," admonished Bancroft, "were glittering implements for the losing of human life, it was taken for granted that no life was safe without such implements." Bancroft further asserted that "weapons invite violence. They are as bad playthings for men as for children." Although who fired the first shot that evening in the canyon at Fish Creek will never be known with certainty, the preponderance of circumstantial evidence strongly suggests the lawmen's responsibility. In the words of Peter B. Merialdo, a descendant of Eureka's charcoal burners, "There was no [Italian War].... As far as my dad had told me, the charcoal burners had no weapons of any kind...and he was quite put out by the fact that [the burners] were slaughtered."[18]

Pondering the ubiquitous violence that pervaded the American mining frontier of the nineteenth century, Mark Twain lamented the premature and brutal deaths of scores of unwary young men who had journeyed to the West in search of fortune. Of the youthful forty-niners who heeded the "call of gold" to California's Eldorado, Twain wondered, "Where are they now?" Yet he seems to know the answer beforehand: "Scattered to the ends of the earth, or prematurely aged and decrepit—or shot or stabbed in street affrays—or dead of disappointed hopes and broken hearts—all gone or nearly all—victims on the altar of the golden calf."[19]

Twain's lament seems a fitting requiem for the five Italian burners who, in the prime of their lives, left their native country and traveled halfway around the world in search of opportunity on the American western frontier. Although they did reach the "promised land," they did not taste the milk and honey America promised, only the bitter sweat of their brawn; they did not saunter city streets paved with gold, but trudged worn trails speckled with charcoal grime. Their journey ended in tragedy in a forlorn ravine outside Eureka, Nevada, thousands of miles away from their home in the Italian Alps. The slain burners were laid to rest in a common yet premature grave, dug in a desolate cemetery, not far from what is today US Highway 50, christened "The Loneliest Road in America." Their unfulfilled dreams lay buried with them. A stony monument inlaid with a memorial plaque bearing their names marks the grave site. Erected in 1983 by the Eureka County Historical Society and its supporters to remember the burners' violent deaths, the shrine is a testament to the cruelty of the ruthless, who, in their voracious pursuit of earthly riches, all too often resort to armed violence to steal another man's dream.[20]

Notes

1. *Leader*, August 21, 1879.
2. *Sentinel*, August 20, 1879.
3. *Leader*, August 20, 1879.
4. *Sentinel*, August 21, 1879.
5. *Sentinel*, August 23, 1879.
6. *Leader*, August 19, 1879.
7. *Sentinel*, August 20, 1879.
8. *Leader*, September 3, 1879.
9. *Sentinel*, August, 21, 1879.
10. *Leader*, August 12, 1879.
11. *Sentinel*, September 3, 1879.
12. Ralf Dahrendorf, *Class and Class Conflict in Industrial Society*, 215–18; Frehner, "Ethnicity and Class," 50.
13. *Leader*, August 11, 1879.
14. *Sentinel*, August 16, 1879; Frehner, "Ethnicity and Class," 43.
15. Robert M. Utley, *High Noon in Lincoln: Violence on the Western Frontier*, 172; Prassel, *Western Peace Officer*, 45.
16. *Esmeralda Star*, February 17, 1864, as quoted in the *Virginia Daily Union*, February 21, 24, 1864, in Roger D. McGrath, *Gunfighters, Highwaymen, and Vigilantes: Violence on the Frontier*, 88; Prassel, *Western Peace Officer*, 107.
17. Rosa, *Gunfighter*, 63.
18. Bancroft, *Popular Tribunals*, 1:121; Merialdo, *Memoirs of a Son of Italian Immigrants*, 2.
19. Mark Twain, *Roughing It*, 839–40.
20. *Sentinel*, July 28, 1983.

Afterword

Perhaps it was an immigrant's longing for the solidarity of his fellow wayfarers in a new land, or maybe a Calabrian's obstinacy to find meaning in his own restiveness, that drew me to those desolate charcoal camps strewn across the Fish Creek Range outside Eureka, Nevada.

I first visited Eureka in March 2004. Taking advantage of my spring break from teaching in Fresno, California, I undertook the long drive over the Sierra Nevada and braved the snow-covered mountain passes that sealed Eureka from the outer world. Eureka was still in the throes of winter, and banks of snow hemmed its wide streets. I realized, belatedly, that my visit had been ill-timed. Eager to discover Eureka's history, I wandered through town in search of remnants of the past. Although the main purpose of my visit was to explore the charcoal country outside Eureka, I promptly realized that any attempt to travel to the area would have been risky and futile. Thus, I opted to visit what was once the newspaper headquarters of the *Eureka Daily Sentinel*, nowadays a museum, instead. Here I would spend two full days poring over stacks of old papers and faded photographs relating the tumultuous history of the "Pittsburgh of the West." Mining the museum files turned out to be enormously productive, widening my perspective on Eureka's past.

I returned to Eureka in August 2007, a more propitious season. Anxious to reach the charcoal country that lay beyond my reach on my first visit, I left Eureka just before midday and headed east on US 50, affectionately dubbed "The Loneliest Road in America." After driving a few miles, I reached the junction with SR20. Here I glimpsed the Fish Creek road sign for the first time, and suddenly I realized that I was now at the crossroad between present and past. I drove on a rough gravel road for a few miles and then turned west, past Fish Creek Ranch, and headed straight toward the Fish Creek Range. While the landscape retreated before my rapidly advancing automobile, out in the distance the stillness of the scenery was broken by the sudden appearance of a band of free-roaming mustangs galloping against the westerly wind, as if intending to show me the way leading to my uncertain destination.

Journeying alone across the stark vastness, and without a trace of civilized man in sight, my trip assumed an almost surrealistic dimension, as if I were pilgrimaging to a far-off shrine. As I made my way through the base of the range, second-growth piñon and juniper trees unfolded on both sides of the dirt road. Scanning the landscape for vestiges of the charcoal days, when scores of Italian charcoal burners scurried about these mountains, I spotted what seemed a miniature stone kiln next to a burn pit littered with shards of charcoal.

As I approached the little stone structure, I realized that it was more akin to a beehive oven for baking bread than a small kiln for making charcoal. After all, bread had been an essential staple food of the Italians' diet for millennia. As I contemplated the ingenious amenity erected in the midst of the wilderness, having presumably stood the test of time, I was stirred by a strong sense of ethnic pride. Even in the harshest of environments, I thought, Italian creativity thrived. Images of hardy charcoal burners gathered around the campfire at the end of another day of toil to warm their bodies and their hearts filled my mind. Echoing through time, I could hear those lonely and brawny men chattering away in their Ticinese (from Switzerland's Canton Ticino region where many burners originated) and Chiavennasco (around the town of Chiavenna, only a few miles south of the Swiss border) dialects, playing familiar card games like *briscola*, singing songs that reminded them of home, perhaps drinking wine to quench their longing for home and dull the anguish of their uprootedness, eager for homemade bread to be shared with their companions. In the absence of the warmth of a domestic hearth, I could picture these rugged young men, who had been reared in a culture that did not frown upon the expression of affection, amusing themselves in boisterous and harmless male jostling during those rare moments of leisure, deepening in this way the bonds of ethnic solidarity and renewing their sense of shared destiny.

As I hiked farther toward the summit of the Fish Creek Range, at a short distance from the little oven, I stumbled upon a row of stones piled upon some desiccated tree trunks stretched across a dry streambed. Clearly, the structure was man-made and not an accident of nature. A few feet from the rudimentary dam, the ground was covered with a thick layer of charcoal scraps tangled in the underbrush, the site of an old charcoal pit. Here and there, withered stumps rose through the grass like crosses in a graveyard. Once I reached the summit, I stood in contemplation of the awe-inspiring vista. Although the harshness of the terrain possessed an elemental beauty of its own, it was a far cry from the pastoral landscape of the northern Italian Alps, birthplace of scores of charcoal burners who toiled in the austere environs of the Fish Creek Range.

As fate would have it, although I was born in the rugged mountains of Calabria, the southernmost region of the peninsula, overlooking the Ionian coast, and was raised in Milan, the most industrialized of Italian cities, I was well acquainted with those northeastern provinces of Lombardy, where many charcoal burners started out. As a teenager I spent countless late-summer days trudging through the thick woods of Valtellina, as the region is known, combing the undergrowth in search of the delectable porcini mushrooms concealed beneath the foliage of an assortment of alpine trees such as oak, chestnut, mountain maple, larch, beech, birch, walnut, and a variety of conifers like fir, pine, and spruce. Not infrequently, on my wanderings through the woods of Valtellina, the silence would be broken by the bark of a truffle dog goaded by his master in search of the underground fungus, a highly valued delicacy. Truffles grew symbiotically with the roots of the local trees. At a higher elevation, where trees grew more sparsely, among shrubs of alpine junipers and dwarf rhododendrons, I would kneel on the rocky terrain to feast on handfuls of plump blueberries.

Indeed, the alpine region of northern Italy was a veritable arcadia abounding with luxuriant meadows, thriving forests, perennial glaciers, limpid waters, roaring cascades, luminous peaks, and radiant snows. Lamentably, this Alpine paradise, with all its majestic beauty and abundant resources, could not sustain a rapidly exploding populace. Competing fiercely for ever-diminishing resources within densely populated medieval hamlets and towns, many were forced to abandon their native soil and emigrate to distant shores in search of better prospects. Here many of them had come, to the wilderness of Nevada's mining frontier, to cut vast forests and to make charcoal for the smelters in Eureka, thousands of miles away from the land that gave them birth.

At the summit I turned west and began the descent toward the site of the carnage. Out in the distance, I gazed at the vastness of Antelope Valley basking in the afternoon rays of a hot August day. The trek downhill was effortless, made easier by a cool breeze that blew toward the mountaintop behind me. About two miles downward, I stopped to glance at a copy of a rudimentary map that marked the route taken by the sheriff's posse to reach the actual site of the shooting, reconstructed by eyewitnesses present at Fish Creek the day of the killings. The map had been included in Grazeola's master thesis and was the only guide I had to lead me to the spot where the incident had occurred, so long ago. Branching off from the main road, on the right-hand side, lay a faintly visible trail that bent sharply to the north. As I strode down the secluded path, I wondered how many had retraced the footsteps of the *carbonari* along this lonely trail since the tragic day of the massacre.

Unexpectedly, I found myself standing in a wide clearing with an open view of the treeless slope below me. A dry streambed enclosed the spot on its northern flank. Not far beyond the narrow waterway, a stone chimney rose stoutly, while a coarse fire pit encircled its base. Above the trail, to the east, robust piñons and junipers graced the slope. The clearing stood out like a bald spot on an otherwise full head of hair. Its interior was covered with a thick circular layer of charcoal, and all around lay old tree stumps still bearing the scars of the sharp axes wielded by the *carbonari*. Indeed, the place exhibited the features of a sizable charcoal camp.

I kneeled reverently and sifted through the dense blanket of charcoal as if they were ancient relics. After all, this was the very charcoal the slain burners had paid for with their lives. I thought it was strange that from such hard trees as junipers and piñons, with their compact wood that rendered them almost impenetrable even to the sharpest blade, such a light and delicate material could be born. Yet the creation of this refined ebony gold demanded herculean toil. In the solitude of this remote canyon, with the wind whistling as it blew across the clearing, one could almost hear, echoing across the gulf of time, the sound of the *carbonari*'s axes shuddering as they hit the rugged trees. Yet the brutal physical exertion their adamant muscles endured could hardly be imagined. With their toil unrewarded and the specter of starvation hovering above their exhausted bodies, like a vulture awaiting its dying prey to surrender, the *carbonari* defiantly ceased their fruitless and backbreaking labor.

Unexpectedly, I found myself sauntering upon the very site of the carnage. The camp had the eerie aspect of a once industrious work site hastily abandoned. It felt as if time had been erased and the *carbonari*, who once had roamed these forests, should reappear at any moment to resume their interrupted work. Gripped by the solitude and stillness of the arcane surroundings, I was stirred at once by feelings of foreboding and serenity. An ethereal aura seemed to shroud the charcoal camp where the burners had fallen, as if to preserve their earthly spirit for eternity. Although the forest dwellers had long since departed, the corner of the forest where the massacre took place appeared to have remained unchanged. Here, where the wind, the sun, and the rain blistered the body and scorched the soul with the same rigor they hardened the earth, I could almost sense the burners' otherworldly presence lingering in the brush. Here, where the desolate frontier stood untamed, in all its rawness, where the footprints of the charcoal burners who once trudged these woods had turned to dust swirling in the winds of time, here upon this patch of earth strewn with blood-stained charcoal, human memory endured.

When I first set out to rescue the memories of the slain charcoal burners and their countrymen from the clutches of time, it was mainly a quest of the mind. But now, as I stood where the burners had fallen, more than 130 years earlier, I was awed by the silence and gloom and mystery of the place, and all the senses were overwhelmed with emotion. Like a surveyor of man's soul peering through the hazy lenses of impartiality, I was attempting to measure the immeasurable depths of the human suffering poured onto this patch of earth so long ago. Like a trusted friend dispatched by the victims' families to this bleak place to express their sorrowful laments and final eulogy, I felt like a herald from a distant land who had journeyed halfway around the world, though belatedly, to pay homage to those young *carbonari* who never returned. It felt like a sort of ancestral veneration journey.

In this remote corner of the American West, the palpable harshness of frontier life becomes irreconcilable with the nostalgia of the mythical West of fiction, where the pioneers' struggle against nature and men is invariably romanticized. After I wandered the Fish Creek Valley for three strenuous days, the odyssey experienced by the Italian charcoal burners so long ago became far more tangible, no longer a tenuous perception but a solid reality undiminished by time, vividly etched in the soil of history. The almost petrified tree stumps, the shards of charcoal scattered through the brush, the stone oven, the rudimentary dam—all were material artifacts left behind by a remarkable people in their unfaltering pursuit of the American dream.

Distant from John Ford's mythical westerns of my childhood days, unfolding in glorious landscapes, where good invariably triumphed over evil, where the fictionalized heroics of the legendary man on horseback instantly transported me to the fabled Old West, was the barren canyon that stretched across the windswept Antelope Valley beneath the blazing sun. Having been raised on generous portions of homemade pasta and a copious fare of American westerns served daily on Italian television during the 1960s, I had been thoroughly beguiled by the frontier morality play reenacted time and time again in countless Hollywood creations, where the downtrodden always found a safe haven and was reborn as a true American in the redeeming embrace of the frontier, an overly romantic vision of the West of the imagination disguised as the West of history.

Equally distant was the desecrated West as seen through the foreign eyes of Italian director Sergio Leone, father of the spaghetti-western genre, in which the excesses of blood spilled on the set were as thick as the heaps of tomato sauce Italians customarily served atop spaghetti. Leone's ostentatious and brutish frontier, redolent of death, doom, and dark humor, garnished by Ennio Morricone's sublime orchestral scores, not only debunked the myth of the American West but glossed over its true past as well. Behind Leone's thin western facade lurked a historical void as vast as the frontier itself. Utterly disassociated from history, Leone's cynical portrayal of the West as a sanguinary and sadomasochistic milieu trivialized the infinitely subtler reality of the human West. Indeed, the blood spilled at Fish Creek was all too real, requiring no feigned goriness to impress the human senses. Perhaps the only likeness the tragedy of Fish Creek bore to the cinematic West was that of the abiding showdown unfolding against a crimson-hued sunset over a desolate canyon, with the strongest contender emerging victorious and unscathed from the violent contest.

Out on the western horizon, the sun was beginning to set, reminding me that soon darkness would reclaim the forlorn site. Although this was not where the slain burners were laid to rest, the place exuded the solemnity of a burial ground. I departed halfheartedly. As I retraced my trek, I realized I was traveling the same dusty road trodden by the sheriff's posse in pursuit of the insurgents more than a century earlier. It was the same thoroughfare on which the wagons laden with the bodies of the dead *carbonari* journeyed back to Eureka. On the eastern flank of the range, beyond the reach of the sinking sun, darkness was swiftly descending upon Fish Creek Valley. The day was done. Here and there, the high beams of an advancing automobile cast long phantasmagorical shadows over the retreating scenery.

The impression of journeying through a landscape inhabited by ghosts was inescapable. Sharing the Native American belief that the spirits of the departed linger in the physical realm they once inhabited, my overwrought southern Italian imagination conjured up haunting images of restless spirits roaming through the darkened valley.

By the time I reached Eureka, the town, with its well-lit Main Street, was deserted. Unable to calm my agitated mood, I walked through the center of town where many of the historic buildings still stood adorned in their old-fashioned motifs. Following the itinerary suggested in the self-guided tour brochure I had purchased the day I arrived in Eureka at Raines' Market, I set out on a lonesome tour of what was once one of the most prosperous mining centers in Nevada.

My solitary tour of Eureka's deserted streets began at the imposing Eureka Courthouse, a two-story brick structure begun in 1879 and completed in 1880 at a cost of thirty-eight thousand dollars. Designed in an unpretentious Italianate turn-of-the-century style, it became the finest courthouse in the state of Nevada after Virginia City's. This house of justice was built shortly after the shooting of the Italian charcoal burners at Fish Creek. I glanced momentarily across Main Street where the elegant Eureka Opera House stood, an amenity built for the enjoyment of the wealthy and a painful reminder of the good life that eluded the poor. Extolling the virtues of the entertainment venue, the November 11, 1880, *Eureka Daily Sentinel* stated, "The building is...to be thoroughly fire-proof, built with masonry (volcanic tuff) walls, brick and iron front, and slate roof. From the basement to dome the new theatre will be furnished as none of the class have ever been in Eureka.... [I]t is bound to be a beneficial and permanent monument to the memory of those who have erected, and who will so soon elegantly furnish the same for the edification of our people."

Among those generous donors who contributed to the financing of the opera house numbered several wealthy Italians, whose enjoyment of opera could be traced back to the old country. During the town's glory days, the Eureka Opera House hosted many famous artists and entertainers, who brought a taste of cultural refinement and diversion to a lackluster mining town. Unlike their affluent and philanthropic compatriots, the charcoal burners almost certainly never caught a glimpse of the opulence and beauty that filled the sumptuous edifice. It must have been a sad irony for the alienated burners to know that Italian operas were being staged in such a remote locale of the frontier, bringing a taste of Italian culture so close to their natural sensibilities, even if blunted by life in the wilderness, only to watch from a distance the opera troupe travel on to entertain eager audiences in yet another boomtown.

Heading in a northwesterly direction from right behind the courthouse, I found myself standing before the *Eureka Daily Sentinel* building. Originally built in 1870 by Archibald Skillman, founder and publisher of the newspaper, it was reconstructed after being destroyed by the town fire on April 19, 1879. Although the stone fireproof building at the rear of the main office was spared, immediately after the conflagration it was so hot that the staff resorted to shrouding themselves in wet blankets and printed a special edition for the next morning. From the printing press housed inside this epic building issued forth a flurry of journalistic reports and inquiries about the charcoal crisis that galvanized public interest throughout the western frontier for most of the summer in 1879. The *Sentinel* building became a museum in 1982; within its vaults are stored the annals of Eureka's eventful career as a prosperous mining burg.

I walked past the Colonnade Hotel, a building erected in 1880 by the Italian Benevolent Society used for social events and regular meetings up to 1890. Half a block north of the Colonnade stood the two-story Sadler House, built by Reinhold Sadler, a German immigrant who became a prominent businessman, contract teamster, rancher, and Nevada governor from 1896 to 1902. Sadler was among the archrivals who opposed the burners' crusade to raise the price of charcoal. Disinclined to face Eureka's inclement weather, Sadler had a tunnel built from the basement of his home to his general merchandise store on Main Street.

Shortly after, I reached what was perhaps the most significant landmark of all, Celso Tatti's saloon. Now converted to a garage, the once two-story building witnessed the genesis of the Eureka Charcoal Burners Protective Association in July 1879. Within its walls more than five hundred exasperated Italian charcoal burners gathered in the saloon owned by their sympathetic countryman to organize a union to leverage a higher price for their charcoal. Although an ethereal silence suffused what was once a lively place of recreation, I could almost hear the angry burners bellow their fierce imprecations at their foes, their courage bolstered by liquor and camaraderie. Here was where the burners first inaugurated their tumultuous movement, where they first uttered their emancipation proclamation, and, also, where the seeds of their demise were first sown.

Not far from the raucous union hall of yesterday stood the Tognini and Company Building, built in 1877 by three Swiss Italian business partners, Joseph Tognini, Ferdinando Bonetti, and Gabriele Zonali. While the building housed the Eureka Billiard Hall Saloon, Tognini and Company was also one of the largest charcoal enterprises in the county. As denoted by the company's trade name, Tognini's financial share of the business predominated. Erected upon what was once the site of the first business establishment in Eureka, known as the Pioneer Restaurant, which consisted only of a canvas tent, the Swiss Italian company stood awkwardly close to Tatti's saloon, hub of the burners' agitation against charcoal monopolies. As I gazed at the two neighboring buildings, I wondered about Tatti's sympathetic gesture toward the distraught burners. After all, according to the tax rolls of 1880, Tatti was ranked the fourth-wealthiest Swiss Italian of Eureka County; furthermore, Tatti's business activities included the charcoal trade. My puzzlement would remain unanswered, one of the countless unknowns concealed between the lines of history.

My furtive wandering through the empty streets of Eureka after dark enabled me to contemplate some of the vestiges of its past history without haste and undisturbed by the glance of its guarded residents. I was now standing before Saint Brendan's Catholic Church, erected in 1874 by Father D. Montiverde for a cost of five thousand dollars. I marveled at the solidity of this house of prayer and wondered how many of the desperate charcoal burners found solace within its hallowed walls. All throughout the unfolding of the charcoal crisis of the summer of 1879, the historical record is utterly silent regarding any involvement of the Catholic church with the plight of the Italian charcoal burners of Eureka, many of whom, undoubtedly, practiced the Catholic faith. I could not help but wonder if Father Montiverde at any time before, during, or after the charcoal uprisings had counseled the reckless compatriots to turn away from violence and to trust in God's providence.

Historically, servants of the church have played an active role in mediating disparate social conflicts in the name of that universal brotherhood that bonds all men, recognized as all God's children, deserving equal respect regardless of their station in life and their place in the world. Was a requiem for the slain burners and the mourners who grieved their sudden death offered within this temple? Were any charitable acts ever bestowed by Eureka's Catholic community upon the destitute burners? Did the fallen burners ever receive their last, though belated, rites? Did holy water anoint the lifeless bodies of the charcoal burners slain at Fish Creek? Did the church bell toll in honor of the deceased burners? Did Father Montiverde accompany the caskets to their final resting place? These disquieting questions lingered in my mind like shadows in the night. Like a woeful soldier returning from the battlefield, longing for the oblivion of sleep to ease his weary mind, I retired to the motel on Main Street where I had been encamped for the last three nights. Overcome with exhaustion, sleep swiftly transported me to a place where the boundary between reality and illusion faded away and where phantoms roamed freely through the forest of the mind.

Early the next morning, I prepared for the last leg of my quest, a visit to the forlorn graveyard where the slain burners had been interred. After a short drive west, past the courthouse up Ruby Hill Avenue, I reached Grave Yard Flat, or, as it was known in the camp's early days, Death Valley. This veritable necropolis, which once boasted nine cemeteries, is now a cluster of five or six graveyards that still receive the living who come to pay respect to those who are no longer, just as eagerly as they embrace those who come, albeit unwillingly, to find their perpetual repose. Laid out as a hallowed mosaic of distinctive tombs, Grave Yard Flat is truly a monument to religious freedom in the heart of the lonesome frontier. Attesting to the divergent religious paths the deceased followed in life, be it Catholic, Protestant, or Masonic, the earthly roads they traveled ultimately brought them to the same final destination, equal, yet separate, in death as in life. Somewhat distinguished in its advanced years for its assorted graveyards, Eureka has been derisively depicted as the frontier town where more inhabitants dwell underground than above it. Yet although the graveyard signifies the final resting place of the departed, it is also the repository of human memory, an authentic history book embossed in the very earth that harbors the physical remains of those gone before.

With trepidation I drove to the bottom of Grave Yard Flat, where, secluded from the rest, lay an almost faded burial site. I walked among the desolate graves, most of them unmarked; a few wooden markers twisted and shriveled by the sun still stood, their inscriptions forever erased into anonymity by the wind. Only a few headstones, cracked, faded, and partly buried in the shifting sands, survived to preserve the identity of those interred below. Abandoned to the elements, this graveyard was dying a slow death; its uncared-for graves, devoid of any remnants of human affection such as flowers or candles or other signs of recent human visitations, seemed to have lain undisturbed since the day they were first dug.

At the northern end, on the edge of the dilapidated cemetery, encircled by a metal fence, stood an imposing rock-strewn monument that marked the common grave in which the slain burners had been interred. Providentially, the grave had been saved from certain obscurity. Had it not been for Albert Biale's unfailing memory of where the charcoal burners had been laid to rest, quite certainly the historic grave would have vanished. As a young lad, Biale used to accompany his grandmother Louisa Morgantini to this spot, where she would place flowers on the grave of the young *carbonari*. That is how Biale remembered the burial site. Over the years Biale endeavored to ensure that someday a suitable marker would dignify the undistinguished grave. Biale's yearning became reality on July 9, 1983. I paused a while to read the inscriptions on the bronze plaque that crowned the stone memorial. The names of the slain charcoal burners were presented in order of nationality, with the Italian burners appearing at the top of the list. The plaque (with spellings not consistent with those generally used in the press) read:

GIOVANNI PEDRONI
MARCELLUS LOCATELLI
TEODORO ZESTA
POMEPO PATTINI
ANTONIO CANONICA
CHARCOAL BURNERS MASSACRED AUG. 18, 1879
BY A SHERIFF'S POSSE SOUTHWEST OF THE
FISH CREEK RANCH
EUREKA HISTORICAL SOCIETY
1983

The stillness of the graveyard was stirred by a cedar-scented breeze that hailed from the wooded hills nearby. I crept reverently around the metal fence and contemplated the memorial from all sides. Its sturdiness rose imposingly from the graveyard floor, as if to proclaim the memory of the souls that dwelled beneath it that the inclemency of the elements and the weathering of the seasons could not erase. The American frontier was such an unforgiving and lonesome place that the prospect of leaving one's bodily remains in its desolate midst frightened even the sturdiest of settlers. As I stood alone in the bleakness of the austere graveyard, I remembered the mournful refrain intoned by a weary settler of bygone days who warned:

> Don't listen to enticing words
> From men who own large groves and herds
> Oh, comrades brave, take warning, pray
> Don't leave your home for the lone prairie.[1]

Before leaving I offered a prayer to the memory of those young charcoal burners who, although I knew only by name, had become as intimate as members of my own family, no longer arcane strangers. Leaving this hallowed plot was harrowing. Here, a few feet below the soil of their promised land, lay the earthly remains of those brave wayfarers who came to make charcoal in the forests, destined to never go back to the land of their nativity. Yet though the burners' physical remains dwelled in this humble graveyard, the true memorial of their tragic death lay thirty miles away, on that patch of earth among the trees of the Fish Creek Range where their lifeless bodies first embraced the ground, consecrating it with their blood.

After traveling so far to retrace the footsteps of those intrepid *carbonari*, my quest ended here, in this deserted graveyard, inhabited by the living memories of those countrymen who came before me. My journey of discovery had come to an end. Melancholically, I departed, leaving behind a world where the past endures. I returned to "The Loneliest Road in America," where restless strangers still travel the solitary highway in search of the dream; then I started my way back, comforted by the conviction that a fragment of Italian immigration history in the American West and a strand of Nevada's heritage had been rescued from oblivion.

Notes

1. H. Clemens, "Oh Bury Me Not on the Lone Prairie."

Author's Notes

When I first began my foray into the history of the Italians of Eureka, I was truly an untrained chronicler, a genuine amateur who longed to recount a gruesome and nearly forgotten incident. As a novice I first approached the subject timidly, as an impromptu suitor whose meager endowments hardly justified his entreaty. Yet as I heartily probed the depths of my passion, I garnered the wherewithal of scholarship along the journey.

Indeed, the writing of this book has been a poignant experience. The subject matter of my ten-year endeavor was not merely the inanimate substance of scholarly research, but a living body of historical material that resonated hauntingly within me. Retracing the faded footsteps of those young Italian immigrants who toiled on the Nevada frontier of long ago was truly a sympathetic quest into the lives of men who, although several generations removed, I regarded as long-lost relatives.

Seeking to write an objective account of a historical tragedy that befell an ethnic minority on the Nevada frontier of the late nineteenth century, I strove to heed Salvemini's warning to the student of history; the Italian chronicler proclaimed, "The historian amputates reality." I will admit that, in breaking the literary silence that surrounded the incident for more than a century, the stealthy bias that naturally arises when an author encounters a personally significant and life-transforming theme tested my impartiality.

Whether I succeeded in distancing myself from the topic at hand sufficiently to let the facts speak for themselves or whether I "amputated reality" will be for the reader to decide. Recognizing that objectivity is an elusive affair perennially suffused by rivalry between the mind and the heart, I aimed toward a sensible symmetry by eschewing both a strictly cerebral approach and an overly demonstrative treatment of the book's content. Yet to define the realization of this overlooked historical event solely as an academic pursuit would be inaccurate. As English historian C. V. Wedgwood once said, "Without passion there might be no errors, but without passion there would certainly be no history."

It was, after all, my intense absorption with the timeless plight of the immigrant that led me to discover the works of Wilbur S. Shepperson, the Nevada historian who wrote lucidly and perceptively about the complexities of the immigrant's experience. Specifically, Shepperson's lament about the century-old neglect of this notable chapter in Nevada history provided the spark that ignited my inspiration, compelling me to attempt the reconstruction of the forgotten tragedy.

One is left to wonder how many other immigrant narratives have yet to be unearthed from the vastness of the American landscape. Probing further into those yet unknown recesses of history will certainly deepen one's understanding of his or her national heritage. Only through a renewed appreciation for the prodigious efforts exerted by the immigrant in its midst will America attain a clearer sense of its historical identity and, ultimately, a reconciliation with its immigrant past.

At a time in history when the United States is confronted by vast challenges to its immigration policy, when its mythical and deep-rooted image as "the promised land" of the world's poor is crumbling, reflecting upon the vicissitudes of the Republic's tumultuous past could prove salutary. To ponder upon the Fish Creek incident is to acknowledge the human suffering often exacted from those who forsook the land of their nativity to seek a better life in America. Fish Creek represents a dim yet sobering reminder that America's gold-paved streets have often glittered not only with the sweat and tears of its huddled masses, but also with their blood.

Appendix A

The Strikers' Defense
The Objects and Designs of the Coal Burners' Association
Eureka, August 14, 1879

Editor Sentinel: Knowing that the sentinel has always been the champion of the rights of the people, I hope you will not refuse to insert the following statement of facts, in justification of the Coal Burners' Association:

Although a great deal has been said about the coal burners' strike, still no one has yet touched the keynote of the question. The matter has been ventilated but partially, and generally in favor of the corporations and contracting middlemen. Only one side of the medal exposed to the unbiased and disinterested public to judge upon. Rumors are being circulated to the effect that the furnaces would shut down, through the cause of this coal burners' strike, to prejudice the people against the most sacred right of the American people, the right of free labor, free speech, freedom of public meeting, unions, orders or societies, but with great care hushing the real motives that may justify a temporary suspension of our furnaces. Not even the slightest hint has been thrown to the judicious public to demonstrate the wrong treatment these poor coal burners have been subjected to through their contractors, who have grown fat and opulent, generally at the expense of the poor producers, while these latter are left in the most dire destitution, and driven to despair to a degree that but two alternatives are left to them, either to starve to death, or to rise against monopoly, their oppressor! (and although it is to be regretted) by a natural instinct of nature and law of self preservation. They have chosen the latter, and though this strike has been going on for a month, yet no lives have been taken or threatened, nor any property destroyed by the consent, will or knowledge of the main body of the association.

The burners' main object is not so much the question of the thirty cents, as it is the abolition of all further contracts and contractors. There is no harm in that, and if everything is well meaning and bona fide on the other side, why don't they grant the burners the rightful demands, join the union and strike for a living price? During the last two or three years the greatest number of these middlemen have arrogated to themselves the arbitrary right of even denying the burners the sight of their coal receipts, contrary to the just and fair custom of former days, when things were conducted in a more satisfactory way for either party; but now they insolently answer "When you have your grocery bill paid then we will settle up business!" Meanwhile the burner works on, for months and years, and when this settlement comes, in nine cases out of ten, the poor burner in reward for his hardship, toil and privations of all kinds, has the pleasure of knowing from his contractor (who is generally also his dealer) that he is yet indebted to him. Is it a wonder, then, if these poor victims of monopoly, driven to the wall by despair, at last gather up the few good impulses left them by nature, and spurred by a famished stomach, rise, demanding a change in the order of things, and an amelioration of their condition? Let the public judge. Let the people draw a parallel of the situation of the contractor, who got rich at easy work, and the miserable, pitiful state of the poor toiler of the forest! Why, these very contractors are to a great extent coal producers themselves, but, being of a very charitable disposition and liberal to prodigality, they don't want to join the Union. They prefer taking twenty-six cents for coal instead of thirty cents. They would rather donate the extra four cents to enrich the wealthy stockholders of the companies. Of course it wouldn't do to join the association whose main by-law reads: "We want to abolish all further contracts." That's what keeps them off. There is more in it by staying out—in plainer words, by managing or monopolizing the coal of the outsiders in the way they have heretofore. These facts ought to be criterion enough to reveal the whole business. This row and trouble about Alpha has been kicked up and magnified to an exaggerated, gigantic proportion in order to arouse the public indignation and have a strong force sent there that might scare the harmless bands, carrying their point at the expense of the State. Here they make believe by their assumed terrible looks that an army of lawless rebels and revolutionary men (worse than a barbaric invasion) threaten destruction at Alpha and all around, while people coming from there know nothing about it, and have to come to Eureka to be informed of that fact.

Enough, gentlemen; throw down your mask, be fair and just, and in atonement for the past be at least humane in time to come. And since you have been made rich by these poor workers, don't try to raise prejudices or talk of sending an army with guns, bullets, etc.; but it better becomes your duty to send an army of cheese and macaroni to quench the hunger of these poor, famished, desperate wretches, who are really more hungry than ill-disposed.

—Veritas

Appendix B

Scoring "Veritas"
A Reply Written in the Plainest of King's English
Eureka, Nev., August 15, 1879.

EDITOR SENTINEL: In your issue of this morning we find an article headed "The Striker's Defense. The Objects and Designs of the Coal Burners' Association." As a preface, permit us to say that the feeling of the author is conclusively proven and shown when he speaks of "strikes." Now, Mr. Editor, what are strikes? Conflicts existing between labor and capital, organizations existing in defiance of law, and in restraint of trade. In any well organized community these strikers are regarded as rioters, disturbers of the peace, and punished as they justly deserve by the law. Who can gainsay this assertion? And we would like to see the man possessing temerity sufficient who is willing to approve the section of an organization claiming that it is right to defy the law, throw a peaceable community into a condition of chaotic disorder, and make a call upon the Governor of State for troops to protect honest citizens in the maintenance of their rights. The writer speaks of contracting middlemen. Who are they? Let him point them out, and not by a sweeping assertion, which has hardly the merit of glittering generality, accuse honest citizens of wrong. Come to the front, Mr. Veritas, and name your men. It is perfectly natural that in times of depression and stagnation of business, idle men, necessarily disturbers of the public peace, seek some plausible excuse to foment other idlers, hoping thereby to derive a benefit from the wreck of the fortunes of good citizens. There is a law governing the business conduct of all men, viz: that of supply and demand. It is said that the coal burners have been persecuted by these "bloodless monopolies." Please let Veritas give dates, facts and particulars. Let him point to a single instance wherein such persecution exists or has existed. Now to be honest, Mr. Editor, with our friend Veritas, we intend critically to resolve into first principles his propositions. In the outset he claims that the furnaces would shut down through the cause of this coal burners' strike, "to prejudice the people against the most sacred right of the American people, the right of free labor, free speech, freedom of public meetings, unions, orders or societies, etc." Bosh, balderdash and nonsense! The writer shows some degree of intelligence, but he has committed a grave blunder. Who has endeavored to stop their free labor? Who has tried to stop their free speech, and who has disturbed their so-called unions? No one. But one thing is certain, and that is that their speech, their unions and their threats have commanded the interposition of the law, and the law must be enforced regardless of labor unions and conspiracies in restraint of trade. Please name the contractor or middleman who has grown fat and opulent. Please indicate the poor devils who have been starved to death under the grinding exactions of the two companies who to-day furnish the health and life of this camp. Every reasonable man knows that the prosperity of the Eureka Con. and the Richmond Mining Companies is the prosperity of every man, woman and child in the camp. Is it to be claimed that in consequence of the organization of a lawless band, calling itself a "union," that these companies should be compelled to run their furnaces, do a losing business, declare "wish dividends," and all for the purpose of catering to the whims and caprices of an organized mob? No, Mr. Editor; there are other fields of labor. Eureka has hitherto sustained the reputation of being law-abiding, and its civil officers have ever been found competent to enforce the law. Strikers don't pay. Take the railroad strikers and the glass-blowers at Pittsburg [sic], Pa. What have they accomplished? Saddled the community with a debt which will take years to remove and themselves, their wives and little ones impoverished and dependent. Lives have been threatened and property has been destroyed, notwithstanding the assertion of our friend "Veritas." Who constitute the main body of the association? The writer seems to be one of them, and knows whereof he speaks. We claim the facts to be, that honest contractors have lost their time, had their property destroyed and their lives threatened by this same "Coal Burners' Association," and that each and every member of this organization was voting under the advice of the majority thereof. Herein consists the conspiracy, and every member guilty of such conduct should be held personally responsible under the law. Your writer shows the most sublime ignorance, when he says that "the burners' main object is not so much the question of the thirty cents, as it is the abolition of all further contracts and contractors." Why not employ the word "exterminate" in lieu of "abolition?" Veritas' good sense will come to his rescue. Who is going to join the Union? The Eureka Consolidated, or the Richmond, or both? Why, they are soulless, and would have no voice at the meetings of the Union. What are the merchants doing here? Helping the furnace companies, or the poor devils whom Veritas claims are starving to death in consequence of the unreasonable exactions of the so-called bloated monopolies who to-day are doing everything in the world for the benefit and welfare of the camp. Let the public judge; we are content to abide by the decision of the public. How can any association claim as their motto "we want to abolish all further contracts?" Can you stop the sun from shining or the wind from blowing?

The row and trouble about Alpha has not been magnified nor exaggerated. Property consisting of over 2,000 bushels of coal, was scattered all over an area of 20 acres. Armed rioters threatened the lives of those who were peacefully and lawfully engaged in the care and transportation of their own property. The Coal Burners' Association or any single rioter thereof, had no right under heaven to interfere with the hauling of this coal, to cut sacks open, or to keep the same on the grounds to the detriment of the owners thereof. Veritas is exceedingly funny in his conclusions, when he speaks of cheese and macaroni as opposed to guns, bullets, &c., but we imagine his levity will not be appreciated by the better class of Italians, who thoroughly understand the meaning of this slur against their countrymen. "Cheese and macaroni!" "Veritas," you have put your foot in it. Your sympathy is not wanted.

—J. Tognini & Co. AND Vanina

Appendix C

Once More
"Veritas" Answers Interrogatories and Closes the Argument.

Editor Sentinel: Please publish the following reply to the card of Messrs. Tognini and Vanina, that appeared in yesterday's Sentinel. I shall not trouble you with further communications, as I believe all points have been answered:

easy points to answer

Point No. 1—Strikes: We don't condemn strikes when imposition has passed all bounds, but we denounce violence.

Point No. 2—Rioters: We are strikers, but no rioters. We recommend the punishment of all trespassers of the law, when proven.

Point No. 3—The contractors, who are they?: Probably those who are liable to resent when pinched where the sore is.

Point No. 4—Let dates and instances be given: Plenty will be given, if compelled to.

Point No. 5—Free Labor: Labor is not free, where receipts are denied to its owners.

Point No. 6—Who has grown fat? Etc.: Those who but a few years ago were burning coal for a living, then willing to enhance the prices, but now leading an easier life, and some others following other business.

Point No. 7—Who have starved to death?: We think a dead hero not worth a cent; antidotes are generally administered while life's breath exists.

Point No. 8—The property of the town depends on the Richmond Consolidated Company, etc.: We agree on this point, but not on the proposition that through these middlemen every cent should return to the same, with our labor thrown in the bargain. Moral: We had money left to pay our debts when there were no contracts, and still the furnaces kept on going as usual. We can't now.

Point No. 9—What have strikers accomplished in Pennsylvania? Etc.: Do not go so far; illustrate your case with home events. The Virginia Miners' Union and our brethren of Ruby Hill will answer as well. At any rate, if strikes fail, that does not prove they are wrong.

Point No. 10—Lives have been threatened and property destroyed, etc.: That has to be proven yet.

Point No. 11—We claim that we contractors have lost our time, our property, and (why not add) our lives, also; We pity you.

Point No. 12—Want to abolish further contracts etc.: We mean contracts carried on as in the past, where one side reaped all the benefits, and the other the toilsome labor. We claim by the same rights of the universal cry, "The Chinese must go!" If there is any right in that. We claim it by the very right our fathers declared, "When in the course of human event, it becomes," etc. By the identical law this country has freed itself from tyranny, injustice and imposition. But we don't propose to raise a war, as you fear, but by refusing to deliver coal unless receipts are given us.

Point No. 13—Who is going to join the Union—the Consolidated, the Richmond, or both?: We don't invite any but the oppressed.

Point No. 14—Can you stop the sun from shining? Etc.: No; but we surmise that our strike will not eclipse it, but the sun will shine even if charcoal is sold at 28 cents with receipts and without contracts.

Point No. 15—Two thousand bushels of coal scattered, etc.: Large deduction, gentlemen, large deduction.

Point No. 16—"Veritas" is very funny, etc.: Yes, so he is, and happy, too, because he advocates a righteous cause, and is willing to take all responsibilities of the great slur thrown at his countrymen, by having introduced in their defense their traditional and characteristic "cheese and macaroni." Lastly, but not leastly, we will conclude by saying: That we admit one point, that we are poor. We cannot afford to hire lawyers or other proficient talents that know it all to keep up a war of pen and ink. We aim to the brief and laconic in this our last issue. "Veritas" is not a professional knight of the quill, but a knight of the camera, and although not so very extensively interested in this coal question, has volunteered his services to the cause in as far as things are kept within the limits of the law, but strenuously defending the rights of any one to claim and obtain a receipt for anything he pays for or disposes of. "Veritas" emphatically denies the slur flashed through "Scoring Veritas" of our friends T. & V. in this morning's SENTINEL that he is in any way connected with the Coal Burners' Association. He knows whereof he speaks, partly by his own experience and mostly by having been chosen by these burners, to fairly submit to the public their grievances, their wrongs and their reasons—in fact the privilege which, in justice to our free laws, should not be denied or refused to any one. So, T. & V., we are quits. We don't begrudge you for your answer; we expected one. It was but the proper course to pursue by both parties. We don't (at least "Veritas" don't) propose to carry on a useless war of polemics, since our aim has been attained. "Veritas" has other business to attend to besides indulging in this "skirmishing." The other side of the medal has been exposed. His task is at an end. To the people belong the sentence. This is our ultimatum.

—Louis Monaco
Alias Veritas, for the Coal Burners.
(*Sentinel*, August 17, 1879)

Appendix D

Bishop & Sabin
Attorneys at Law
Eureka County, Nevada

Eureka, Nevada, Aug. 24th 1879
Col. Geo. C. Lyon,
Carson, Nevada

Dear Col.
I should have reported to you the condition of affairs here sooner had I deemed it very necessary. Of course everything is supposed to be normal unless we hear something to the contrary. At time of my last telegraphic advice I deemed our War over. And concluded to wait a day or two longer before writing. Our Papers have kept the public advised of the status of all parties and their reports have been very correct. I had relieved all men on duty here the evening of the 17th, not deeming it necessary to detain them further, or that their services would be required. On the morning of the 18th I ordered fifteen men and a Com. Officer on duty here, at the Armory and ordered the Co. at Ruby Hill to hold themselves ready for instant duty. The companies responded promptly, and if necessary I could have put 70 to 100 armed men on duty within an hour. I was of the opinion however that the Sheriff could control the whole matter and insisted that he should do so, assuring however that if it became absolutely necessary myself and men would support him. Of course on the 19th and 20th, the days succeeding the homicides, there was considerable feeling here among the Italians, some approving the action of the Sheriff and others condemning. The *Jews*, always a patriotic self-sacrificing lot of cusses were, some of them, profoundly stirred, and fearful lest the solid pillars of the Constitution be toppled over and in the wreck of matter and the crash of worlds they would find no places left to which to tie clothes lines on which to hang the precious old "clo" and this was especially true of those who were copping for the Italian trade in the future. But the solid sentiment of all of the best men in the City, is that the Sheriffs men did their duty and no more, one thing is certain, there is an abiding conviction here that if a like emergency again arises that the action of the Sheriff will be repeated,

only perhaps to a greater extent, that our Military Companies if called upon will promptly respond.

There a few men here, conservative men all of them, good men too, Hillhouse, Cole (Cole Judge) and all of that political stripe who are wonderfully exercised over Constitutional Law. Who loves the State so well that they would see it thrashed, choked and shot to death by a mob and find no power to save it? It is but the repetition of the old story. We heard it in full chorus in 1861. The same men who in '61 were so shocked that the Nation could live when some one said it must die, are now equally shocked that means were found to protect good men and hold a mob in check. I suppose it will always be so. Examination of the men, Italians, charged with conspiracy and riot, is now going on and will probably continue some days. But I feel confident, there will be no more armed interference by any of the coal burners, or others, and should there be I am confident it will be quelled. I have thought it much better that the Civil authorities control this whole matter if possible and while I have been aware that the Shff. greatly wanted me to order out, my men and take charge I have refused to do so until the disturbance should pass beyond his power to control. I was a little solicitous lest the Governor should deem the matter more serious than it really was and return from Bodie sooner than he otherwise would. Please remember me to the Governor and assure him that our sentinels are out and that we will preserve order at the Camp, not damage the Constitution or Bylaws in the slightest particular.

Believe me Col.
Yours truly
G. M. Sabin

George M. Sabin to George G. Lyon, private secretary to Governor John H. Kinkead, August 24, 1879 (copy in James A. O'Neill Papers, Nevada Historical Society, Reno).

Bibliography

Primary Sources

Archivio Storico Diplomatico del Ministero degli Affari Esteri (ASDMAE). Rappresentanza Diplomatica Italiana a Washington (1861–1901). Rome.

Bechtel, Dale. "When the Swiss Made America" (radio broadcast). New York, May 11, 2009. http://www.swissinfo.ch.

Bonnifield, M. S., and T. W. Healy, comps. *The Compiled Laws of the State of Nevada in Force from 1861 to 1900*. 2 vols. Carson City, NV: Charles A. V. Putnam, State Printer, 1873.

Eureka County Recorder's Office. Deed Index. Eureka, NV.

Ferrario, Ercole. Conference at the Instituto Lombardo di Scienze e Lettere, June 4, 1868. Presented in *Considerazioni intorno all' emigrazione che avviene nel circondario di Gallarate* [Considerations regarding emigration from Gallarate and surroundings]. Rendiconti (Reports)—Istituto Lombardo, Academia di Scienze e Lettere. Vol. 1. Milan, 1868.

Freshfield, Douglas William. *Italian Alps: Sketches in the Mountains of Ticino, Lombardy, the Trentino, and Venetia*. 1875. Reprint. N.p.: Elibron Classics, 2005.

Giovinco, J. P. "The Ethnic Dimension of Calaveras County History." Unpublished manuscript, 1971. Calaveras Heritage Council, Altaville, CA.

Grand Jury Minute Book. A, no. 18. District Court of Eureka County, NV.

McCracken, Robert D. "Eureka Memories: A Series of Interviews with Fourteen Individuals and Families in Eureka, Nevada, 1993." Eureka County History Project, Eureka County, NV, 1993.

Merialdo, Peter B. *Memoirs of a Son of Italian Immigrants, Recorder and Auditor of Eureka County, Nevada State Controller, and Republican Party Worker*. Edited by Mary E. Glass. Reno: University of Nevada Oral History Program, 1968.

Milani, Ernesto R. "Genoa, Wisconsin and the Civil War: The Guscetti Brothers Fight for Their New Country." Ecoistituto della Valle del Ticino of Cuggiono presented at the thirty-seventh conference of the American Italian Historical Association, Annapolis, MD, November 4, 2004.

Nevada State Census, 1875. N.p., n.d.

Nevada State Legislature. *Appendix to the Journals of the Senate and the Assembly (1875): Fifth Biennial Report of the State Mineralogist for the Years 1873–1874*. N.p., n.d.

———. *Appendix to the Journals of the Senate and the Assembly, Eighth Session (1877)*: Census of the Inhabitants of the State of Nevada. Vol. 1. N.p., n.d.

———. *Appendix to the Journals of the Senate and the Assembly, Ninth Session (1879)*. N.p., n.d.

———. *Appendix to the Journals of the Senate and the Assembly, Tenth Session (1881)*: First Biennial Message of Governor Kinkead, Governor of Nevada, Delivered to the Legislature, January 4, 1881. Carson City: J. W. Madull, Superintendent, State Printing, 1881.

———. *Appendix to the Journals of the Senate and Assembly, Tenth Session (1881)*: First Biennial Message of the Adjutant General of the State of Nevada; Report of the Brigade Commandant. N.p., n.d.

———. *Journal of the Assembly, 1879*. N.p., n.d.

New Mexico Statutes (1905). N.p., n.d.

"Report of Meeting of the Richmond Consolidated Mining Co. (Dec. 3, 1872)." *Mining World* (December 7, 1872).

Sabin, George M. Letter to George G. Lyon, private secretary to Governor John H. Kinkead, August 24, 1879. Copy in the James A. O'Neill Papers, Nevada Historical Society, Reno.

Scott, Patricia A. "Obituaries published in the *Pioche (NV) Daily Record*, 1872–78." Database, Lincoln County Nevada Heritage Collection. http://www.nvgenweb.org/lincoln/PDRobits.txt:2010.

US Department of the Interior, Census Office. *Statistics of the Population of the United States at the Tenth Census (1880)*. Washington, DC: Government Printing Office, 1883.

Newspapers

Carson City (NV) Morning Appeal
Daily Alta Californian (San Francisco)
Daily Nevada State Journal
Esmeralda Star (Aurora, NV)
Eureka (NV) Daily Leader
Eureka (NV) Daily Sentinel
Gold Hill (NV) Daily News
New York Times
Reno Daily State Journal
San Francisco Chronicle
San Francisco Evening Bulletin
Virginia City (NV) Chronicle

Other Sources

Amfitheatrof, Erik. *The Children of Columbus: An Informal History of the Italians in the New World*. Boston: Little, Brown, 1973.

Andrews, Thomas G. *Killing for Coal: America's Deadliest Labor War.* Cambridge, MA: Harvard University Press, 2008.

Bancroft, Hubert Howe. *History of Nevada, California, and Wyoming, 1540–1888.* Vol. 25 of *The Works of Hubert Howe Bancroft.* San Francisco: History, 1890.

———. *Popular Tribunals.* Vol. 36 of *The Works of Hubert Howe Bancroft.* San Francisco: History, 1887.

Barkan, Elliott R. *From All Points: America's Immigrant West, 1870s–1952.* Bloomington: Indiana University Press, 2007.

Billington, R. A. *America's Frontier Heritage.* Albuquerque: University of New Mexico Press, 1974.

Clemens, H. "Oh Bury Me Not on the Lone Prairie" [Deadwood, Dakota Territory, 1872]. In *Songs of the Cowboy,* edited by N. H. Thorpe. Boston: Houghton Mifflin, 1921.

Cochran, Thomas C., and William Miller. *The Age of Enterprise: A Social History of Industrial America.* New York: Harper, 1961.

Conde, Alexander de. *Half Bitter, Half Sweet: An Excursion into Italian-American History.* New York: Charles Scribner's Sons, 1971.

Courtwright, David T. *Violent Land: Single Men and Social Disorder from the Frontier to the Inner City.* Cambridge, MA: Harvard University Press, 1998.

Dahrendorf, Ralf. *Class and Class Conflict in Industrial Society.* Stanford, CA: Stanford University Press, 1959.

Demaris, Ovid. *America the Violent.* New York: Cowles Book, 1970.

Earl, Phillip I. "Murder at the Opera House—This Was Nevada." *Panorama* (January 30, 1997).

———. "Nevada's Italian War." *Nevada Historical Society Quarterly* 12, no. 2 (1969).

Egleston, Thomas. "The Manufacture of Charcoal in Kilns." *Transactions of the American Institute of Mining Engineers* [Eureka County, NV], no. 8 (1880).

Elliott, Russell R. *History of Nevada.* Lincoln: University of Nebraska Press, 1993.

Emmons, David M. *The Butte Irish: Class and Ethnicity in an American Mining Town, 1875–1925.* Urbana: University of Illinois Press, 1989.

Fell, James E., Jr. *Ores to Metals: The Rocky Mountain Smelting Industry.* Boulder: University Press of Colorado, 2009.

Folkes, John Gregg. *Nevada's Newspapers: A Bibliography, a Compilation of Nevada History, 1854–1964.* Reno: University of Nevada Press, 1964.

Frehner, Brian. "Ethnicity and Class: The Charcoal Burners' War, 1875–1885." *Nevada Historical Society Quarterly* 39, no. 1 (1996).

Giovinco, Joseph P. "'Success in the Sun?': California's Italians during the Progressive Era." In *Struggle and Success: An Anthology of the Italian Immigrant Experience in California,* edited by Paola A. Sensi-Isolani and Phylis Cancilla Martinelli. New York: Center for Migration Studies, 1993.

Grazeola, Franklin. "The Charcoal Burners War of 1879: A Study of the Italian Immigrant in Nevada." PhD thesis, University of Nevada Press, 1969.

Hacker, David J. "A Census-Based Count of the Civil War Dead." *Civil War History* 57, no. 4 (2011): 306–47.
Halaas, David Fridtjof. *Boom Town Newspapers: Journalism on the Rocky Mountain Mining Frontier, 1859–1881.* Albuquerque: University of New Mexico Press, 1981.
Hilton, Mike. "The Split Labor Market and Chinese Immigration, 1848–1882." *Journal of Ethnic Studies* 6, no. 4 (1979): 99–108.
Hollon, W. Eugene. *Frontier Violence: Another Look.* New York: Macmillan, 1974.
Hulse, James W. *The Nevada Adventure: A History.* Reno: University of Nevada Press, 1969.
———. *The Silver State: Nevada's Heritage Reinterpreted.* Reno: University of Nevada Press, 1991.
Limerick, Patricia N. *The Legacy of Conquest: The Unbroken Past of the American West.* New York: W. W. Norton, 1987.
Lingenfelter, Richard E. *The Hardrock Miners: A History of the Mining Labor Movement in the American West, 1863–1893.* Berkeley: University of California Press, 1974.
Masterson, W. B. (Bat). "Famous Gun Fighters of the Western Frontier." *Human Life* 4 (January 1907).
McGrath, Roger D. *Gunfighters, Highwaymen, and Vigilantes: Violence on the Frontier.* Berkeley: University of California Press, 1987.
Mendez, Antonio J. *The Master of Disguise: My Secret Life in the CIA.* New York: William Morrow, 1999.
Molinelli, Lambert. *Eureka and Its Resources.* Reno: University of Nevada Press, 1982.
Mother Jones. *The Autobiography of Mother Jones.* 3rd ed. Chicago: Kerr for Illinois Labor History Society, 1977.
Murbarger, Nell. "Charcoal: The West's Forgotten Industry." *Desert* 19, no. 6 (1955).
———. "Forgotten Industry of the Frontier." *Frontier Times,* n.s., 39, no. 3 (1965).
Myron, Angel. *History of the State of Nevada.* Berkeley, CA: Howell-North, 1958. Photo reprint edition of Oakland: Thompson and West, 1881.
Oberbillig, Ernest. "Development of Washoe and Reese River Silver Processes." *Nevada Historical Society Quarterly* 10 (Summer 1967): 6–43.
Paher, Stanley W. *Nevada Ghost Towns and Mining Camps.* Berkeley, CA: Nevada Publications, 1970.
Prassel, Frank R. *The Western Peace Officer: A Legacy of Law and Order.* Norman: University of Oklahoma Press, 1972.
Reichman, Frederick Wallace. "Early History of Eureka County, Nevada, 1863–1890." Master's thesis, University of Nevada, 1967.
Rohrbough, Malcolm J. *The Land Office Business: The Settlement and Administration of American Public Lands, 1789–1837.* New York: Oxford University Press, 1968.
Rolland, David. "Switzerland to West Marin (Part 2 of 10)." Canonica Club of North America, September 6, 2007. http://camonica-club.blogspot.com/2007/09/switzerland-to-west-marin-part-2-of-10.html.

Rolle, Andrew. *The Immigrant Upraised: Italian Adventurers and Colonists in an Expanding America.* Norman: University of Oklahoma Press, 1970.

Rosa, Joseph G. *The Gunfighter: Man or Myth?* Norman: University of Oklahoma Press, 1969.

Salvetti, Patrizia. *Corda e sapone: Storia di linciaggi degli italiani negli Stati Uniti.* Rome: Donzelli Editore, 2003.

Schiavo, G. *Four Centuries of Italian-American History.* New York: Center for Migration Studies, 2000.

Scrugham, James G. *Nevada: The Narrative of the Conquest of a Frontier Land.* Vol. 1. Chicago: American Historical Society, 1935.

Sensi-Isolani, Paola A., and Phylis Cancilla Martinelli. *Struggle and Success: An Anthology of the Italian Immigrant Experience in California.* New York: Center for Migration Studies, 1993.

Shepperson, Wilbur S. *Restless Strangers: Nevada's Immigrants and Their Interpreters.* Reno: University of Nevada Press, 1970.

Sobel, Robert, and John Raimo, eds. *Biographical Directory of the Governors of the United States, 1789–1978.* 4 vols. Westport, CT: Meckler Books, 1978.

Spence, Clark C. *British Investments and the American Mining Frontier, 1860–1901.* Ithaca, NY: Cornell University Press, 1958.

Stern, Norton B. "The Jewish Community of Eureka, Nevada." *Nevada Historical Society Quarterly* 25, no. 2 (1982): 101–8.

Turner, Frederick Jackson. *The Frontier in American History.* New York: Henry Holt, 1920.

Twain, Mark. *Roughing It.* Scituate, MA: Digital Scanning, 2002. e-book.

Uhlmann, John, and Peggy Heinrich. *The Soul of Fire.* Pompano Beach, FL: University Books, 1987.

"Understanding the Stress Response." *Harvard Mental Health Letter* (March 2011).

Utley, Robert M. *High Noon in Lincoln: Violence on the Western Frontier.* Albuquerque: University of New Mexico Press, 1987.

Winzeler, Judith K., and Nancy Peppin. *Eureka, Nevada: A History of the Town.* N.p.: Nevada Humanities Committee, 1982.

Woolley, Dale E. *The Dameles and the American Curly Horse.* N.p.: Limited Publications, 1993.

Wren, Thomas. *A History of the State of Nevada: Its Resources and People.* New York: Lewis, 1904.

Young, Otis E. *Western Mining.* Norman: University of Oklahoma Press, 1979.

Zeier, Charles D. "Historical Charcoal Production near Eureka, Nevada: An Archeological Perspective." *Historical Archeology* 21, no. 1 (1987).

Index

Page numbers in *italic* indicate illustrations.

Abrams, Robert, 195
Adams, Jewett W., 150
African Americans, 9
Aiello, John, 24
Alpha, 110–11, 113, 250, 253
American dream, pursuit of, 238
American history, charcoal burner struggle parallels in, 116–17
American independence, 116
Anderson, Thomas G., 24
Anglo-Americans as westward movement protagonists, 5
Anglo-Saxon dominance, immigrant threat, perceived to, 32
Anglo workers, 1–2, 19–20, 116
anti-Chinese sentiment, 1–2, 19–20
antiforeign hysteria, 32
anti-Italian sentiment, 68
Antivill, Bronda, 183
armed conflict, deliberation element during, 165–66
arrest warrants, flawed, 76–77, 130, 131, 160, 184, 193
Arrivey, Thomas: as charcoal burners' trial witness, 191; charcoal loading and hauling efforts aided by, 190; Fish Creek Massacre, account of, 132–33, 138, 227; Fish Creek Massacre, role in, 128, 132, 134, 174; murder charge against, 188; unlawful conduct before and after Fish Creek, 171; as untrained gunman, 165
Ashim, Sol, 47
Asian immigrants, 32
Austrian Empire, 120, 121

Baer, George F., 51
Baker, George, 56
Baker, G. W., 98, 183, 188, 196
balance of power, 19
Bancroft, Hubert Howe, 93, 223, 231
Barkan, Elliott Robert, xii
Barrilis, Diego de: charcoal burners, dealings with, 208–10; coal burner numbers reported by, 53; in Eureka, 206, 207; Fish Creek Massacre, intercession following, 200; Fish Creek Massacre, statements concerning, 203, 204–5; Fish Creek Massacre investigated by, 212; inquest demise predicted by, 209–10, 220
Bassetti, Guido, 44, 70, 81n33, 195
Bassetti, James: arrest warrant for, 76–77; background of, 70, 81n33; Cassani ranch incident, involvement in, 75; as indicted striker, 193; Sadler, R. dealings with, 192; trial of, 183
Bassetti, Louis, 70, 81n33
Batista, Milito, 189
Batistta, Dullenella, 183
Beatty & Laspeyre (law firm), 183
Biale, Albert, 243
Biales, 17
Bianca, Diola, 190–91, 192
Bianca, Parola, 183
Bigelow, Jesse, 33
Bigelow's Eureka Opera House, 45–46
Bishop, A. C., 56, 123, 147–48
Bishop, W. W.: charcoal burners' trial, involvement in, 183, 196; charcoal crisis, communication concerning, 98; as

Eureka Republican, 56; mining assets invested by, 56; posse members' trial, involvement in, 188, 196
black mahogany, 29
Blanc, Albert, 53, 208
blast furnace, 10
Bondio, Angelo del: arrest of, 106, 126; Cassani ranch incident, involvement in, 75; as CBPA president, 70; as indicted striker, 193; Sadler, R. dealings with, 192; trial of, 183
Bonetti, Ferdinando, 18, 241
Boston Massacre, 1770, 116
Botto, Gus, 33
Bradley, Lewis, 97
Brennan, Johnny, 33
Brown, R. E., 46
Brown, Robert: charcoal burners' trial, involvement in, 180; as charcoal burners' trial witness, 190–91; charcoal transport wagon stoppage, 66–67, 68; death, 172; Fish Creek Massacre, account of, 162–63; Fish Creek Massacre, role in, 128, 129, 134, 155, 156, 174; lawsuit against CBPA by, 70; murder charge against, 188; shooting, alleged of P. Pattini, 215; threats, alleged to kill, 183; threats allegedly made to kill, 187; unlawful conduct before and after Fish Creek, 171–72; as untrained gunman, 165
Broy, C. L., 196, 197
Burlingame, Jose, 101
Burlingame, J. S., 46, 83
business, laws favoring, 96
business class, 225–26, 230
business ethic, 55
business leaders, charcoal burners criticized by, 74–75
Butler, C. J. R., 99
Butte, Montana, Irish community in, 64

California: Italian immigrant experiences in, 6–7; ore shipping to, possibility of, 94; smelting operations in, 63, 65
California Gold Rush, 7
Camp Douglas (temporary prison), 127

Canepa, John, 18
Canonica, Antonio, 147, 164
Canton Ticino, 120, 121
capital, 61, 111, 251
capitalism: defense of, 113; laissez-faire, 37, 55, 56, 58, 109; unbridled, 229–30
capitalist class, 55
capitalistic hegemony, 61
capitalists, native, 57, 60n39
Capitol Market, 18
Carpenter, C. C., 196, 197
Caschina, Matteo, 8
Cassani ranch incident, 75–77
Catholic Church, 242
Causey, M. L., 77
central Europeans, 9
Cesanoli, G. (Giovanni), 126, 183
chain immigration, 17
charcoal: consumption of, 40; cost increase, 1, 19, 34, 35, 65; demand for, 10, 12, 19; measuring system for, 27–28; millwork dependent on supply of, 143
charcoal burners: artifacts and legacy, 234–35, 238; attitudes toward, 78–79, 92; businessmen attitude toward, 112–13; on charcoal pit, 146; charcoal team transport obstructed by, 61, 64, 66; charges against dropped, 218, 221, 222; daily life, 234; deaths (Fish Creek Massacre) (see Fish Creek casualties); deaths on the job, 30; debts incurred by, 26, 40, 48, 63, 71–74, 250, 255; dehumanization of, 111; descendants of, 223, 231; discriminatory practices against, 106; dwellings, 28; economic conditions, 25, 26–27; economic slump impact on, 39; employment opportunities for, 24–25; experience, importance of, 14; experience prior to immigration, 16; financial vulnerability of, 51, 54; illiteracy, 73; as independent agents, 54; intentions of, 227–28; internal strife, 49; Italian diplomacy impact on, 210; Italian envoy attitude toward, 208–9; Italian envoy meeting with, 207–8; living conditions, 25, 31–32; marketplace competition impact on, 38; missing,

187; occupation change by, 114; outlaw tactics, 64, 69, 80, 225, 226; overproduction by, 40–41, 105; plight of, 249, 250; production, interference with, 62, 66; radicalization of, 64; release on bail, 222; remittances allegedly sent abroad by, 75; revolt by, 64; rioting by, 74–75, 80; smelters, direct dealings sought with, 73, 110; spokesmen for, 72–73, 109–11, 114–15, 116–18; stand taken by, 123; struggle of, 116–17, 122, 225, 228; teamsters, dealings with, 73; treatment *versus* posse member treatment, 188; unionizing by, 44–46, 49; wages, 25, 26, 144; weaponry, 215, 227–28; working conditions, 25, 30, 86, 110; work stoppage, potential of, 45, 48 (*see also* charcoal stoppages)

charcoal burners' strike: defense of, 110, 115, 116, 249–50, 256; media coverage of, 89

charcoal burners' trial: accused, list of, 183; characters, blemish on, 218–19; grand jury decision, 218–23; grand jury inquest, 197, 198; Italian consul involvement in, 198; legal representation, 183, 195–96; overview and key players, 180–83; posse's murder case combined with, 196; press coverage of, 186; proceedings, 182–87, 189–95; public opinion concerning, 177

Charcoal Burners' War, xi, 52, 152

charcoal bushel, determining, 27–28

charcoal camp: raid of, 64–65, 68; remains of, 236–37

charcoal crisis: after Fish Creek Massacre, 208; deepening of, 79–80, 90, 101; diminishing seriousness of, 152; escalation of, 87, 126; intraethnic dimension of, 230; legal aspects of, 95; local response to, 102–3; press coverage of, 240; public opinion concerning, 94; reports of, 100–102, 104; resolution of, 225, 228; smelter operator views on, 103–4; smoldering of, 125

charcoal dealers, commentaries by, 111–13

charcoal dispute, 1879: attempts to defuse, 117; deterioration, 105; in Fish Creek Massacre aftermath, 176–77, 222; Kinkaid, J.'s characterization of, 97

charcoal industry, 24–25, 39

charcoal manufacturers, payment received by, 26, 28

charcoal pits, 234, 235

charcoal price: charcoal burners' defeat over, 222; charcoal burners' trial testimony concerning, 181, 183, 184, 185, 193; dispute over, 3, 44–45, 47–49, 53–55, 61–63, 71, 72–73, 86, 106, 144, 220, 229, 241, 249, 250; drop, factors affecting and impact of, 39–41; factors affecting, 27, 28, 34; factors limiting, 55; as incidental issue, 110; increase, adaptive measures, 35–38, 65; increase obtained, 69; lowering sought for, 2; media coverage, cessation of, 49–50; pricing structure, 25–26; stability sought for, 20

charcoal production: dangers of, 30, 31; interference with, 62, 66; Italian monopoly over, 2; overproduction, 40, 41, 103; pace of, 25; processes, 12–14, 25, 29–30; reduced, potential result of, 55; stoppage, 236–37

charcoal quantity, factors determining, 31

charcoal rancher, profile of typical, 83, 91n1

charcoal shipping receipts, concealment from charcoal burners, 27, 48, 49, 86, 185, 186, 193, 222, 250, 255, 256

charcoal stoppages: actual *versus* reported, 101–2; analysis of, 104; burner motives behind, 63–64, 84–85, 86; at Cassani ranch, 75–77; CBPA-Eureka Consolidated agreement followed by, 66–68; charcoal burner trial testimony concerning, 185–86, 187, 190–91, 192, 193–94, 195; circumstances leading to, 61; commentaries on, 110–11, 253; in Fish Creek district, 77–78; after Fish Creek Massacre, 176–77; governor's views on, 97; at Hansen, P.'s ranch, 83–84, 126; impact of, 64–65; law enforcement response to, 86–90; at Newark, 78; posse murder trial testimony concerning, 215; production, interference with, 62; public opinion concerning, 62, 63, 68, 92, 93; reports of, 92, 98–99; at Roberts Creek, 83;

sporadic, 125; as tactic, 225, 227; at Tognini, J.'s ranch, 78, 105; at Torre, J.'s ranch, 84, 172; at Willow Station, 172

charcoal strikers: anonymity, attempts at, 107, 130; arrest of, 106, 126; arrest warrants for, 76–77, 128, 129–30; attack on, 227; guerilla-style skirmishes, 128; harassment campaign, 227–28; legal treatment of, 198; nonviolent conduct of, 128; statements issued by, 89

charcoal supply, 3, 103

charcoal transport: dangers of, 31; obstruction of, 61, 64, 66; prices and pricing of, 46, 73–74; railroad transport, pros and cons of, 31, 36–38, 112; rising cost of, 34; town merchant involvement in, 73

"charcoal war" (term), 52

Chase, R. L., 196

Chinese: businessmen, intermediary class of, 57, 60n39; ethnic bourgeoisie, dynamics of, 57, 59–60n39; in Eureka, 19; social status of, 9

Chinese immigration, opposition to, 182, 198–99n12

Chinese laborers: as charcoal makers, 19; expulsion of, 19, 20, 256; mistreatment of, 116; provisioning of, 57, 59–60n39; timber harvested and fuel produced by, 1–2

civil disobedience, 117

Civil War, 8

claim jumping suits, 198

class conflict, 61, 229

class *versus* ethnic loyalties, 230

"coal war" (term), 79–80

coke, 35–36, 55

Colonnade Hotel, 240

Colorado, mining officials' hiring practices in, 24

commerce, 95–96

Comstock, unionization in, 46, 58n7

Comstock Lode, 7–8

Comstock social pyramid, 9

Congress of Vienna, 1815, 120

conspiracy (defined), 95

constitutional law, 167

consumer goods, purchase orders redeemable for, 26

Contract Labor Law, 1864, 8

contractors: commentaries by, 111–13; critique of, 115–16; padrone system, participation in, 24; wealth *versus* worker poverty, 110

Cordano, G. B.: arrest of, 126; charcoal price negotiations, involvement in, 48, 54; as indicted striker, 193; Sadler, R. dealings with, 192–93; trial of, 183

Corichino, D., 126

Cornforth, E. N., 183, 186–87, 191, 192

corporate America, attitude concerning unionism, 51

corporate irresponsibility, 96

court interpreters, 117, 196, 213

Courtwright, David T., 171

Cromer, L. W. (Lawrence Washington): background, 183; as Eureka Republican, 56; as judge (charcoal burners' trial), 126, 183, 184, 190; as judge (posse members' trial), 188; Simpson, J. B. dealings with, 172, 189

Dameles, 17

Dave Keane Mountain, 125, 225

Davis, A. E., 19, 20

de Barrilis, Diego. *See* Barrilis, Diego de

Declaration of Independence, 219

Defendetia, Garcia, 183

deforestation, 2, 34

del Bondio, Angelo. *See* Bondio, Angelo del

Delume, Andrew, 185

de Paolis, 17

Dequili, Louis, 186

Diamond Mountain, 29

district court, 168

Donnelly, H.: business as usual reported by, 85; business transaction concluded with, 54; charcoal crisis, views on, 104; charcoal price increase rejected by, 45; Molinelli, L. relationship with, 69; position modified by, 66; posse member bond posted by, 196; smelting, plans to continue, 103

Douglas, Tommy, 127
Doutrick, Frank, 196
dwarf cedar, 29

Earl, Phil, xii, 125, 129, 190
eastern European Jews, 9
Eco d'Italia, L', 8, 16
economic depression, 74
economic downturn, 25, 55, 65
economic hegemony, 228–29
economic recovery, uneven benefits of, 25
economic resources, 56
economics, relationship to politics, 97
Emmons, David M., 64
Eseere, John, 30
ethnic bourgeoisie, 56–57
ethnic cohesion, geographic dispersal as obstacle to, 57, 230
ethnic discord, 229
ethnic hatred (Italy), xii
ethnic hostility, 23, 25
ethnic labor force, 56–57
ethnic minorities, 5, 247
ethnic prejudice, 7
Eureka, Nevada: charcoal burner seizure, false report of, 92–93; charcoal making in, 16; county status granted to, 10; development and expansion of, 1; development of, Italian immigrant role in, 17; fires, 222, 240; immigrants in, 1, 16; mineral outcroppings at, 9; mines, 11; as mining camp, 141; past and present, 233, 239–45; as smelting district, 143; societal structure lacking for, 32–33; threats, alleged to burn, 187
Eureka and Its Resources (Molinelli), 9, 17–18
Eureka and Palisade Railroad, 145
Eureka authorities, attitude toward Italian consul, 205
Eureka Charcoal Burners Protective Association (CBPA): Cassani ranch incident, involvement in, 75–76; challenges faced by, 51; character of, 53; charcoal price demands made by, 47–48, 53–55, 61, 65–66, 71; charcoal stoppages, position on, 67, 75–76, 93; critique of, 252, 253; Eureka Consolidated, dealings with, 67; founding of, 3, 44, 46, 55, 61, 84, 241; goals of, 61, 65–66, 86, 249–50; internal dissension of, 69, 70, 71, 84; Italian envoy meeting with representatives of, 207; lawsuit against, 70; leadership, 46–47, 69, 70–71, 79; measures, difficulty of implementing, 71; meeting places of, 18, 44, 45–46; officers on trial, 195; recruitment efforts and membership, 51–53, 101, 256; Sadler, R. conversations with members of, 192; spokesmen for, 109; violence rejected by, 62
Eureka Consolidated Mining Company: California smelters, potential contract with, 65; CBPA, dealings with, 67; charcoal price, statements concerning, 48–49, 62, 88, 144; charcoal rate increase agreed to by, 19, 64–65, 66, 69; charcoal rate increase rescinded by, 74; charcoal stoppage impact on, 85; charcoal supply, 103; defense of, 112; Eureka mineral production increase noted by, 10–11; legal disputes, involvement in, 181–82, 197–98, 220; management of, 45; ore shipments to California, possible by, 94; smelter shutdown planned by, 104–5
Eureka Courthouse, 239
Eureka Daily Sentinel, 50, 233, 240
Eureka Italians: economic predicament faced by, 6; ethnic solidarity lacking among, 229, 230; Fish Creek Massacre and inquest, opinion concerning, 168, 180; historic treatment lacking on, xii; Italian consul, communication with, 203, 204–5; Italian diplomatic aid sought by, 200; Italian government, attitudes toward, 210; San Francisco Italians sympathetic to, 201; statistics on, 1; Swiss consul, communication with, 203
Eureka non-Italians, San Francisco Italians criticized by, 202
Eureka Opera House, 45–46, 239–40
Eureka smelter, charcoal produced by, 34

Eureka State Military Armory, 127
Eureka Teamsters Association, 46
Europe, charcoal-producing regions of, 14

Fall River strike, Massachusetts, 111
Farrell, Marion, 170
Fell, James E., Jr., 10
Ferretti, George, 194
"fight-or-flight" response, 166
firearms, indiscriminate use of, 231
fires, 31, 222
Fish Creek casualties: burial place and monument, 242–45; dead identified, 147, 164; funeral procession, 175–76; killing, 125; memories of, 237; requiem and monuments, 231–232; wounded, 187; wounds of those slain, 164–65, 227
Fish Creek charcoal dispute, 40, 46
Fish Creek coroner's inquest: incompleteness of, 166–68, 220; jury composition, 174–75; jury's verdict and reactions to, 167–68, 173–74; medical analysis, 164–65; witness testimony, 154–64
Fish Creek district, 77–78
Fish Creek Massacre: aftermath of, 118, 147–51, 152–53; attempts to prevent, 117; burners' accounts not heard, 168–69; business as usual during week of, 85; cinematic West compared to, 238–39; circumstances leading up to, 231; coal burning occupation numbers at time of, 53; coal crisis culminating in, 230; firearms use and skill during, 165–66; grand jury hearing to probe, 102; historic significance of, 248; Italian accounts of, 138–40, 209, 218, 227; Italian envoy attitude concerning, 208–10; law enforcement role, analysis of, 173, 189; overview of, xi, 3, 125; prelude to, 63, 128–30; press coverage of, 200–201, 202; public opinion concerning, 148–50, 169–70, 176, 178, 212–13; reinvestigation, hypothetical, outcome of, 221–22; reports of, 130–140; silence surrounding, xi–xii; site of, 237; violence prior to, 33
Fish Creek Range, visit to, 233–35, 236–38, 239

Fobeli, Natali, 185–86
Foley, M. D., 98
Ford, John, 238
foreign-language newspapers, 8
Foreign Miners Tax, 1850, 7
foreign speech, American attitudes toward, 32
forty-niners, jobs serving, 7
Frehner, Brian, 57, 122, 229, 230
freight business, 36–39, 112
freight company owners, 26
freighting companies, 26
Freshfield, Douglas William, 16, 21–22n1
From All Points (Barkan), xii
frontier: burial in, 244; capitalism in, 56; law enforcement in, 173, 188–89, 230–31; myth *versus* reality, 238; violence pervading, 231
frontiersman's code of honor, 171
frontier thesis, 5
fuel, 1–2, 35–36
furnace shutdowns: action to prevent, 100, 103; retaliation, threatened in event of, 187; threats and rumors, 49, 65, 109–10, 249, 251

Garden City (general store), 18
Gardner, J. C., 193–94
Garibaldi Hotel, 18
Gaspari, Giuseppe, 217
Gentili, Georgeta, 183
Genzoli, Estelle, 16, 17, 21n1
Gibellinis, 17
Giovinco, Joseph, 6
gold, 7
Gold Hill, 46, 58n7
Gorman, Fred: arrests made by, 191, 214; charcoal burners escorted by, 126; charcoal loading and hauling efforts aided by, 190, 192; as Eureka Republican, 56
graft, 26, 225
Grave Yard Flat, 242–45
Grazeola, Franklin: CBPA, burners affiliated with estimated by, 79; CBPA early leadership, commentary on, 69; charcoal burner charge dropping, analysis by, 221;

Index

Fish Creek shooting, analysis of, 160, 162, 165; master's thesis, xii–xiii, 236; riot law interpretation analyzed by, 95
Grimm, Charley, 78, 101, 106
Guilded Age, 55

Halaas, David Fridtjof, 50
Hansen, Pete, 83–84, 93, 101, 126
hardwoods, 31
Haskell, D. A., 197
Haskell, S. P., 147, 164, 175
Hausman, Joseph, 47, 52, 68, 69–70, 184
Headley, H. T., 98, 99
Heinrich, Peggy, 30, 31
Hickok, Wild Bill, 166
Higby's Station, 77
Hillhouse, A. M. (Adelbert Milton): charcoal burners' trial, legal defense by, 183–84, 195; as Eureka Republican, 56; Fish Creek coroner's inquest, participation in, 162, 164, 166–67, 174; legal defense by, analysis of, 167–68
Hillhouse, Cole and Laspreye (legal team), 195
Hillhouse & Cole (law firm), 183
Hilton, Mike, 56–57
Hinckley, J. L., 196
History of Eureka (Molinelli), 204
Hollon, Eugene W., 173
honor, violent defense of personal, 171
Hulse, James W., 10, 97

immigrant labor, 11
immigrants: American attitudes toward, 5–6; experience, complexity of, 247–48; narratives, unearthing, 248
immigration chain, 23
immigration policy, challenges to, 248
impartiality, testing, 247
Indignation Committee (San Francisco), 201–2
individual responsibility, 96
industrialization, 58
interethnic conflict, 228–29
international business community, 17
Invernozzi, Antonio, 195

Inyo County, 27–28
Irish community, 64
Italian Alps, 16, 21n1, 232, 235
Italian Benevolent Society, 240
Italian bourgeoisie, 58, 114
Italian business community, 16, 18–19
Italian charcoal burners: economic predicament of, 6; legal representation, independent lacking for, 210, 256; literature on, xii; occupational ladder, bottom of, 229; recruitment and hiring of, 20–21; Swiss merchants, conflict with, 121; unfulfilled dreams of, 231–32
Italian charcoal ranchers, 83, 91n1
Italian consulate: advice given by, 203, 204–5, 212; establishment of, 7; Eureka visit by representatives of, 205–8; Fish Creek Massacre, statements concerning, 203–4, 208–10; intercession, impact of, 210; San Francisco Italians' committee independent of, 201; united front, image cultivated by, 205
Italian emigration, 3, 4–5, 235–36
Italian ethnic community, 56–57, 230
Italian explorers, 6
Italian government, 210
Italian immigrants. *See also* Eureka Italians: acculturation process, 57; American attitudes toward, 5–6, 31–32, 33, 68, 92; charcoal making experience of, 16, 21–22n1; class antagonisms between, 85–86, 109, 112–113, 114, 115, 122; descendants of, 16, 17, 21n1, 22n4; economic inequality, 57; employment, 17; ethnic distinctiveness of, 33–34; ethnic solidarity, 117, 200, 229; Fish Creek Massacre, accounts of, 138–40; Fish Creek Massacre and inquest, opinions concerning, 168–69, 173–74, 176; frontier experiences of, 6–7; geographic distribution of, 57; hierarchical order among, 113; history, remembering, 245; isolation, 31–32, 57; legal bias against, 33; occupations dominated by, 16; retracing footsteps of, 247; in San Francisco, 200, 201–2, 205; upper class, 229; upward mobility, 57–58; West,

largest community in, 200; xenophobia against, 2
Italian immigration to U.S., history of, 6–7
Italian Jesuit missionaries, 6
Italian-owned businesses, 18
Italian press, Fish Creek Massacre accounts by, 139–40, 202
Italians, northern, 9
Italian strikers, legal treatment of, 198
Italian-Swiss border, 120
Italian unification movement, 121
Italian urbanites, geographic distribution of, 57
Italian War, xi, 219, 231
Italian witnesses: anonymous, 138–40, 209, 218, 227; in posse murder trial, 213–17
Italy, 4–5

Jefferson, Thomas, 219
Jesuit missionaries, Italian, 6
"John Doe warrant," 76–77, 130, 131
Johnson, H., 197
Jones, John E., 181
Jones, R. P., 10
Joseph, Billy, 172, 189
juniper, 29, 31, 236
jury, balanced, selecting, 197–98, 213

Kaye, Henry, 77
Keen, David, 194
Kemp, H. R., 197
killing, legal justification for, 171
kiln burning, 12–14, 29–30
King, John Henry, 171
Kinkead, John H.: advisors, 140; background, 95; burners' revolt, views on, 97; charcoal crisis, communications received concerning, 88, 92, 102, 103, 104, 125, 181; charcoal measuring law approved by, 28; Fish Creek Massacre, opinion of, 150–51; militia deployed by, 93, 97, 98, 99, 100, 229; as mining interests supporter, 97; secretary of, 167, 258
Kyle, Matthew: at Alpha, 75, 76; attorney for, 162; bond filed by, 213; as charcoal burners' trial witness, 194–95; charcoal crisis, response to, 67, 87, 88–89, 127–28, 129, 151–52, 228; charcoal crisis described by, 92, 98, 100, 101; charcoal striker arrests made by, 106, 126, 128; as Eureka Republican, 56; Fish Creek action advice given by, 135; Fish Creek action defended by, 207; Fish Creek Massacre reported to, 137, 177; Fish Creek Massacre scene, trip to, 131; Italian envoys, dealings with, 206–7; Kinkaid, J., communication with, 88, 99, 102, 125; posse, bond for executed by, 188; posse sent to charcoal camps by, 3, 90

labor: capital, relationship with, 61, 251; demands, typical, charcoal burners' demands compared to, 53, 54; disputes, 1; exploitation of, 55–56, 57; as impersonal term, 111
labor-management conflicts, 96
labor market, ethnic and racial segmentation of, 16
labor shortage, 8
labor surplus, 23
laissez-faire capitalism: critique of, 109; curbs on, 37; features of, 58; post–Civil War promotion of, 55, 56
Lambert Molinelli & Co., 18
Lamoureux, George W.: Cassani ranch charcoal stoppage experienced by, 75, 76, 77; CBPA, views on, 69; charcoal crisis, communication concerning, 98; as Eureka Republican, 56; posse member bond posted by, 188, 196; Rich, M. connection with, 128, 129, 170; strikers, dealings with, 79; teamsters' union meeting attended by, 46; wagon teams at Fish Creek, 134; Wren, T. involvement with, 182
Las Animas, Colorado, 24
law breaking as tactic, 64, 225, 226, 230
law enforcement, 3, 189, 212–13, 230–31
lawlessness, 8, 173
law officers: bonds imposed on, 213; criminal backgrounds among, 231; murder

trial, 213–18; public opinion concerning, 222; weaponry, 228
lead, 41, 65
Leader, 50
Leone, Sergio, 238
life, right to, 219–20
Ligurian immigration to California, 6
Limerick, Patricia, 5, 56, 96
Locatelli, Marcelino, 147, 164
Locke, John, 219
Lombardy (region), 120, 235
Lucca, Joseph, 213, 214
Lyon, George, 140, 151, 167, 257–58

Maginni, Joseph: as CBPA president, 47; CBPA resignation by, 68, 69–70; coal price goal stated by, 53; national origin, 122; as striker leader, 190
Mannion, James H., 195
Marconi, Gregorio, 195, 215–16, 217, 218
Margorali, Giovana Angelo, 30
marketplace, 112, 222
Martin, William: attempted murder, alleged of, 214; Fish Creek Massacre, role in, 128, 129, 134, 155, 174, 228; murder charge against, 188; unlawful conduct before and after Fish Creek, 170; as untrained gunman, 165
Martinoli, Giuseppe: Cassani ranch charcoal loading, warning against endorsed by, 76; as CBPA vice president, 70; charcoal stoppage involvement, alleged of, 183, 186; as indicted striker, 193; release on bond, 195; town burning allegedly threatened by, 187; trial of, 183
Mason, J. F., 87–88, 102
Master of Disguise, The (Mendez), 16, 21n1
Masterson, William Barclay "Bat," 165
McCracken, Robert D., 16, 17, 21n1, 22n4
McDonald, teamster, 154
McKay, Alex, 194
McKee, H. B., 77, 106
McKee, H. J.: charcoal stoppages experienced by, 195
McKenney, L. C., 50

Mendes, Joseph, 196, 197
Mendez, Antonio J., 16, 21n1
mercantile establishments, overcharging at, 26
Merialdo, Bernardo, 17
Merialdo, Peter B., 231
Merrill, George W., 162, 196
Mexicans, 9
military assistance, 88
Mills, W. O., 197
millwork, 143
mine laborers, wages of, 25, 26, 144
mine owners, 96
mineral economy, 23
mineral market, weakening of, 41
mineral ore, railroad transport of, 36, 145
mineral output, decline in, 223
mineral production, 8, 11, 19, 55
Miners' Protective Association: founding of, 46, 58n7
miners' unions, 46, 58n7
mines: Italian envoy visits to, 206; shutdown of, 223
mining, decline in, 34
mining frontier, violence pervading, 231
mining industry: burner action impact, potential on, 63; capitalist ideology prevalent in, 55–56; dominance of, 49; in Eureka County, *141*; leaders as politicians, 97; negotiations, failed with, 63
Mint Act, 1873, 55
Molinelli, Lambert: CBPA resignation by, 68, 69–70, 204; as CBPA vice president, 47, 68; charcoal burners' meeting attended by, 44; as compromised individual, 204; Italian diplomatic communication with, 203–4; motives of, 68–69; newspapers described by, 50; office, meeting in, 206; works by, 9, 17–18, 204
Monaco, Louis: background, 145; Bishop, A. C., dispute with, 123; charcoal burners, loyalty to, 121; charcoal burners' meeting attended by, 44; charcoal burners' predicament described by, 63, 210; as charcoal burners' spokesman, 116–18, 255–56;

charcoal burners' union involvement of, 47; as court interpreter, 117, 196; Fish Creek coroner's inquest, participation in, 167; Fish Creek Massacre, account of, 139–40, 202; immigration to U.S., 120; Italian consul communications translated by, 203; national origin, 119; as photographer, 18, 118; political views, 121, 122–23; professional reputation, 118; pseudonym used by, 115, 117 (*see also* Veritas (pseudonym)); *Sentinel* praised by, 214; as social critic, 118; as working-class spokesman, 115–16

Montiverde, Father D., 242

Moore, James P., 197

Morgantini, Gabriel, 18

Morgantini, Louisa, 243

Morrison, R. K., 197

Mother Jones, 58

mountain mahogany, 31

mule teams, ore hauled by, 142

Native Americans, 9

nativists, 32

natural resources, plunder of, 55–56

Negrini, Giuseppe, 215, 228

Negrini, Joe, 186–87

Nevada: demographic composition of, 16; immigrants in, 7–8; statehood, 8

Nevada Militia: deployment of, 93, 94, 97–98, 99–102, 107; intervention in strikes, 96; need for questioned, 103; request for, 99, 102, 125, 181, 226, 229; sheriff's authority reclaimed from, 90

Newark, 78

newspapers: charcoal price dispute, coverage of, 49–50, 51; corporate ownership and control of, 50; union strength reports by, 52–53

New Town Ruby Hill, *141*

Noce, Angelo, 213

northern Italians, 9

northern Italy, 16, 235–36

Oberbillig, Ernest, 10

Oberfelder, Max, 197

Old World occupations, 7

ore: abundance of, 24; production, 40; shipping to California, possibility of, 94; transport of, 142

Pacific Coast region, 6

padrone system: burner-teamster dealings and debt postponement under, 73; charcoal burner subordinate status in, 54, 86; ethnic bourgeoisie and, 57, 59–60n39; internal dynamics of, 105; Italian immigrant influx due to, 23–24; overview of, 17

Paher, Stanley W., 40

Pajorola, Tom, 183

Pastorinos, 17

Patterson, W. M.: as charcoal burner trial witness, 184–85; coal stoppage experienced by, 83, 84, 106, 126

Pattini, Michael, 187–88, 189

Pattini, Pompeo: charcoal stoppage involvement, alleged of, 183; death of, 147, 164, 186, 215, 217; threats allegedly made by, 186–87; trial for death of, 187–88; weapon carried by, 215, 228

payment, flawed system of, 26

peasants (Italy), 4–5

Pedroni, Eunice, 217

Pedroni, Giovanni: charcoal stoppage involvement, alleged of, 183, 186; death of, 147, 164, 165, 186, 217; town burning allegedly threatened by, 187

Pennsylvania coal regions, 11

Piccola, Louis, 193

pine, 31

pine-nut trees: as charcoal source, 28

Pine Station, 83–84

Pinola, Luigi, 183

Pinoli, L. (Luigi), 126

piñon, 31, 236

pit burning, 12, 13, 29, 30, *146*

Plater, John E., 197

politics, relationship to economics, 97

Porter, J. A., 197

Porter, Jim: Fish Creek shooting, participation in, 128, 129, 134, 155, 174;

murder charge against, 188; as untrained gunman, 165
posse: action taken by, 133, 134, 135, 139, 140, 156, 157, 158, 166; aggressive intentions of, 226–27; arrest of, 189; bond posted for, 188–89, 196; charges against dropped, 218, 220; deaths at hands of, 167, 169; dispatch of, 3, 90, 97; grand jury praise for, 219; Italian consulate statements concerning, 208; leadership of, 161, 162, 172–73; legal representation for, 162, 163; legal victory, 180; members forming, 128–29, 170–73, 174; murder trial, 180, 187–89, 196, 212, 213–18; plan, 131; public opinion concerning, 169, 170, 173, 178, 212; raising, 87, 88, 102; route taken by, 236; standard of conduct for, 137; sureties posted for, 168; as unskilled gunmen, 165; weaponry, 159, 226
Powell, J. C., 197
Prassel, Frank R., 173, 188, 189
press, charcoal crisis public perceptions shaped by, 94
prisoners, transfer of, 127
private property, preeminence of, 219, 220
Probert, Edward, 38, 49, 197–98
Progressive Era, 6
property rights, 219, 220
prospecting, 16, 211n1
Proti, Angelo, 70

Quadro, Domenico, 102, 213–14, 218

Radetsky, Joseph, 120
Radoni, John, 195
railroad: charcoal transport by, 31, 36–38, 112; construction of, 145; economic impact of, 11, 36–38; strikes, 252; transcontinental, 19
Railroad Saloon and Store, 18
ranching, 17
Rapp, Antone, 186
Ratazzis, 17
Ratti, Nicola, 70–71
Raum, Ed, 87
Rebaleatis, 17
Reilly, Tom, 176–77

Remington W. H., 196–97
Republican politicians, 55, 56
Restless Strangers (Shepperson), xi
Reynolds, Budd, 106
Rich, Marshall: as charcoal burners' trial witness, 191–92; charcoal loading and hauling efforts aided by, 190; Fish Creek, injury at, 133, 137; Fish Creek Massacre, account of, 154–58, 161, 162, 226; Fish Creek Massacre, role in, 128, 129, 131–32, 134, 136, 137, 174; murder charge against, 188; Pattini, P. allegedly killed by, 217; pistol allegedly drawn on, 215–16; unlawful conduct before and after Fish Creek, 170–71; as untrained gunman, 165
Richmond Consolidated Mining Company: charcoal pricing, position on, 61–62, 65, 66, 69, 144; charcoal stoppage impact on, 85; charcoal supply, 103; defense of, 112; Eureka mineral production increase noted by, 10–11; lawsuits against, 197–98, 220; legal counsel for, 181–82; management of, 38, 44–45, 118; operations, environmental impact of, 142; refinery built by, 12; smelter shutdown planned by, 104–5
Richmond smelter, 34, 38–39, 40, 65
Rickard, Richard: business strategy of, 35; charcoal price increase rejected by, 44–45; as Eureka Republican, 56; Italian envoys, dealings with, 206; Molinelli, L. relationship with, 69; position modified by, 66; Wren, T. involvement with, 182
Riley, Thomas, 77
rioting (defined), 95
Risorgimiento, 4, 121, 122
Roberti, P., 18
Roberts Creek, 83
Robinson, E. M., 99–100, 101, 103
Rock, A. D., 197
Rockies, silver-lead ore in, 10
Rodono, G., 183, 193
Rogantinis, 17
Rohrbough, Malcolm J., 96
Rolle, Andrew, 6, 32, 122
Rosa, Joseph G., 166

Rosetti, C. (Consbandise), 183, 186–87
Rosetti, Giuseppi, 183
Ruby Hill, 36
Ruby Hill Miners' Union, 55
rural Italian labor force, 57

Sabin, George M.: charcoal crisis, response to, 151; as Eureka Republican, 56; Fish Creek Massacre, account of, 140, 257–58; Lyon, G., correspondence with, 167, 257–58; militia deployment, conditions requiring stated by, 107; militia deployment, participation in, 100, 187; as Nevada Militia general, 97, 98, 99; posse members' trial, involvement in, 188; prisoner relocation ordered by, 127; reputation following Fish Creek Massacre, 152–53
Sacco, Ferrario, 206, 212
Sacco and Vanzetti drama, xi–xii
Sadler, Reinhold: building constructed by, 240–41; CBPA, views on, 69; charcoal burners' demand opposed by (price), 3, 181; charcoal burners' trial, involvement in, 180–81, 182–83, 184; as charcoal burners' trial witness, 192–93; charcoal crisis, communication concerning, 98, 181; charcoal dispute, involvement in, 79; charcoal price negotiations, involvement in, 48, 54; charcoal stoppages experienced by, 77; charcoal transport contract with, 66–67; examination of, 216; posse member bond posted by, 188; teamsters' union meeting attended by, 46; threats, alleged to kill, 183; threats allegedly made to kill, 187
Sadler House, 240–41
sagebrush, 31
Saint Brendan's Catholic Church, 242
saloon keeping, 17
San Francisco, 6, 200–201
San Francisco, Italian consulate in. *See* Italian consulate
San Francisco Italians, 200, 201–2, 205
Scrugham, James G., 93
Second Brigade (Nevada Militia), 92, 97, 125–26

Sentinel, 50, 233, 240
Shepperson, Wilbur S., xi, 17, 23, 247–48
Sholderer, W. M., 18
"shoot first" philosophy, 166
Siddle, Maximillian, 185
silver, 9–10, 34–35, 41, 55, 65
silver-lead ores, 9–10
Simpson, J. B.: brushes, prior with law, 172, 189; charcoal stoppage, attempt to prevent by, 77; charcoal stoppage perpetrators sought by, 76, 84, 87; charcoal striker arrests made by, 106, 126; Fish Creek arrest mission of, 128, 129, 130, 131, 132, 133–34, 135–36, 137, 138, 139–40, 158–59, 160; Fish Creek Massacre, account of, 158–62, 163, 164, 166; Fish Creek Massacre, role in, 155, 156, 157, 158, 163–64, 172–73, 174, 189, 226, 228; Marconi, G.'s life spared by, 216; murder charge against, 188; public opinion toward, 212
Sincerity (pseudonym), 72–73, 109
Sine, Jacovio, 183
Skillman, A. (Achibald), 50, 197, 240
smelter operators: burner inability to deal with, 73; charcoal crisis, views on, 103–4; charcoal delivery payments made by, 26; economic interests, furthering by, 27; shutdown planned by, 104–5; teamsters, relationship with, 27; timber scarcity impact on, 34–35
smelting activity: burst of, 19; environmental degradation caused by, 11, 142; increase in, 24; overview of, 34; peak of, 40
smelting companies, 41
smelting industry, 48, 55, 62, 84–85, 103
smelting technology, 9–10, 11
Smith, George, 194
Smith, G. H.: charcoal loading and hauling efforts aided by, 190; Fish Creek shooting, participation in, 128, 129, 132, 134, 155, 174; murder charge against, 188
Smith, J. W., 131, 154, 174, 176
Smith, M., 196
social class, 229
social conflicts, church mediation of, 242

Soul of Fire, The (Uhlmann and Heinrich), 30
south-central European immigrants, 32
southern Italians, xii
Stewart, Oliver, 32
stone kilns, 29, 234
Stone Saloon, 18
Storey, Hank: charcoal striker arrests aided by, 106; Fish Creek Massacre, account of, 131, 132, 133, 137, 138; Fish Creek shooting, participation in, 128, 129, 134, 174; murder charge against, 188; weapons confiscated by, 195
strikes: critique of, 111, 251, 252; defense of, 255
Strozzi, Pete (Peter): coal stoppage experienced by, 83, 101, 186; as Italian charcoal rancher, 83, 91n1; threats, alleged to kill, 183, 187
Strozzi, Severino: arrest of, 84, 106, 126, 185; as CBPA treasurer, 71; charcoal stoppage, participation in, 83, 184–85; release on bond, 195; trial of, 183
supply and demand, law of, 40–41, 112, 225, 251
survival of the fittest, 222
Swiss consulate, 203
Swiss immigrants, 16
Swiss-Italian border, closure of, 121
Swiss-Italian immigrants, 121–22, 230, 241
Swiss Italians, Italians distinct from, 119–20
Swiss merchants, 121
Switzerland, neutrality of, 120

Tarabino brothers, 24
Tatti, Celso, 122
Tatti, Celso's saloon, 3, 18, 44, 241
teamsters: charcoal burner dealings with, 73; charcoal burners' trial, testimony in, 183, 184–85; charcoal manufacturers paid by, 26, 28; deputation of, 129, 174; economic interests, furthering by, 27; graft system devised by, 225; railroad transport *versus* protecting interests of, 36–37,

112; smelter operators, relationship with, 27; unionizing by, 46; wages, 26
Thoma, G. H., 131, 164
Thompson, W. H., 195
Ticinese immigrants, 120
Ticino-Lombardy border, 120
Ticino region (northern Italy), 4
timber, 1, 28–29
timberland scarcity, 34
Tognini, Cristoforo Guiseppe 'J. C.', 16, 21n1
Tognini, Joseph: building constructed by, 241; capitalism, unbridled favored by, 229–30; charcoal burner casualties under, 30; charcoal burners' claims held by, 54; charcoal burners' demand opposed by, 3; charcoal crisis, commentary concerning, 111–13; charcoal crisis, communication concerning, 98; charcoal delivery stoppage ordered for, 104; charcoal dispute, involvement in, 105; charcoal price increase opposed by, 229; charcoal shipping receipt access allegedly not refused by, 186; charcoal transport, involvement in, 73; as court interpreter, 196; as freight business contractor, 36; as Italian charcoal rancher, 83, 91n1; national origin, 122; posse member bond posted by, 188, 213; ranch belonging to, 78, 185, 186; threats allegedly made to kill, 183, 187; as wealthy Italian mogul, 56; written commentary, 251–53
Tognini and Company Building, 241
Tognini & Co., 98
Toomey, Joseph: attempted murder, alleged of, 214; Fish Creek Massacre, account of, 163–64; Fish Creek Massacre, role in, 128, 129, 133, 134, 135, 155, 156, 158, 174, 228; murder charge against, 188
Torre, John: charcoal stoppage experienced by, 84; on grand jury, 196, 197; hotel owned by, 18; as Italian charcoal rancher, 83, 91n1; posse member bond posted by, 188, 196, 213; as wealthy Italian mogul, 56
Torre, Joseph, 73
trade laws, 95–96

transcontinental railroad, 19
transportation costs, inflation of, 2
Treasure City, 8, 16
trees, harvesting and cording of, 31
Turner, B. J.: charcoal crisis described by, 92, 98, 100; Kinkead, John, communication with, 88, 99, 102, 125
Turner, Frederick Jackson, 5–6
Twain, Mark, 231
Tybo, 20
Tybo Consolidated Mining Company, 20

Uhlmann, John, 30, 31
unemployment, 23, 39, 64
union activity, risky nature of, 51
unionization in Nevada, 46, 58n7
unspecialized labor, 7–8
Utley, Robert M., 230

Vanina, Joseph: capitalism, unbridled favored by, 229–30; charcoal burners' claims held by, 54; charcoal burners' demand opposed by, 3; on charcoal crisis, 98, 111–13; charcoal delivery stoppage ordered for, 104; charcoal price increase opposed by, 229; charcoal transport, involvement in, 73; as freight business contractor, 36, 39; national origin, 122; saloon owned by, 18; teamsters' union meeting attended by, 46; as wealthy Italian mogul, 56; written commentary, 251–53
Vebala, Antone, 183
Veritas (pseudonym): anonymous authors, other compared to, 217; charcoal burners championed by, 249–50; commentary by, 109–11; critics of, 111–13, 251–53; Fish Creek Massacre, account of, 139–40, 202; Fish Creek slain, examination of bodies of, 166; identity of, 115, 118–19; intraethnic bigotry condemned by, 230; response to critics, 114–15, 255–56

Victor Emmanuel II, King of Italy, 4
Vigilante Committee, 33
vigilantism, 33
violence: attempts to prevent, 88; charcoal burner temptation, possible toward, 49, 62–63; charcoal stoppages without, 67, 77–78, 84; denunciation of, 255; over charcoal price, 70; prelude to, 80; social order, restoring by, 32–33
Virginia & Truckee Railroad incident, 1879, 96

Watchfulness (pseudonym), 216–17
Wedgwood, C. V., 247
West: ethnic minorities in, 5, 230; fiction *versus* reality, 238–39; inequality in, 56; law enforcement in, 230–31; lawlessness of, 173; social flexibility in, 122
westward movement, 5
White, Fred, 185
Whitehill, H. R., 11
Williams, James, 164
Williams, John, 10
Willow Station, 66
Winkelreid, Joe, 183
workers, communal action by, 61
working class, 55, 58, 61
Workingmen's Protective Union of Central Nevada, 20
Wren, Thomas: anti-Chinese views, 182; background, 181–82; charcoal burners' trial, involvement in, 183, 196; coroner's inquest, participation in, 162, 163; as Eureka Republican, 56; posse members' trial, involvement in, 188, 196

Yerington, Henry, 96

Zarger, Joseph, 70
Zerli, Theo, 147, 164, 165
Zonali, Gabriele, 241